NO HAIL, NO FAREWELL

A *Cass Canfield* BOOK

By Louis Heren

NO HAIL, NO FAREWELL

THE NEW AMERICAN COMMONWEALTH

NO
HAIL,
NO
FAREWELL

Louis Heren

HARPER & ROW, PUBLISHERS
New York and Evanston

FIRST EDITION

LIBRARY OF CONGRESS CATALOG CARD NUMBER: 71-95964

Contents

To

CASS CANFIELD

who persuaded me to write something longer than a

newspaper column

NO HAIL, NO FAREWELL

1963

There was no hail and farewell when President Lyndon Baines Johnson returned to Washington on November 22, 1963, with the body of his predecessor. That night at Andrews, the air force base outside Washington, one was hardly aware of the new president as the coffin and pallbearers were lowered from Air Force One on a fork-lift truck. Those who were there must have known that power had passed from John Fitzgerald Kennedy, that the former vice-president was now the thirty-sixth president of the United States, but the grief and shock of the senseless assassination was such that there was no immediate recognition of his new authority. Somehow it was still assumed to belong to the dead man. Nor was there an assertion of authority. Johnson stood back modestly after being rudely thrust aside by some of the Kennedy men. Eventually he went to the microphones and said, "This is a sad time for all people. We have suffered a loss that cannot be weighed. For me it is a deep personal tragedy. I will do my best. That is all I can do. I ask your help—and God's."

It seemed that few were listening. The country had not accepted the death of Kennedy, let alone the succession. The

White House was still the Kennedy home. Johnson had essential business to conduct that night. None knew if the assassination was the result of a conspiracy, domestic or foreign. Most members of the cabinet, who had been on their way to Japan, were still airborne somewhere between Honolulu and Washington. The nation's defenses had to be alerted, foreign reactions studied, and the FBI ordered to Dallas. It was an intensely critical situation, but Johnson worked that night in his old vice-presidential office. He went home to sleep in Spring Valley, a residential section in northwest Washington, where he lived until after the funeral. The fate of the country was in steady hands, but few knew it. Fewer cared. Clustered about millions of television screens, most Americans were involved in the death and burial of Kennedy to a degree unimaginable before the age of electronic communications. And they were involved in his life. Continued coverage from Friday to Monday, from morning to night, demanded more than the ceremony of presidential death could at first provide. Thousands of feet of film were shown, of Kennedy on the campaign trail, at home, as president, and even speaking in Texas a few hours before he was killed. No man, living or dead, had ever been given such concentrated exposure.

I think it is worth recalling those seventy-two hours, because they help to explain at least part of what later happened during the Johnson administration. The fact that they spanned a weekend, a miserable winter weekend when bad weather prevented most outdoor activity, ensured the massive national audience. There was nothing else to do, even if one wanted, except to watch television and become part of the mourning multitude. Habits of a lifetime were in abeyance in millions of homes. The reluctance to accept the new president was thus sustained even when Kennedy's body lay in state, first in the East Room of the White House and afterward under the great dome of the Capitol. Then the heads of state and government from the four corners of the world began to arrive to pay their respects. They reminded Americans of the power and the glory of their country and perhaps gave them a new sense of pride—but a special kind of pride, for the dead president.

As the great drama mounted toward its climax on Monday, the day did not begin anew in spite of the evidence of the clocks. All through the bitterly cold night a vast crowd waited patiently to pay homage at the Capitol. Midnight was meaningless, but at some time during that night the pride became deeply personal. Jacqueline Kennedy, indomitable and beautiful in her grief, went back to the Rotunda to pray again for her husband. She had earlier listened there with her family to the eulogies of the chief justice of the United States, the speaker of the House of Representatives, and the Senate majority leader, but pride of family did not demand of her this time to bring the children. Her favorite of Kennedy's brothers, Robert, who in happier times had shielded her from the ebullience of the family, stood back in the shadows of the statues of other assassinated presidents, Lincoln and Garfield. The slow moving column of mourners came to a halt. When this last personal communion was over, she arose, still poised, and looked wonderingly into the eyes, some blinded with tears and others merely curious, of those waiting people. Then slowly and as a president's wife she walked down the steps with her brother-in-law.

In the cold night air she at first dismissed her car and began to walk down Pennsylvania Avenue, along which less than three years previously she had ridden in triumph with her husband after the inauguration. Perhaps too many memories came crowding, perhaps the uselessness of this last visit became apparent; silently the black car came up again, surrounded by watchful Secret Service agents, and she was gone. When dawn came up over the Potomac, thousands were still waiting outside the Capitol to pay their last respects. They had begun to move through the Rotunda at about six thousand an hour, but the line still lengthened. It stretched for more than a mile at one time, and the pace was quickened. At nine o'clock—perhaps soon after the dead president's son, John, had awakened for his third birthday—the great gates of the Capitol were closed. There were protests and scuffling, but the police soon put an end to the unseemliness.

The last sad ceremonial began soon after ten on a still cold but brilliantly sunny morning. Inside the gleaming Capitol the Senate had briefly met to pass a resolution of sympathy for Mrs. Kennedy. Outside, the reds and blues and blacks of the cortege arranged themselves on the broad plaza. Soon afterward Mrs. Kennedy emerged from the White House accompanied by her brothers-in-law and sisters-in-law, her nephews and nieces. The seven black cars made their way through silent crowds to the Capitol, and minutes later Mrs. Kennedy, lightly veiled, walked slowly up the huge white steps into the Rotunda again. There she briefly knelt, before the bronze casket was carried out into the sunshine. Then out again to watch it, draped in the Stars and Stripes, on the shoulders of men of the armed services. Arms were presented and "Hail to the Chief" was played by the Marine Band as the coffin came into view, and to solemn music it was borne slowly down the steps to the caisson. There was a brief pause while the procession formed, and then with muffled drums the lumbering caisson jolted forward and began to move slowly down the street, casting a long shadow.

It was a martial and dignified scene, yet somehow with none of the arrogance of militarism. In the lead, the Marine Band stepped out bravely. The national flag fluttered slightly ahead of the caisson, the presidential flag behind with a prancing horse, saddled but riderless and with reversed boots in the stirrups. Then to the White House, where the concourse of famous men was waiting. Mrs. Kennedy dismounted from her car and on foot, behind the caisson, led them to St. Matthew's Cathedral for the Low Mass. They were the most distinguished company of dignitaries ever assembled in the 187 years of the Republic; Johnson was lost in the crush.

After the service, Cardinal Cushing of Boston in his brilliant robes led the procession from the church. As the band played "Holy God, We Praise Thy Name" little John, in a sky-blue coat to match his sister's, stepped forward for a moment and put his hand to his forelock as if in salute. And so the slow procession moved away on the long drive to a grassy slope below the old Custis-Lee Mansion in Arlington National Cemetery. From there the grave of President Kennedy would look down, for as long as this Republic could expect, across the Potomac River to the Lincoln Memorial and the city he completely dominated for so few years.

It was the last formal act of the tragedy that began in Dallas, Texas, three days before, and after the prayers of the burial service there was nothing left to be said. The other branches of American government, Congress and the judiciary, had delivered their eulogies, and it was the turn of the armed services to provide military honors. The American forces are no less jealous of their prerogatives than others, but they were generous to the last and gave the main military exercise to a troop of Irish Army cadets to perform. Their presence with the Black Watch pipers from Britain, at the special request of Mrs. Kennedy, was perhaps recognition not only of Mr. Kennedy's origins but also of the first origins of this country.

The Arlington National Cemetery is part of a tract of six thousand acres granted in 1669 to one Robert Howson, who sold it for six hogsheads of tobacco. In the mansion above the president's grave, built by the adopted son of George Washington, General Robert E. Lee resigned from the Union Army to command the Confederate forces in the War Between the States. In a way, the history of much of the world as well as the United States was there on that day. The Emperor of Ethiopia, who had appealed in vain to the old League of Nations and was now secure in a world system that, in the final test, depended upon this Republic; the President of West Germany and a prince from Japan, whose countries enjoyed a renascence because of the generosity of this Republic; and the Duke of Edinburgh and the Prime Minister of Britain, President de Gaulle, the King of the Belgians, the Dutch Consort, and others representing the most powerful alliance for peace in the history of mankind because of the leadership provided by this Republic.

The awful power that made all this possible was not much in evidence. Fifty fighter aircraft, representing the components of this Union, roared overhead. They were followed by Air Force One, the president's personal aircraft, which had taken him to Vienna for that fateful meeting with Khrushchev, to London,

7

Paris, Berlin, and Rome in pursuit of interdependence, and finally to Dallas and back again. But on the ground, among the oaks and dogwoods, in the hard cold light of a North American autumn, only the bright-colored cloth of ceremonial was to be seen; the Marine Band in the once-hated red coats, the army special forces in green commando berets, the blues of the navy, air force, and coast guard. As the caisson came slowly up the hill with the men of religion, or rather of the many religions that had found freedom in this land, the air force bagpipe band played a lament—a Negro, wearing the kilt, at the big drum.

Members of Congress and their wives stood in a half circle below the grave, and protocol broke down when the foreign dignitaries arrived en masse. The pomp and circumstance of most of the world was caught in an egalitarian crush, and the more determined came to the fore, among them, inevitable perhaps, President de Gaulle and Mr. Mikoyan. The widow, supported by the Kennedy family, among them the late president's mother, took up a position at the right of the grave with the White House staff and the press in the rear. Cardinal Cushing, his gaunt voice again a surprise as it issued from his medieval face, said the burial service, and Mrs. Kennedy and the two Kennedy brothers lit what was to become the eternal flame. Taps sounded, and the final formality was over.

That night, the remains of President Kennedy were lowered into the grave. An appropriate memorial would later be raised, but it would not be the memorial that Kennedy would have wanted. He had wanted to be a great president whose name would rank with Washington and Lincoln, and much endeavor had been cut short by the assassin. But if his work was to be completed by his successors, especially the search for peace at home and abroad, he would be given his rightful place in American history. Then this grave, in view of the memorials to the great presidents, would be splendidly appropriate for the time being; he was among a brave company.

I wrote as much on November 25, numb from the cemetery cold and drained of all emotion. I recall it here to suggest how the grief and pride of those three days became a collective

8

national experience, shared also by foreigners, surely unprecedented anywhere in the world and at any time in history. Again unprecedented, the new president was more often than not excluded. In monarchies, heralds announce, "The king is dead, long live the king." Continuity not only exists but is seen to exist. Ancient ceremony elevates the crown prince immediately to the throne, often months before the formal coronation. At the funeral he takes precedence even before the widowed queen. Her personal grief is respected but is not allowed to draw public attention from the king who now reigns.

Such ceremony does not exist in the United States. There are no heralds extraordinary. The Constitution only requires that the successor president takes the oath or affirmation of office. It does not designate where the ceremony should take place or who should be the administering officer. Johnson had taken the oath in a cabin of Air Force One parked off the runway of Love Field in Dallas. He was the lawful successor, but the circumstances of Kennedy's death and the three days of televised sorrow and ceremony combined to deny him immediate recognition. They did more. During those days the Kennedy legend was wrought before the television cameras and firmly established by them. The legend was to become a great political property that gave Robert Kennedy's presidential ambitions an assumed legitimacy of succession. It is not too fanciful to suggest that on that grassy slope in Arlington National Cemetery began a chain of events that led inexorably to the bitter rivalry between Johnson and Kennedy, to Johnson's decision not to run for office again in 1968, and to the second Kennedy death.

That was Johnson's initiation to the presidency, unnoticed and alone, and five years later he retired from office again with no hail and farewell. The nation seemed only too glad to get rid of him, to see him return to Texas, where the assassin's bullets had literally shot him into the White House. What happened in between is the subject of this book, but looking back on those tragic three days one can perhaps see a few of the beginnings of his eventual departure, again unnoticed and alone except for a few faithful friends.

I am not suggesting that the funeral ceremonies of John F. Kennedy were somehow contrived for maximum political profit. Nothing could be more ridiculous. For Americans, lacking the continuity the crown has given to Britain, the death of a president has always been a very disturbing experience. The continuity of presidential rule is assured by the vice-president, and behind him stand in the prescribed order of precedence an adequate number of surrogates from the Congress and the cabinet. But the uncertainty of death is infinitely greater than in monarchies such as Britain, where all power is vested in Parliament and where the prime minister and not the king rules. Moreover, the relationship between the president and people can be direct and personal. The sorrow at his passing is thus all the deeper. It was always so, not only for Lincoln, but also for Garfield and McKinley, the other murdered presidents, and others such as Franklin D. Roosevelt. Even the death of Harding, natural if sudden, in the Palace Hotel in San Francisco, was the occasion of national grief. Millions watched the train that carried his body back to Washington and then to its final resting place in Marion, Ohio.

The journey to Washington took four days, and the train stopped at a hundred towns and railroad crossings. Flowers were strewn on the tracks, and impromptu choirs sang "Lead, Kindly Light." Work stopped. In lonely places on the plains farmers lighted the track with the headlights of their cars, and conclaves of the Ku Klux Klan held midnight services under flaming crosses. More than 300,000 lined the track in Chicago. Harding's body also lay in state in the East Room of the White House and in the Rotunda of the Capitol. During the short drive up Pennsylvania Avenue, the caisson stopped while children sang "Nearer, My God, to Thee." There were eulogies, and at noon, with the sounding of taps on the Capitol steps, the entire country maintained a great silence.

The scandals of the Harding administration were not then widely known, and Kennedy was certainly the better man. He was not the great president claimed by his many friends. His administration had been too short. For all his surface *élan*, he was a cautious man, very much aware of his tiny popular majority in the election. He made many mistakes, beginning with the Cuban invasion and his unprepared meeting with Khrushchev in Vienna. He had gone apparently expecting to persuade the leader of the other superpower to exercise restraint in Berlin and elsewhere until he had settled in office. Khrushchev mistook this for weakness, and the suggestion was brutally swept aside. It was to prove a bad mistake, but determined to reassert his presidential authority, perhaps even his manhood, Kennedy took the fatal step of involving American troops in the Vietnam war as advisers. He overreacted to the Soviet threat to Berlin by calling up army reserves. He was responsible for one of the biggest steps forward in the arms race when he ordered hundreds of Minuteman missiles and a fleet of Polaris submarines. Yet the old caution was evident in his reluctance to introduce civil rights legislation.

There was, of course, another side to the man. His inauguration after the stodgy Eisenhower years was like a breath of fresh air. The dangerous implications of his inaugural speech were not immediately evident, and the rhetoric stirred many young souls. He had served with distinction in the Second World War and as president had come to represent the generation which had provided the junior officers for that war. This was the generation moving into positions of power and influence in appointed politics, the mass media, the foundations and the centers of special learning at the great universities. There was no generation gap, except perhaps with the elderly. His generation was vigorous, in tune with the times, and eager to improve them, and as president he was their most distinguished representative. More than that, he was seen as the instrument of change. There were the mistakes and the prevarications, but he understood much of what was required. He was a great educative force, and his speech at the American University in Washington, D.C., led eventually to the signing of the partial nuclear test-ban treaty, the first step toward disarmament.

Looking back on those thousand days many remember them as a golden age, and in some ways they were. They seemed to

No Hail, No Farewell

hold the promise of a bright future, but subsequent events suggested to me that they were in fact the end of an age. The English look back to the first decade of the century, to before the First World War, when everything seemed possible. In poetry, if not in chronology, Rupert Brooke's "Grantchester" was perhaps the prologue. Wilfred Owen's "Anthem for the Dead" was certainly its harsh epilogue or requiem. History is said not to repeat itself. Certainly a direct transatlantic comparison cannot be made because the unseen changes in the United States at that time were far more fundamental. The age of American innocence was passing as thousands of young people were lining up to serve in the Peace Corps. Even as the 1964 Civil Rights Act was passed, and many more well-intentioned youngsters were flocking southward to help in the rehabilitation of the Negro, the black activists were moving from integration to separatism. On many campuses, white militants were beginning to question the very moral and constitutional foundations of American society. The politics that had created the Republic and sustained it for more than 180 years were being rejected along with institutionalized religion and accepted morality. Within a few years the Peace Corps was to be dismissed as square, and the nation's cities would be in flames and its campuses in ferment.

Kennedy, had he lived, perhaps could have led the country through these convulsions to a new and better order, as some people claim that the 1954 school desegregation order of the Supreme Court would have been more successful if Eisenhower had given leadership. If this is correct, Kennedy's death was a greater tragedy than the cruel snuffing out of a vigorous life. Robert Kennedy's conviction that there was a torch to pick up and that only he could carry it would have to be taken more seriously. Being a European I am not so sure that man can be master of his own fate to that degree, especially in a pluralistic society such as the United States. If John Kennedy was admired and trusted by many, he was also disliked by a large suspicious minority. His kind of politics and appeal could be divisive. But if no more than a good man died in Dallas, the belief that

12

Kennedy was, or could have been, a great president sustained the legend wrought before the television cameras during that weekend.

The grave became a place of pilgrimage, visited every year by tens of thousands of the curious and those who could not forget, or refused to forget, the promise of his thousand days. One could not avoid the impression that the thirty-fifth president was well on his way to deification. There was a lot of morbid nonsense in this, especially in the talk of a vanished Camelot. Kennedy, with his wry and somewhat self-deprecating humor, could not easily have seen himself in such a state or place, but the legend grew. The intensity of emotion could not, of course, be sustained, but before Robert Kennedy declared his candidacy for the Democratic presidential nomination the phenomenon had become a potent political force that did much to undermine the Johnson administration. For that reason the explanations are worth examining. They varied. There were suggestions of national atonement, but for what? For giving birth to Lee Harvey Oswald, the assumed assassin, or to John Wilkes Booth, and other forgotten presidential assassins such as Charles Guiteau? It seems unlikely, but there is no place for historical analysis when a people, or some of its youth, wants a genuine folk hero. There was place perhaps for resentment against the fates but not over what was largely accepted as his martyrdom. Again it would be useless to ask what he was martyred for. Resentment continued to smolder, however, and must be assumed to explain, at least in part, the widespread rejection of the findings of the Warren Commission's report on the assassination.

The commission and the report were to have served the continuity of presidential rule and the rule of decency as well as investigate and explain all the facts beyond reasonable doubt, but it appeared to have done none of these things. The question marks had not been dimmed by sorrowful oblivion but loomed larger with the suggestions of conspiracy and official silence. It was arguable that the commission failed to answer all the questions, or was too aware of the other causes it served, but the

13

alternatives were too horrifying to contemplate. To accept some of the theories would be to believe that somehow the chief justice of the United States, the FBI, the Secret Service, leading members of Congress, and Johnson had entered into a monstrous plot to keep the truth from the public.

The fact that Johnson was from Texas kept some suspicions alive. There was even a play written, in which a thinly disguised Johnson played Macbeth to Robert Kennedy's Hamlet. This was part of another phenomenon which suggested that the assassination in Dallas could only be atoned by electing another Kennedy to the presidency. I am sure that it was not engineered, but it sustained the Kennedy legend, and of course there was the constant talk by Kennedy supporters of a restoration and a return to Camelot. With the falling apart of the old order, the legend became a political property beyond compare. If this now sounds unseemly after the second Kennedy death it was clear that Robert both believed and used the legend. In keeping the flame alive, he never lost his sense of proprietorship over it. It was his, and only his, to use. The assumption was that it would eventually carry him into the White House. Instead, it led to another assassin's bullet fired by yet another alienated man like Lee Harvey Oswald in another rootless, unstable city like Dallas.

Johnson could not have known in 1963 what was to come to pass in 1968, but he must have had some intimation of this threat to his authority. Certainly he was soon to show his profound distrust and dislike of Robert Kennedy. This antipathy went back to 1960. As Theodore White was to write in *The Making of the President* (1964), "There is only one bitter, inescapable appreciation of American politics which the two men —Kennedy and Johnson—share: the knowledge that Lyndon Johnson was never able before 1964 to become President on his own ... the Kennedys opened power to him." They did indeed, although it could be fairly argued that they did no more than reciprocate. John Kennedy probably could not have been elected in 1960 without Johnson on the ticket. Each owed the other a great deal.

Johnson's decision surprised a good many people, but there were good reasons why he settled for the second place on the ticket after being denied the presidential nomination. His short campaign had demonstrated that national politics was very different from congressional politics and that as a southerner he had less chance than a Catholic of being elected president. He had little to lose. With a fellow Democrat in the White House, the Senate leadership could not be the powerful post it had been for him under Eisenhower. There were other factors that swayed his southern advisers. They did not like a Catholic heading the ticket but hated the Republican candidate more. This was especially true of the late Sam Rayburn, the Speaker who had ruled in the House of Representatives as Johnson had ruled the Senate. They had together decided the fate of countless bills over whisky glasses. If for Rayburn the willing exchange of such power for the oblivion of the vice-presidency at first seemed a foolish or willful thing even to contemplate, he did not like Richard Nixon. His ferocity as hatchet man for Eisenhower in the 1952 and 1956 campaigns had left deep scars.

There was opposition within the party. The liberals were appalled, although their candidates for the vice-presidential nomination would not have added much to the ticket. To some of the Kennedy men, especially the Irish Mafia with their strong connections with northern machine bosses, southerners were almost anathema. They were not to be considered beyond delivering the not-so-solid southern vote. More telling later, Robert Kennedy was incensed. The fight for the nomination had been rough, and somebody in the Johnson camp had spread the rumor that his elder brother was suffering from Addison's disease. Whether he was or not, and it is still debatable, the rumor was a nasty one. There was no evidence that Johnson was responsible, but the younger brother never forgot. There was another unfortunate incident. After approaching Johnson, John Kennedy had doubts, largely because of what appeared to be an incipient liberal revolt. His brother was sent to sound him out again, but before they met John Kennedy again changed his mind and telephoned Johnson to reaffirm his place on the ticket.

What happened when the younger brother eventually met Johnson in his hotel suite is not fully known, but Johnson was apparently convinced that Robert Kennedy tried to get rid of him despite his brother's intentions.

Johnson must have been reminded of much of this on the flight back from Dallas when the Kennedy men seemed to turn their anger against him. The next day in Washington, one of them even canvassed the idea of denying him the presidential nomination at the 1964 Democratic national convention. Such behavior seems inexplicable. They were in a state of shock, but no more than Johnson. He had been catapulted suddenly and cruelly from obscurity—and few public offices can be more obscure than the vice-presidency—into one of the world's most exposed and demanding positions. At a time when the circumstances of Kennedy's death were still unclear, when the first national requirement was national unity, few appeared to be less aware of what was at stake than the former presidential assistant who immediately explored the possibility of a ticket for 1964 headed by Robert Kennedy and Senator Hubert Humphrey. He and his like should have known how desperately Johnson needed their help. The presidency is a very personal office, and when a new man enters 1600 Pennsylvania Avenue for the first time he finds only the cops and cooks and an executive clerk. Even the files have been emptied because presidential papers are personal property and not state papers. Within an hour after the news of Kennedy's assassination had reached Washington, McGeorge Bundy, the special assistant for national security affairs, had ordered all files closed. During that long weekend, Johnson had remained in the vice-presidential suite in the Executive Building while the presidential office was stripped, and with the removal of each filing cabinet he needed all the help that could be given.

Before his first presidential day was out Theodore Sorensen, another senior member of Kennedy's staff, tendered his resignation. He was supposed to have said that he had invested over ten years in Kennedy's career, and now the investment was gone—gone as surely as though he himself had been the victim in Dallas. The investment in fact paid off, in book royalties and a law partnership, but when his country needed him most he was reluctant to help a man he disliked. Fortunately there were other Kennedy men who instinctively knew what was required. The press secretary, Pierre Salinger, knew, and with swollen eyes went on helping reporters with ruthless energy. McGeorge Bundy knew. Thank heavens, because he also intimately knew the vast networks of alliances and overseas commitments, communications and control centers, the intercontinental ballistic missiles in their underground silos and the procedures required to fire them. More than the secretary of state and the secretary of defense, he was equipped to advise the new president in the event of an emergency. Even the Russians knew, and sent to the FBI all the information they had of Lee Harvey Oswald's stay in the Soviet Union.

Johnson knew, and refused all the resignations until he had settled in his new office. He also knew that no other men, not even old friends accustomed to treading the corridors of power such as Abe Fortas and Clark Clifford, could give him the necessary support. No others had sat with Kennedy at the center of the web of command and decision and could give substance to the contrived reality of continuity. There were a few apologies from some of the Kennedy men afterward. Their first instinctive reactions, selfish and unheeding, perhaps reflected the harsh reality of American politics and power, but they also indicated the greater challenge to Johnson. These men had held immense power and influence only at the pleasure of Kennedy. The shots at Dallas had brought all this and the reflected glory to an end. Johnson was eager for their help, but they were Kennedy people, men who had hitched their wagons to the family star, and there were two other brothers. Their instinctive reactions revealed the enormous strength of the Kennedy family, American political princes, who, as the great territorial magnates in medieval times could rival and threaten the king, were to challenge Johnson.

The real hero of that weekend was Johnson. Unnoticed, even ignored, he instinctively knew that the American people would have to be rallied when the shock of the assassination wore off.

He knew that his first duty was to achieve national unity and demonstrate the continuity of presidential rule. At first sight, he was not the ideal choice for this central role in a great national drama. It was not only his vanity, deviousness, and secretiveness, which were well known to anybody connected with Congress. As James MacGregor Burns was later to remark, "All strong presidents have such qualities. Roosevelt was vain, devious, thin-skinned and had a passion for secrecy. These are all the standard weaknesses of great leaders. All great leaders are vain. The faults are part of the price of being a successful politician. A president is vain by definition. You just don't get to be president by being a wallflower. Any great leader is a built-in showoff."

I am not so sure, but Roosevelt was also a patrician and the record suggests that, given a choice, the plebeians of modern America prefer a man who can bring dignity to the presidency. Roosevelt, Eisenhower, and Kennedy fitted this role. Truman, who also succeeded to the office from the vice-presidency, did not, but his mixture of pluck and humility had its own appeal. Johnson was a down-to-earth man, who was known at times to be coarse in his habits and speech. Afterward, when the tide of opinion was flowing strongly against him, many remembered how he bared his stomach in public to show the scars of his gall bladder operation. His friends said that the criticism was unfair. They recalled that a woman reporter had asked him what the presidency had done to him, and said that he only wanted to show that he had been scarred in more ways than one. Perhaps, but baring his midriff even to a tough Texan woman was an unseemly and coarse act. Roosevelt would never have displayed his leg braces, or Kennedy his back support.

He was a Texan, and the Lone Star state was not the most popular in the Union, even before Dallas. Reports of the vulgarities of its *nouveaux riches* may have been exaggerated, but they were widespread. Its politics were thought to be Byzantine, its right wing Neanderthal. The Texan congressional delegation was generally dedicated to the defense of the oil-depletion tax allowance, and some of its members were creatures of the oil and gas barons. After the Harding administration, Americans were also more alert to honesty in government, and the assumption was that Texans cut corners in their pursuit of a fast buck. Johnson's personal fortune raised many eyebrows. He had entered Congress with no money and the dowry his wife brought him was insignificant even in those Depression days. By 1960, he was a millionaire many times over, and the source of this sudden wealth was said to be his influence with the Federal Communications Commission, which allowed him to operate a television station in Austin, Texas, under the most favorable conditions. He consorted with men such as the late Senator Kerr of Oklahoma, who placed the accumulation of great wealth before his senatorial duties. In his five-gallon hat, Johnson was regarded, I think quite unfairly, as a typical product of Texas, at least of the Texas of popular imagination. If he was typical, Texas was a great deal better than the political and social caricatures, but the assumptions told against the man and the state.

The curse of the South was also still upon him, the curse that since the Civil War had denied the presidency to its political sons. The South has produced some superb senators and congressmen for good and bad reasons. If they represented states and districts that were rotten boroughs, the safe tenure these guaranteed ensured long periods of service and immense experience often denied to northerners. Many southern states are poor, and politics attract intelligent men who elsewhere might have gone into industry. The aristocratic aura of the south is often spurious, but nevertheless it has produced men dedicated to the highest ideals of public service, except civil rights. Johnson was no aristocrat, spurious or otherwise, but unlike many of his kind he was no racist. Attachment to the remnants of that peculiar institution, if for no other reason than to ensure reelection, was one reason why the southern curse lingered on into the late twentieth century and why Johnson aroused further suspicions, but only a few months before Dallas he had delivered a civil rights speech which went far beyond the cautious position of the Kennedy administration. He was absolutely sincere.

19

Johnson was also a superb politician whose experience, in dealing with the executive as well as Congress, was probably unsurpassed. He was in and out of the White House during his years as Senate majority leader and certainly understood the intricacies of the federal system of government. He was well advised on the large issues. He counted some distinguished men among his friends, and if they were not much help in explaining the more intimate workings of presidential power, they nevertheless provided him with perspective and wise counsel. The obvious two, whose names I have already mentioned, were Fortas and Clifford. Fortas was a successful lawyer, and subsequently an associate justice of the Supreme Court, who without fee defended the helpless and in so doing helped to humanize the law. Clifford, who had served Truman and had helped to draft the Truman Doctrine, was another lawyer whose advice was sought by great corporations. I can remember having a drink with one of them two or three days after Dallas, and within one hour he was twice called to the telephone to advise the new President. Men, even Presidents, do not have such friends unless they themselves have some claim to distinction. One must assume that Johnson had gifts which they recognized, but Fortas and Clifford stayed in the background. The country was more aware of Johnson's staff assistants, and on the whole they did not look impressive. They enhanced the assumption that he was not much more than a regional politician most comfortable in the company of provincial hacks and sycophants. Again appearances were misleading. Men such as Bill Moyers and George Reedy were sterling characters, and of course the best of the Kennedy men had remained to serve their country.

One of them, John Kenneth Galbraith, afterward wrote that by a large margin Johnson was the most experienced figure in American political history. What follows was taken from a pamphlet written for the 1964 campaign, but allowing for the understandable hyperbole of such literature is not without truth.

During the Kennedy years he, of course, shared in the making of legislative strategy although the post of Vice-President affords little practical leverage on legislative matters. The real test came earlier. For eight years from the beginning of 1953 to the end of 1960 he was first Senate Democratic Minority Leader and then the most effective Majority Leader of modern times. From 1954 on, President Eisenhower no longer had a Republican majority in Congress. Historians will almost certainly agree that this was no misfortune, for instead he had Lyndon Johnson. The Senate worked well in these years and it worked because Johnson led . . . no other contender for the Presidency in our history has had such a comprehensive public career . . . it is surely apparent that Lyndon Johnson measures up for the post. Certainly no one measures up better in our time. Certainly few have measured up better in our history. . . .

The professor was to change his tune later, and in 1968 a petition for Johnson's impeachment was circulated when his leadership was seen to be too vigorous. The petition, the work of a body known as Citizens for Governmental Restraint, charged that he had usurped the constitutional powers of the Senate in foreign affairs, of the Congress in the power to declare and wage war, and of the People by insidiously eroding their civil rights. Nevertheless, in November 1963 it was leadership that was most required, as Johnson knew. He assumed the role as soon as Kennedy was buried. For instance, at the reception given for the foreign dignitaries who attended the funeral, he said that unity would be the password of his administration abroad. Later he told the assembled governors of the states that it would be continuity at home. "I think that continuity without confusion has got to be our password and has got to be the key of our system. I intend to tell Congress that we intend to honor the commitments we have made. . . ." He spoke, even then, of civil rights legislation, but Johnson's greatness was that he recognized in those dreadful, apprehensive days that only a display of presidential continuity could hold the nation together until national equilibrium returned.

He was then still living at his home in Spring Valley, where I happen to live, and the crying need for such words was apparent when he was escorted to and from his old vice-presidential office. The city was possessed by an apprehension bordering on fear. I can remember hearing the wail of many sirens the night he received the foreign mourners and governors, and going to a window with my children saw the presidential car speed by with a protective screen of Secret Service and police cars. The Secret Service agents stood up in an open car with pistols, rifles, and submachine guns leveled at the windows of my decorous middle-class street. I felt that they would have fired if one of my children had waved. For a brief moment I saw their anguished and blazing eyes, and then they and Johnson were gone up the hill like a colonial governor moving through a restless province.

He was in fact a new and untried President of the United States moving through a world made restless by grief and apprehension because much of it was now dependent upon him for their security. The rest—the Soviet Union, Eastern Europe, and the third world—was surely no less anxious. This Johnson also knew, and that day had sent a message to the members of the armed forces.

Our Constitution provides for the orderly continuity of the civil offices of our Government. In the transition brought upon us by tragedy, there is no interruption in the continuity of that commitment to strength, steadfastness, and selfless sacrifice which has kept us free and the world at peace. As you stand your guard of freedom and peace, you may know that the policies and purposes of your country are unchanged and unchangeable in seeking honorable peace, the friendship and alliance of free nations and the building of a responsible world. . . .

Two nights later, November 27, Johnson went to Congress to call for national unity and reiterate the promise of continuity in domestic and foreign policies. I can remember him walking through the chamber on the balls of his feet and with that High-Noon half smile on his long face. Later the recollection of his Texas accent was to offend or amuse many people, but not that night.

He told the joint session that the ideas and ideals which Kennedy had so nobly represented would be translated into effective action.

From his chamber of representative government, let all the world know and none misunderstand that I rededicate this government. . . . On the 20th day of January, in 1961, John F. Kennedy told his countrymen that our national work would not be finished "in the first thousand days, nor in the life of this administration, nor even perhaps in our lifetime on this planet. But," he said, "let us begin." Today in this moment of new resolve, I would say to all my fellow Americans, let us continue. This is our challenge—not to hesitate, not to pause, not to turn about and linger over this evil moment, but to continue on our course so that we may fulfill the destiny that history has set for us.

He spoke up courageously for civil rights, although the applause instantly became less enthusiastic.

We have talked long enough in this country about equal rights. We have talked for one hundred years or more. It is time now to write the next chapter, and to write it in books of law.

He spoke with equal sincerity on the need for understanding and mutual respect.

The time has come for Americans of all races and creeds and political beliefs to understand and respect one another. So let us put an end to the teaching and the preaching of hate and evil and violence. Let us turn away from the fanatics of the far left and the far right, from the apostles of bitterness and bigotry, from those defiant of law, and those who pour venom into our nation's bloodstream. . . .

The prepared text of his speech delivered, Johnson paused and then went on:

And on this Thanksgiving eve, as we gather together to ask the Lord's blessing, and give him our thanks, let us unite in those familiar and cherished words:

> "America, America,
> God shed His grace on thee,
> And crown thy good
> With brotherhood
> From sea to shining sea."

Again there were to be sneers afterward, but then I, a foreigner, could not but be deeply moved by his simple patriotism.

Such were the unifying effect of those familiar words and his sure belief in their promise. The next day, in a special Thanksgiving message, Johnson continued to call for unity and understanding. He said that in spite of their grief, Americans had much to be thankful for. Harvests were bountiful, factories productive, and defenses strong. There was peace, and the good will of the world was pouring in. "But more than these blessings, we know tonight that our system is strong—strong and secure. A deed that was meant to tear us apart has bound us together. Our system has passed—you have passed—a great test. You have shown what John F. Kennedy called upon us to show in his proclamation of this Thanksgiving: that decency of purpose, that steadfastness of resolve, and that strength of will which we inherit from our forefathers." He went on to recall that each of the five presidents he had served and known had found their greatest burden to be the unthinking hate and division of their countrymen. He asked Americans to think on these things. "God made all of us, not some of us, in His image. All of us, not just some of us, are His children."

Neither the speech to the joint session of Congress nor the Thanksgiving message will be compared with the Gettysburg Address, but they were entirely appropriate. The nation began to live again. In Washington, the cabinet agreed to stay on. Congress and the bureaucracy resumed work. The flags flew at half staff, but Johnson had successfully demonstrated the magnificent strength and continuity of the American political system. There were, of course, regrets for the dead president. I am not referring to the phenomenon already reported, but to personal judgment of journalists and those who spend most of their time in and about the White House. For all the alarums—the Cuban invasion, the resumption of nuclear testing in the atmosphere, and the missile crisis—the brief Kennedy years had been fun. There was substance to the legend. Kennedy had responded to ideas, and for all their solemn nonsense about objectivity most good reporters, and the White House attracts many, are first interested in ideas. Kennedy could request the *New York Times* to remove their correspondent from Saigon because his honest reporting raised doubts at home about the wisdom of American policy there. He could put others of us in the doghouse when we offended, but most of us were engaged. The assumption was that the Johnson years would be dull; efficient, no doubt, but dull. We were wrong in more ways than one.

For instance, there is a presidential tradition known as the First Hundred Days. This expectation of intense initial activity is in fact not old, at least not by American political standards. My reading of American history suggests that it began only with Franklin Roosevelt, who surely had cause for fast action, and was ignored by Truman and Eisenhower. Kennedy had his first hundred days, but not with entirely happy results. Johnson raised no such expectation, if only because, with Truman, he had succeeded to the presidency in unhappy circumstances. Nevertheless, his vigorous and successful leadership extended beyond pulling the country together, and far beyond the traditional hundred days. Later, in private conversation, he was to brush aside talk about a hundred days and honeymoon periods. As he saw it, after more than thirty years in Washington, a capable president had a nine-month period, nearly three hundred days, in which to get his legislative program enacted. His leadership and circumstances actually gave him at least five hundred days, to the end of the 88th Congress and well into the next, and he was active from the beginning.

There were the inevitable chores of a new president, such as addresses to departments and agencies of the executive branch; and unusual ones such as the appointment of the Warren Commission to investigate the assassination of Kennedy, and the presentation of an award to the Secret Service agent who might well have saved Johnson's life at Dallas. He spoke to the AFL-CIO executive council and the Business Council. He flew to New York to attend the funeral of Herbert Lehman. His first press conference was very informal, with coffee served in his office. He said that McNamara, the Defense Secretary, would go on to Vietnam after attending the ministerial meeting of the North Atlantic Council in Paris. He announced that congressional hearings on the civil rights and finance bills would begin in January, and that the West German chancellor and British prime minister would soon come to Washington. He was concerned about unemployment: it was much too high. He supposed that he had had about ten appointments a day since succeeding to office. He ran through the budget and in so doing displayed an insider's knowledge rare among presidents. He was obviously comfortable in the seat of power and enjoying it immensely.

In a message to the North Atlantic Council, Johnson promised to keep the equivalent of six American divisions in Europe as long as they were needed. The next day he addressed the General Assembly of the United Nations, promising the full power of the United States in the joint effort to eliminate war, disease, poverty, and illiteracy. He established the committee on the economic impact of defense and disarmament, announced his intention to reduce the number of military installations, and took the first steps to ensure that the closing of the Studebaker plant would not ruin the town of South Bend, Indiana. Down at the Texas ranch for Christmas, Johnson conferred with the secretary of state, the director of the Central Intelligence Agency, and members of the White House staff. So it went on, with a rush that seemed to carry all before it. Before he exchanged New Year's greetings with Khrushchev, he had settled into a routine, which ought to have been crushing for a man who had suffered a heavy heart attack, but which was maintained until the end.

Awakened at 6:30 with the newspapers and government papers, Johnson ate breakfast in bed and worked in his office for four hours. Then there was a swim, a light luncheon, and a nap, and back to the office until 8:00 P.M. and often after dinner. He quickly grew to enjoy the ceremony of the presidency and protested less about meeting visiting troops of boy scouts, women's organizations, and pulpits of Baptist ministers. The Tuesday luncheon with the secretaries of state and defense in the private dining room upstairs also quickly became an institution. Johnson's special assistant for national security affairs was always in attendance, and the luncheons for the most part replaced the formal meetings of the National Security Council. The arrangement was considered successful even by McGeorge Bundy, the special assistant, who was a perfectionist.

Johnson's early approach to foreign affairs was very tentative. He had had little prior interest, was uneasy in the presence of diplomats of the old school, and soon decided that he did not want to receive ambassadors frequently. But again before the New Year was out, Johnson also decided that he would be his own secretary of state. He admired Rusk as much as McNamara and once said that he wished he had McNamara's command of facts and Rusk's eloquence. He perhaps felt at home with Rusk because he had also been a poor southern boy, born on a dirt farm in Cherokee county, Georgia. The Secretary was then also very good with Congress, but Johnson was too positive a man to delegate authority, as Eisenhower had to Dulles. The first indications were that his approach to foreign affairs would be cautious. He said that the American people must be made to realize that there could be no victory or defeat in many conflicts and issues.

Nevertheless, in those early days most of his formidable talent and energy was devoted to domestic issues. His belief in a nine-month mandate exerted a powerful discipline. As he saw it, there was much to be done and only nine months in which to do it. Even then, he was putting the moral force of the presidency behind the civil rights bill. There were talks with labor, business, and religious groups, and the first thoughts were given to organizing and keeping united the great coalition that was to succeed in enacting the bill in 1964. The genesis of the antipoverty program was a long conversation at the LBJ ranch at Christmas with Theodore Sorensen, a holdover from Kennedy's staff, and Moyers. Johnson said that the program must be dramatized as Franklin Roosevelt dramatized the New Deal. He agreed with Sorensen that the State of the Union message provided the best platform, and presumably the decision was then made to deliver the message at night, when millions would be watching their television screens as other millions had listened to Roosevelt's fireside chats. The great problem was not to raise expectations too high, and Sorensen pointed to the danger of the programs' being dismissed as a gimmick in an election year. There was also too little time to work out an effective program before November 1964. Johnson teetered on the edge of decision, and then decided to go ahead.

Those few brief weeks between Kennedy's assassination and the end of the year were decisive for the United States. It survived the assassination with small internal damage mainly because of Johnson's leadership, but there were the beginnings of his rivalry with Robert Kennedy. Preparations were also made for the great legislative victories of the final session of the 88th Congress, but at the cost of paying too little attention to Vietnam. This lack of attention, first by Kennedy and then by Johnson, was responsible for what was to become the longest war in American history and the third costliest in lives lost. We have it from one of his biographers that Kennedy never really gave his full attention to Vietnam. In those early weeks, when it may have been still possible to avoid the commitment of American divisions, Johnson's full attention was devoted to civil rights and the antipoverty program. Perhaps it could not have been otherwise, especially in view of the optimism of McNamara, but the shots that killed Kennedy were to have consequences undreamed of by the miserable man who fired them.

1964

There were many changes in Washington after the New Year was celebrated, in spite of the call for continuity. Kennedy had frankly enjoyed the monarchical side of the presidency, and the dignity and trappings he had brought to the White House were quickly discarded by Johnson. There was no recital of eighteenth-century music under the chandeliers of the East Room when Ludwig Erhard paid a state visit. Instead, the West German chancellor was entertained at the ranch, and there was a barbecue and a rendering of "Deep in the Heart of Texas" in local German. Cousin Oreole and other kissing cousins, and not a busload of Nobel Prize winners, were on hand. Johnson talked with Sir Alec Douglas-Home, the British Prime Minister, of his Hereford cattle, which he preferred to the Scotsman's Ayrshires, and afterward danced with almost every woman in the room. It was like a Saturday night hop in a small town, but with little bars set up in the corners of the room to dispense Cutty Sark and Jack Daniel's. The heat was terrific, and a sweating Johnson abandoned his partner without apology to open a window.

Other changes were more obvious to the man in the street. After dark the great dome of the Capitol was bathed in brilliant light while the White House stood in the shadows, as if not to draw attention to itself. The more malicious said that power other than electricity had been switched to Congress, or that this was the first administration to make a virtue out of working in the dark. The facts were that Congress had just happened to extend the period of floodlighting of the Capitol, and Johnson had switched off unwanted lights to dramatize the need for government economy. Frugal by upbringing, he knew the value of example and publicity. There was also a better relationship between the executive and legislative branches.

This improved relationship was Johnson's most notable achievement after establishing the continuity of the presidency. Nineteen sixty-three had been a bad year on the Hill, although the 88th Congress had convened with more than the customary flurry of hopeful expectation. The Democrats had avoided the usual losses of a majority party in a midterm election. The Republicans had only gained two seats in the House of Representatives and had actually lost three in the Senate. Kennedy had gained both credit and confidence for his handling of the Cuban missile crisis in 1962, and the thaw in the cold war had continued. The limited nuclear test-ban treaty had been negotiated and ratified, and the hot line installed between Washington and Moscow. Kennedy and the Democratic leadership had looked forward to a solid year of legislative achievement, but as hopeful expectations go these went quickly. The most intense Negro drive for civil rights since the Civil War became the dominant domestic issue, and not the tax cut Kennedy had wanted to stimulate economic growth. The old coalition of southern Democrats and Republican conservatives rushed to defend their prejudices, and apart from the race issue one would have thought that they loved high taxes. The first session was long and frustrating, longer than any since 1950, when the Korean War began. Action had not been completed on the civil rights bill or the tax cut when Kennedy died.

Much of this immediately changed under Johnson, and although it was an election year the final session of the 88th

Congress established an impressive record. The most important piece of legislation was the Civil Rights Act, the like of which had not been enacted since Reconstruction. The rights it asserted for Negroes and other oppressed minorities had, of course, long been enshrined in the Constitution. The Thirteenth, Fourteenth, and Fifteenth Amendments, all ratified after the Civil War, ought to have been sufficient. They were not, alas, and the 1964 act was in fact an enabling law for the federal government to enforce these and other existing rights. There were eleven titles. They were concerned with voting rights, access to public accommodations and facilities, school desegregation, and equal employment opportunity. There was provision for legal enforcement. The life of the Civil Rights Commission was extended and its powers increased. The Community Relations Service was established to help resolve civil rights problems. The government was also empowered to deny funds to jurisdictions participating in federally assisted programs which were found guilty of discrimination.

The 1957 act, the first civil rights law in more than eighty years, had authorized the U.S. attorney general to seek court injunctions against those obstructing or depriving citizens of the right to vote. The 1960 act was designed to help Negroes and other minorities to vote, and also provided penalties for violence and mob action intended to obstruct court orders. They were useful but inadequate, and in spite of campaign promises Kennedy announced in 1961 that he would not seek stronger legislation. He said that there were sufficient laws on the books, which was demonstrably untrue. It was a political decision, reached because Kennedy did not want to endanger his welfare program by risking the anger of southern Democrats. There was also the argument that much could be achieved by executive action, an argument that proved to be too optimistic.

In any case, the Negroes were aroused and rallied behind leaders such as the late Dr. Martin Luther King, Jr. There were the freedom rides, sit-ins, and other nonviolent demonstrations. There was also the violence of white mobs and the brutality of southern policemen. Much of this was seen on millions of television screens, and a consensus supporting reform began to form. In June 1963 Kennedy submitted a broader bill, and through the summer civil rights supporters of both parties in the House managed to establish sufficient bipartisan support. The bill was reported out of the Judiciary Committee on November 20, but had not been cleared by the Rules Committee for floor action when Kennedy was killed.

A few days after the assassination, Johnson said that nothing could more eloquently honor Kennedy's memory than the earliest possible passage of the bill. He again pressed for action in his 1964 State of the Union message, and soon afterward the bill was sent to the floor of the House under an open rule. After ten hours of debate, the bill was to be read, title by title, for further debate and amendments. The bipartisan coalition was led by Emanuel Celler, the chairman of the Judiciary Committee. The strategy was devised by the White House, the Justice Department, the Democratic Study Group, interested Republicans, the major Negro organizations, and religious and labor groups. More than 120 amendments were offered by the southerners, but few were accepted, and on February 10 the bill was passed by a vote of 290 to 130.

The battle in the Senate was much harder. The conservative Judiciary Committee was bypassed by taking up the House bill, but filibusters against far-reaching civil rights legislation had always been effective in the past. Hubert Humphrey was chosen by Johnson to manage the bill, and he kept in close touch with religious groups and wooed the minority leader, Everett Dirksen. The senior Republican senator from Illinois was at first opposed to a strong bill, but without his help Republicans from the small western states traditionally opposed to cloture would not have been won over. The required two-thirds majority would have been impossible.

Humphrey's organization was reminiscent of a drive for the presidential nomination at a national convention, complete with floor captains in charge of the various titles. Their staffs met every evening, and each morning they met again with men from the Justice Department. There were also regular meetings with the religious and Negro groups who maintained a constant and effective lobby in and out of Congress. There was the occasional slip-up, but a quorum was nearly always available. The filibuster went on for three months but with not too much acrimony or too many late sittings. Humphrey was determined to avoid trouble, and southern motives were never questioned. He was solicitous to Dirksen, who began to enjoy his new role of being a civil rights hero. Two months after the filibuster had begun, Dirksen told reporters: "Civil rights is an idea whose time has come. Let editors rave at will and let states fulminate at will, but the time has come and it can't be stopped." There was some restlessness among his more conservative friends, but the inevitable amendments had been worked out by Humphrey and Dirksen, in Dirksen's office, and the minority leader was more than content to be the hero. The vote was taken for cloture on June 10, and the filibuster was defeated by a vote of 71 to 29.

Before the vote was taken, Richard Russell of Georgia, the southern captain, said that the bill would grant unbridled power to appointed officers of the government. It went to the very heart of the constitutional system, and the arguments for it were communistic. Dirksen this time quoted Victor Hugo's line in full: "Stronger than all the armies is an idea whose time has come." Humphrey said that the Constitution of this country was on trial. The question was whether there would be two kinds of citizenship or one. This rhetoric did not, of course, sway the debate and bring to an end what William Proxmire of Wisconsin described as the granddaddy of all filibusters. (He claimed too much, in fact. The filibuster against the 1846 Oregon bill went on for two months and a 1922 ship subsidy bill for seventy-five days, but the fifty-seven days of the 1964 debate were long enough.) But the time had come for action, and Russell made the fundamental error of pursuing a strategy of all or nothing. He might well have offered a compromise and weakened the bill before Dirksen's conversion. Humphrey had also been trained by Johnson almost since they were elected to the Senate together in 1948. Johnson had then explained to him that the way to get on in the Senate was to go along: to know its members, and not attack them, to know their strengths and weaknesses. As a liberal leader, Humphrey was to become indispensable to Johnson, and that summer, directing the fighting from his office like an intellectual French general above the battle, he earned the right to run in the fall as vice-presidential candidate.

Above all, the credit must go to Johnson. He did not appear to play much of a part. There were the weekly meetings with congressional leaders and the occasional exhortation, but he avoided a public display of power. This was necessary because of his old faith in consensus politics. He also needed southern votes for other bills, but behind the scenes he pulled strings and marshaled forces as he had done as senate majority leader. Then he had probably been the most effective majority leader in its long history. The knowledgeable have agreed that only two of his predecessors had comparable authority. Nelson Aldrich, an imperious Republican patrician from Rhode Island, had had great power because then he alone appointed members to standing committees. Joseph Robinson, an Arkansas Democrat, had exercised the personal authority that can crown long service. Johnson had had neither, but his hunger for power and his immense knowledge of the strengths and weaknesses of his colleagues were an unbeatable combination. Now the quarterback had become the coach. More than that, as president he could command forces off the field, and there can be no doubt that it was he who held the vast national coalition together.

The Civil Rights Act and the $11.5 billion tax-reduction measure were the highlights of what was to have been Kennedy's legislative program, but Johnson put his own L.B.J. brand on them. For instance, the Civil Rights Act was much stronger than its original draft, and other bills were not badly mauled. He also made a start on his own program, beginning with the Economic Opportunity Act. It was the first blow struck in the war against poverty and authorized ten programs under the supervision of an Office of Economic Opportunity, which became part of the White House Office. Among them were the Job Corps, the "domestic peace corps" (VISTA—Volunteers in Service to America), and the community action program. Much of this was to be criticized later, as will be seen, but these were some new departures of considerable promise.

In his usual expansive way, Johnson said, "This has been a year without precedent in the history of relations between the executive and legislative branches of our government. This session of Congress has enacted more major legislation, met more national needs, disposed of more national issues than any other session of this century or the last." He stopped just short of comparing it favorably with the Continental Congress. It was also the year when the New Frontier gave way to the Great Society. The Johnson slogan was first heard in May at the University of Michigan when Johnson said, "In your time we have the opportunity to move not only towards the rich society and the powerful society, but upwards to the Great Society. The Great Society rests on abundance and liberty for all. It demands an end to poverty and racial injustice, to which we are totally committed in our time." It also depended upon peace, and as Johnson spoke his advisers in Washington knew that the war in Vietnam was going badly, that nothing could stop the North from overrunning the South except the intervention of American troops.

In spite of this thunder from across the Bay of Tonkin (there was also trouble in Laos) Johnson was flushed with success and fully confident of his strength. There was general recognition that a strong president was in the White House and was firmly in control of the situation. His popularity ratings were impressively high, higher than Kennedy's at a comparable period, and he managed to engender a sense of national unity and confidence the like of which few could remember. Much was due to the belief that he was a president who got things done, a splendid American accolade. Apart from the legislative record, he had settled a railroad dispute under terms that were to last for many years. He had persuaded the Russians to reduce production of fissionable material for nuclear weapons. There was also some hoopla, which many people found amusing, and which at least suggested a return to a recognizable America. Cowboys once again came riding up Pennsylvania Avenue. In the rose garden of the White House, they shouted the ridiculous noises expected of their trade by a television generation brought up on late cowboy movie shows. The cabinet again attended ball games as well as Shakespearean plays. Kennedy and the shame of his assassination seemed forgotten except by the faithful.

If the White House still looked gloomy after nightfall (LBJ now stood for Light Bulb Johnson) the days were brightened by Johnson's energy and informality. Some people were worried by memories of his heart attack and the lack of a vice-president, but Johnson's frequent appearances at the gates of the White House to shake hands with tourists delighted many. His movements about town were unpredictable. He dropped in unannounced for lunch at the home of one woman reporter, and often went to the Hill. "Where are we going?" shouted one police motorcyclist as the presidential car roared through the White House gates one night in late April. "Where, indeed," muttered a photographer who earlier that month had pursued the president over the plains of Texas at an estimated speed of ninety miles an hour. One day he was off to Chicago, the next he visited five depressed towns in Appalachia, and that week went twice to New York. Fatigue became a serious professional hazard for the White House press. It was not only the sudden dashes across the United States, but also the constant appearances of Johnson from his office or the Cabinet Room to commune or joke with them.

In comparison, the Kennedy administration began to look very staid. Then press conferences had been very formal affairs held in the State Department auditorium and announced well in advance. Kennedy would spend most of the day with his staff preparing for them. In between, Pierre Salinger, the press secretary, would put a "lid" on news so that reporters could get their lunch or see their families. In those early Johnson months press conferences were held almost at any time and anywhere, from a haystack to the presidential office with coffee or beer served. Few reporters dared leave the West Lobby, where, between brief periods of intense activity, they slumped in leather club chairs until the last dim light was switched off and they could stumble home to deserted families.

The contents of these exchanges with Johnson were also different for those accustomed to Kennedy's soliloquies on war and peace and other great issues. Announcing the railroad settlement, Johnson referred to a little girl in Illinois who asked him to keep the trains running because she wanted Grandmother to attend her First Communion. With the railroad executives and union bosses simpering in the background, Johnson said, "Cathy May, tonight I am pleased to tell you that the railways are going to continue to run without interruption." There were more appearances on the sidewalk outside the White House to be photographed with relatives or flustered tourists, and the great state occasions became even more informal. King Hussein of Jordan found himself dancing with a reporter from a Jewish weekly, the daughter of a rabbi, while Johnson, the most energetic dancer east of the Pedernales river, performed his nightly chore of dancing with all the ladies in the ballroom.

Some observers were apprehensive as to what distinguished foreign guests thought of this Jacksonian approach, but at home the support he enjoyed seemed solid. He was commended by the press pundits, Lippmann, Reston, Krock, and Alsop. The great corporations were solidly behind him. If the Daughters of the American Revolution thought that his disarmament measures were sinful, another pillar of small-town society, the U.S. Chambers of Commerce, announced its willingness to cooperate. After six months in office, it seemed that Johnson was well on the way to becoming the president of all the people. His earthiness, the drawl, the cornpone humor, the frequent quotations from the lesser Scriptures, and the modest presence of country cousins produced blushes for the national image in the common rooms of eastern universities, but the sentiment was genuine and certainly appreciated by many. Moreover, he talked honestly about the poor and not about the disadvantaged. For him they were people to be helped and not abstract problems to be solved. He was equipped with obvious advantages: his flair for congressional politics, his sure understanding of government machinery, and a populist background less corrupted than it is for most southern politicians. His wife was handsome and shrewd, and he delighted in his two daughters. He belonged to a church that had little dogma apart from belief in God and which permitted him to attend all churches of his choice. Thus he appeared to be the epitome of consensus politics, and a widespread feeling was that Johnson was in the White House and all was well with the world.

Certainly the economy was booming nicely. Many whites felt that they had done their duty by the blacks, and the white backlash had not set in. Robert Kennedy was only slowly recovering from his grief. Johnson had kindly sent him on a special mission to mediate between Malaysia, Indonesia, and the Philippines. Kennedy had not yet made known his political ambitions and was still at the Justice Department. There were indications that Johnson was keeping a wary eye on him, but nothing to suggest the great challenge that was to come. Apart from Vietnam and Laos, there was in fact little to suggest that all was not well with the world. Progress toward European unity, so long an objective of American foreign policy, had, of course, been halted by President de Gaulle's veto of British membership in the common market. Impatience with the French president was growing. There was despair on the seventh floor of the State Department, where the French rejection of Britain was seen as an anti-American act. There was also de Gaulle's independent course within NATO, his scorn of the United Nations, his recognition of China, and his refusal to participate in the disarmament conference. But the Franco-American balance sheet was not yet all one-sided. France stood firm in Berlin, as it had during the Cuban missile crisis of 1962. The Algerian war had been brought to an end, French foreign aid was considerable, and the *rapprochement* with West Germany had for the time being weathered the Kennedy jealousy.

The old affection for France was still strong. Lafayette and Yorktown were still part of the sentimental attachment, and there were also the literary memories of Fitzgerald, Hemingway, and Stein and youngsters' artless dreams of Paris in the spring.

The euphoria was further enhanced by the beginnings of a new debate on foreign policy. William Fulbright, chairman of the Senate Foreign Relations Committee, was questioning some of the basic attitudes. His main thesis was that a complex and fluid world situation was developing, and that the United States was failing to adapt itself. It was clinging to old myths in the face of new realities. Roswell Gilpatric, a former under-secretary of defense, suggested a 35 percent cut in defense spending before the end of the decade. Adlai Stevenson called for a policy of peaceful change and improvements in the United Nations peace-keeping machinery. Johnson joined in the debate. Conceding the relative diminution of American power in a changing world, he acknowledged that the United States could no longer "mash a button" and command the nations of the world to its bidding. Fulbright was not satisfied. American attitudes were still seen to be schizophrenic. The understanding of the nuclear age and the harsh requirement of nuclear discipline had certainly produced a degree of political sophistication worthy of the second half of the twentieth century. Yet, as he saw it, Cuba and Panama had aroused a latent jingoism unworthy of the late nineteenth century, and China still revived a distasteful form of McCarthyism. He spoke of cant and inconsistency in the American moral approach to foreign affairs. This caused some displeasure, of course, but in Washington at least there were men who were beginning to think of possible change, from reducing the garrisons on the distant frontiers of the so-called free world to accommodation and détente.

The country was also thinking of the presidential election. The Goldwater phenomenon was yet to come. He was but one of several candidates for the Republican nomination and had done poorly in the first primary. There in New Hampshire, Henry Cabot Lodge, who had not campaigned and was serving

as ambassador to South Vietnam, had beaten both Barry Goldwater and Nelson Rockefeller. The assumption was that Johnson
would be the Democratic candidate. He was expected to win,
but the attractions and demands of a presidential election were
as powerful as ever, and those rumblings of distant thunder
went largely unheard although more bombers were sent to Vietnam. They were supposed to be flown by South Vietnamese
pilots, but American instructors had long been flying over
bombing targets. In May, Johnson asked Congress to appropriate an additional $125 million and rededicated the United
States to the Vietnam struggle. "By our words and deeds in a
decade of determined effort we are pledged before all the
world to stand with the free people in Vietnam. Daily they face
danger in the cause of freedom. Duty requires, and the American people demand, that we give them the fullest measure of
support. The Vietcong guerrillas, under orders from their communist masters in the North, have intensified terrorist actions
against the peaceful people of South Vietnam. This increased
terrorism requires increased response."

The words were duly published but with little or no comment.
The country was not ready even to admit the possibility of
another war, but there were no demands for the withdrawal of
American advisers sent by Kennedy. Casualties were few, and
presumably the majority, if they thought of Vietnam at all, had
decided that Kennedy's policy would be successful. In fact,
small attention was given to Vietnam. It was just one of those
problems that face great nations which take upon themselves
the responsibility of maintaining world peace. The British had
done it for more than a century, and now it was the turn of the
United States. Some saw Vietnam as another Northwest Frontier, the scene of many a novel and movie in which dashing
British officers and picturesque native troops had defended
India against the Russian bear. There were the occasional excitements, but official assurances placated the anxieties aroused
by press reports from Saigon of a worsening situation.

In fact, the situation was a good deal worse than the reporters
thought. Kennedy's measures were quite inadequate, and the

40

time was fast approaching when the United States would have to review its commitment. Years later, after Johnson had left the White House, one of his senior advisers said that it was already too late by the summer of 1964. Speaking with the benefit of hindsight no doubt, he said that the last opportunity for the United States to get out of Vietnam was in 1963 when President Ngo Dinh Diem refused to liberalize his regime. Indeed, Madame Nhu, the wife of Diem's brother, Ngo Dinh Nhu, complained of American behavior in Saigon. Diem's refusal to cooperate with American advisers was sufficient cause to remove them and the commitment. The USIA threatened to reduce military aid, but Kennedy appeared on television and called for "changes in policy and perhaps in personnel." This was seen as an open invitation to South Vietnamese generals to overthrow the government. Kennedy was thought only to want the removal of Diem's brother, but the South Vietnamese president was assassinated. In the *New York Times,* James Reston wrote, "It was like the head of a foreign government announcing publicly that President Kennedy was pursuing a losing policy, was out of touch with his people, but might make amends by firing Bobby." Kennedy again appeared before the television cameras and announced that he would not reduce aid because that was how China was lost. He accepted the validity of the domino theory, which had it that all Southeast Asian countries would topple like so many dominoes if South Vietnam collapsed. It would improve China's position for a guerrilla assault on Malaya, and also give the impression that China and communism were the wave of the future in Asia. To avoid this was the objective of the American commitment in Vietnam.

No matter if the domino theory was true or false (and there was small reason to regard the North Vietnamese as Chinese puppets), its public acceptance was a serious matter. Not only was an opportunity to withdraw the modest commitment made by Eisenhower missed, but the commitment was increased. The survival of an unrepresentative regime in a distant and divided Asian country became one of the first objectives of American national security policy. More than that, the Kennedy regime

41

began to ponder the possibility of an armed American intervention. A Vietnam war game was soon afterward played by representatives of the White House, the State and Defense Departments, the Central Intelligence Agency, and other interested agencies. It was played largely with statistics and calculations provided by McNamara's computers. The conclusion was that an American army could not be committed in Vietnam before the infrastructure was vastly improved. The construction of new ports, airfields, and roads was called for. While there is no evidence that hard decisions were made then, planning to improve the infrastructure was pursued with some urgency.

After Kennedy's assassination, the Van Minh junta had been deposed by General Nguyen Khanh, but McNamara insisted that progress was encouraging, and went on to emphasize the American commitment. "The survival of an independent government in South Vietnam is so important to the security of all of Southeast Asia and to the free world that I can conceive of no alternative other than to take all necessary measures within our capability to prevent a communist victory." This was the kind of advice Johnson received within two months of succeeding to the presidency. Soon after another war game was held. It was assumed that the necessary ports and airfields were available, and the conclusion was that 500,000 American troops could win the war in three months. Half a million men was, of course, an impossible figure politically. Apart from the election campaign, Johnson—and for that matter, any of the recent presidents—would not have considered committing so many troops in what was still a minor war. But McNamara's young men, the whiz kids, had applied their slide rules to the problems of guerrilla war. Not one of them had any personal experience. Few had heard a shot fired in anger, but they decided it was a matter of ratios. A good deal was heard of ratios over Washington dinner tables that year. I can remember talking about them with Rostow at a party given in the West German embassy for Willy Brandt, the then foreign minister. I do not remember meeting Brandt on that occasion because of those ratios.

Walt Rostow, who had served under Kennedy and remained

under Johnson, had it that the British had discovered when fighting the communist uprising in Malaya that it took ten men for every single guerrilla fighter to win the war. That was the basic ratio for victory. The Americans and the South Vietnamese could not provide enough men—or so it was thought at the time—but there were the factors of fire power and mobility. As I recall, each was given a factor of three. There were other factors, which I have now forgotten, but American industrial power and technical ingenuity, and not men, would provide the correct ratio. I had in fact spent a great deal of time in Malaya, when I was the *Times* correspondent in Southeast Asia. I protested, as I was to do on a number of occasions. The British had not fought a military campaign, but a police action. If the ratio was ten-to-one in the British favor, the majority were simple Malayan policemen who assured the security of the settled areas. Military operations were rarely above the battalion level, more often one company of infantry or less. There were no tanks or bombers. It was a contradiction to talk about winning the hearts and minds of the South Vietnamese if they were to be exposed to bombing raids, artillery concentrations, and mass descents of troops in helicopters. Rostow sneered. I was old-fashioned, like Hilsman. Roger Hilsman, who had had some guerrilla experience, had recently been dismissed from his job as Assistant Secretary of State for Far Eastern Affairs. Rostow said that I did not understand the new strategy or the capability of helicopters and defoliation agents.

I did not mind the sneer. Correspondents expect them from government officials the world over, especially when they have had actual experience of situations that are presented to officials as paper problems. This had been especially true in Kennedy's Washington, where New Frontiersmen who had rarely ventured beyond the Boston-Washington axis regarded me as an unreconstructed British imperialist. I could never follow the logic, it being clear that I was born a cradle radical, but I digress. Much more important was the fact that most of the generals did not share this confidence, but they were ignored because they suffered from the so-called Korean syndrome. This came from the belief, painfully reinforced by the Korean War, that American troops should not be committed on the Asian mainland. For them the reasoning was self-evident. The landing of American troops in Vietnam might lead to Chinese intervention, as it did in Korea, and the United States could not hope to raise a fraction of the men which China could put into the field. A war with China could only be won with nuclear weapons, and even then the remnants of the Chinese armies could retreat to the mountains as did the communist forces to Yenan during the Civil War. Older men in the State Department believed that involvement in Vietnam could lead to Soviet intervention elsewhere. They had not forgotten the anxieties of 1950, when Korea was thought to be a diversionary action intended to weaken the defenses of Western Europe. There was also the possibility that American action could reunite the two communist giants. Dean Rusk, the Secretary of State, was afterward to lead the civilian hawks, but at the time he saw only the danger of war with China. I can remember reporting this at the time and being dismissed as irresponsible and unnecessarily timid.

Perhaps I was. The war-games theory has relevance in superpower relations. The likelihood of a violent Soviet response to the landing of American troops had already been considered, and dismissed. The Russians understood the disciplines required to maintain nuclear stability and had also lost interest in Vietnam. The best diplomatic reporting from Moscow, and the American embassy was very good, said that Khrushchev had conceded North Vietnam as belonging to the Chinese sphere of influence. This was correct at the time, although that also was to change after Khrushchev's departure. There were doubts at first about China. Peking was in an unpredictable mood, and experience showed that Chinese leaders had small respect for the opinions of mankind. It was recognized that a large continental power such as China had a legitimate concern for its frontier areas and the political coloring of contiguous countries. For this reason, after all, the United States had reacted sternly to Castro and Soviet missiles in Cuba.

There were those who argued that Vietnam was a natural

buffer state which should not be dominated by any large power. The old colonial name, Indo-China, was a sufficient reminder that here two great civilizations met. Those within the administration who took a conceptual view of the world and history looked for some kind of eventual regional balance. They argued that India, and countries such as Thailand, Malaysia, Indonesia, and the Philippines, should be strengthened in order to provide a counterbalance to the enormous weight of China. Others argued against the domino theory and said that a Vietnam united under Hanoi would not constitute a threat to regional or world peace. The Vietnamese, they said, had traditionally no love for China. Ho Chi Minh would quickly emerge as an Asian Tito once the nationalist goal of independence and unity completed the long and violent transfer from French rule.

These were powerful arguments against landing American troops, but there were counterarguments. In more ways than one, Vietnam was not Korea. It also shared a border with China, but it was a natural barrier of mountains difficult for motorized troops to penetrate in large numbers. I can remember sitting in McNamara's office one afternoon, and he pointed out on a map only one or two passes which large masses of troops could use. He did this to prove the unlikelihood of Chinese intervention, but the same held good for forces trying to invade China from the south. In any case, there was no question of American troops moving into North Vietnam. To that extent, American intervention in Vietnam would be more limited than that in the Korean War. Moreover, China was not so confident as in 1950. Apart from the Korean experience, Peking had had more than a decade of economic failures and disappointments. Its armed forces were badly equipped. There was small reason to believe that China would, or could, react violently.

One had to agree, but in the early summer of 1964 there were forces more powerful than logic moving inexorably toward intervention. To understand the situation, it is necessary to revise most of one's notions of the balance of power and influence in Washington. Hawks and doves were be found in the strangest places. As indicated, most of the generals and men such as Rusk were opposed to intervention. The air force, as wild-blue-yonder as ever, naturally thought that the war could be won with air power. General Maxwell Taylor, who had succeeded Lodge as ambassador and proconsul in Saigon, seemed to favor bombing but was vague about the probable results. The bombers could make infiltration more difficult by striking at the Ho Chi Minh trail and the training and marshaling areas. Hanoi would be reminded that it could not fight the war unscathed, and that it stood to lose more than it could ever hope to win. The first was arguable. The infiltration routes and training areas were not four-lane highways or established military posts. The bombing of South Vietnamese villages had failed to reduce the Vietcong forces, but nevertheless many believed that a miserable Asian nation such as North Vietnam could not stand up to a determined American assault from the air.

Taylor was regarded as a liberal general, a man who had resigned his commission in protest against the postwar dependence upon nuclear bombers and bombs, and the hawks came mainly from the liberal wing of the administration. In fact, this was not exactly a reversal of historical roles. The Civil War and American intervention in the Second World War, one could argue, were at least in part due to liberal agitation. One could also argue that the fate of Vietnam was hardly comparable to saving the Union or Western Europe, but not in the light of the liberal-technocratic ideology of 1964. The legacy of the containment policy remained a conditioning of men's minds against conceding territorial gains to the communists. Also the liberals had reacted strongly against Khrushchev's thesis on the validity of so-called wars of national liberation. In January 1961 the Soviet leader explained the communist attitude to subversive aggression as follows: "Now a word about national liberation wars. The armed struggle by the Vietnamese people and the war of the Algerian people serve as the latest examples of such wars. These are revolutionary wars. Such wars are not only admissible but inevitable. Can such wars flare up in the future? They can. The communists fully support such wars in the front rank with the peoples waging liberation struggles."

In historical terms, Khrushchev had only found a new label for the so-called people's war, as fought in Greece, the Philippines, and Malaya, but in Kennedy's Washington the speech was read as a declaration of a new phase of the East-West struggle. Already alive to the dangers of subversion, Kennedy then reorganized the Special Forces as an elite group trained to fight such aggression on its own terms and ground. After the Cuban missile crisis of 1962 liberation wars were also seen to be a sin against the new theology of the nuclear stability of the two superpowers. Khrushchev had been clearly shaken by the narrow escape from the nuclear confrontation both sides wished to avoid. The assumption had grown that he wanted to establish a status quo between the superpowers, but Khrushchev continued to support the idea of liberation wars, and this led to a new war theory in Washington. Small wars were seen to be potentially dangerous to American national security because in the event of the interests of the superpowers becoming involved they could bring about a nuclear confrontation. To avoid taking the world to the nuclear brink again, it was necessary for the United States to intervene in such wars before they became global confrontations.

There were other factors. General Vo Nguyen Giap, the North Vietnamese commander in chief, said, "South Vietnam is the model of the national liberation movement of our time. If the special warfare that the U.S. imperialists are testing in South Vietnam is overcome, then it can be defeated anywhere in the world." Marshal Lin Pao, the Chinese Defense Minister, said that liberation wars waged in numerous parts of the world could deplete the strength and bring about the ultimate defeat of the United States. These statements and others were seen to be a larger threat and a challenge from China. Peking had to be taught a lesson before it was too late. Finally, few officials could contemplate the thought of withdrawal. National pride and apprehension of communist intentions, both understandable perhaps, combined to make withdrawal unthinkable. McNamara's whiz kids were also full of confidence. They had helped to prove that nuclear war was too serious for the generals. They were convinced that the new liberal-technocratic authority could also triumph in guerrilla warfare. Victory could be plotted with slide rules and computers.

Their earlier confidence was reflected by McNamara in his annual defense statement before the House Armed Services Committee at the beginning of the year. After claiming success for American measures, he said, "We felt that a start could be made in reducing the number of U.S. military personnel in Vietnam as their training missions were completed." This hard-nosed confidence, reinforced by the Cuban missile crisis, was a factor no less decisive than calculations of Chinese and Soviet intentions. McNamara was to rue that statement afterward. Even when he spoke there were many ominous indications that things were going badly in Vietnam, but the larger confidence remained undented. Indeed, within a few months the first fateful decision was made. I do not mean that Johnson decided in March or April to commit troops more than a year later. Johnson was no warmonger, and he and his advisers saw a number of steps short of war. Kennedy had earlier threatened to use force to stop North Vietnamese infiltration of Laos. A conference was held in Geneva, and the 1962 agreement was signed. The agreement was subsequently acknowledged to have been a failure, but in 1964 it was thought to be reasonably effective. Johnson prepared for a similar display of American determination to defend South Vietnam. While the Defense Department prepared for the worst, Michael Forrestal and William Sullivan, two assistants to Averell Harriman, who negotiated the Laos agreement, were ordered to draw up a draft declaration.

It took the form of a congressional resolution and expressed determination to take all necessary steps in defense of freedom. The resolution was intended to serve more than one purpose for Johnson. He hoped that it would deter North Vietnam. It would provide him with the necessary authority to act if Hanoi was slow to be deterred. He must also have had the presidential election in mind. Goldwater had criticized him for his "no win" policy, and the charge had rankled. The opportunity to act on all fronts was provided by the Gulf of Tonkin incident.

According to the official version, the destroyer U.S.S. *Maddox* was attacked on August 2 by three North Vietnamese PT boats while sailing in international waters. The State Department sent a stern protest to Hanoi, warning that there should be no misapprehension as to the grave consequences that would inevitably result from any further unprovoked action against American forces. Two nights later two destroyers, the *Maddox* and the *C. Turner Joy*, were attacked. The PT flotilla was driven off with the help of carrier-borne aircraft, and American retribution was immediate. Johnson said on television the same night that four North Vietnamese PT-boat bases and an oil-storage depot had been attacked. McNamara afterward claimed that twenty-five boats were destroyed for the loss of two American aircraft. The same day Johnson also requested the congressional leadership to facilitate the prompt passage of a resolution making clear that the government was united in its determination to take all necessary measures in support of freedom and the defense of peace in Southeast Asia. The resolution is worth quoting in full.

Whereas naval units of the Communist regime in Vietnam, in violation of the principles of the Charter of the United Nations and of international law, have deliberately and repeatedly attacked United States naval vessels lawfully present in international waters, and have thereby created a serious threat to international peace;

Whereas these attacks are part of a deliberate and systematic campaign of aggression that the Communist regime in North Vietnam has been waging against its neighbors and the nations joined with them in the collected defense of their freedom;

Whereas the United States is assisting the peoples of Southeast Asia to protect their freedom and has no territorial, military, or political ambitions in that area, but desires only that these peoples should be left in peace to work out their own destinies in their own way: Now, therefore, be it

Resolved by the Senate and House of Representatives of the United States of America in Congress assembled, That the Congress approves and supports the determination of the President, as Commander-in-

Chief, to take all necessary measures to repel any armed attack against forces of the United States and to prevent further aggression.

SECTION 2. The United States regards as vital to its national interest and to world peace the maintenance of international peace and security in Southeast Asia. Consonant with the Constitution of the United States and the Charter of the United Nations and in accordance with its obligations under the Southeast Asia Collective Defense Treaty, the United States is, therefore, prepared, as the President determines, to take all necessary steps, including the use of armed force, to assist any member or protocol state of the Southeast Asia Collective Defense Treaty requesting assistance in defense of its freedom.

SECTION 3. This resolution shall expire when the President shall determine that the peace and security of the area is reasonably assured by international conditions created by action of the United Nations or otherwise, except that it may be terminated earlier by concurrent resolution of the Congress.

The joint resolution was passed unanimously by the House on August 7, and in the Senate only two dissenting votes were cast, by Senator Wayne Morse of Oregon and Senator Ernest Gruening of Alaska. It is worth recalling that both were defeated when they ran for re-election in 1968. It is also worth noting that Senator Fulbright, who subsequently became the most persistent critic of the war, was the floor manager of the Senate bill. He afterward complained of being misled, but there was nothing ambiguous about the text of the resolution. It approved and supported the president's determination to take all necessary measures, including the use of armed force. He was the chairman of the Senate Foreign Relations Committee, which heard testimony from the secretary of state and the chairman of the Joint Chiefs of Staff. His investigating authority was in no way hampered by the requirements of national security. The record shows that with the exception of Morse and Gruening there was no congressional opposition to the resolution. Some Democrats preferred to think of a political solution and spoke of neutralizing the area, but many more in both parties sounded very warlike in their impatient remarks.

Johnson afterward said in private that the resolution was like

Grandma's nightshirt—it covered everything. It certainly did. Subsequently there were doubts as to the veracity of official reports of the two incidents. The Senate Foreign Relations Committee held hearings in 1968, when Fulbright read into the record the report of Captain John Herrick, the commander of the destroyer task force. It read, "Review of action makes many recorded contacts and torpedoes fired appear doubtful. Freak weather effects and over-eager sonarman may have accounted for many reports. No actual visual sighting by *Maddox*. Suggest complete evaluation before any further action." McNamara said that Admiral U. S. Grant Sharp, the Pacific naval commander, was convinced that an attack had occurred and that the reports were evaluated for four and a half hours, but there were other questions. Why were the destroyers in the area? The defense secretary insisted that the prime purpose of the *Maddox* was to observe North Vietnamese naval activity and that American naval ships "played absolutely no part in, and were not associated with" South Vietnamese naval attacks on northern coastal installations at that time. Fulbright read another message from Herrick, in which he said that his patrol would possibly draw enemy PT boats away from the South Vietnamese operations. In a third message, he reported that North Vietnam considered his ships to be enemies directly involved in the South Vietnamese operations and "have already indicated their readiness to treat us in that category...." The transcript of the closed hearings was censored, but it was thus established that the *Maddox* and the *C. Turner Joy* were not subjected to unprovoked attack. There was provocation, thoughtless or otherwise, and the immediate retaliation against the PT-boat bases suggested that Johnson had been waiting for such an opportunity.

This emerged much later. At the time, few questioned the wisdom of that response or the need for the joint resolution. The significance of the resolution was obvious, however. Similar expressions of congressional approval and support had been passed during the crises of 1955 in the Formosa Strait, in 1957 in the Middle East, and in Cuba in 1962. Congress knew what it was doing. So did Johnson. He had already taken the basic political decision that South Vietnam must be defended, and could be defended without Chinese or Soviet intervention. The joint resolution provided him with the necessary congressional approval to resort to the use of armed force when necessary.

The evidence available also suggests that he knew that American troops would have to be landed if South Vietnam was not to be overrun. In spite of McNamara's optimism, the political instability in Saigon was matched by military reverses in the field. Slowly but surely the Vietcong were taking over much of the countryside, and total collapse was only a matter of time. Johnson knew it and yet went on insisting that the survival of South Vietnam was essential to vital American security interests. These statements were obviously a warning to the public, but his intention was blunted by equally frequent remarks that only the South Vietnamese could save themselves. Those who knew that the war was going badly and that the South Vietnamese could not save themselves began to doubt his good faith. Those who hoped that the war would emerge as a campaign issue thought that he was placing his political future, another four or eight years in the White House, above the national interest. Certainly Johnson delayed the final decision until after the election, but at the time I could not escape the impression that Johnson thought that a show of force would stop further aggression from the North. He could not believe that Asian peasants in black pajamas and armed only with captured or primitive weapons, as they were at the time, could stand up to a well-equipped American army.

This is a personal view, but it is supported by the emphasis the joint resolution placed on repelling attack against American forces. Johnson could not bring himself to believe that American bases would be attacked after the retaliatory action which followed the Gulf of Tonkin incident. The disbelief was certainly shared in varying degree by many of his advisers. The fact that the French army had failed and that it was a good army brilliantly led by a great general was of little consequence. In 1954 they represented a hated colonial power fighting a genuine nationalist movement. The suggestion that the Vietcong was the Vietminh under another name, and was still a nationalist movement, was brushed aside. They were now communist aggressors, supported by North Vietnam, a foreign country. Until the very end, administration spokesmen refused to accept the obvious; that the struggle was a civil war in spite of the temporary truce lines between the two halves of the country. Indeed, the boundary was little more than a piece of international legal fiction, and the authority of the Saigon government was not much more. Large areas of the countryside had been under Vietminh or Vietcong control since before the defeat of the French. Many village chiefs appointed by the Diem regime had refused to live in their appointed villages. Much of the government, the only kind of government most Asian peasants know, had been in communist-nationalist hands for years.

This did not impress the ideologues in Washington. As for the 1954 defeat, it was Frenchmen who had lost, not Americans. This chauvinistic attitude was not, of course, particularly American. All great powers have been guilty of it in their heyday, the French and British no less than the Americans. Nevertheless, the corruption of superpower was very much in evidence. Few countries in the past have involved themselves in another country whose government was on the point of collapse. To be fair to Johnson and his advisers, the distant past was dictating the future. They believed, and with good reason within the correct historical context, that the Second World War could have been avoided if Britain, France, and the United States had stood up to Hitler when the Rhineland was occupied. Rusk especially was to return to this repeatedly over the years. They believed that the lesson had been learned and well applied in Greece and Korea. There were obvious differences between these countries and Vietnam. Greece had a legitimate if shaky government. Korea was defended under the United Nations flag, with many European and Asian allies. Nevertheless, Vietnam was also seen to require American strength, courage, and leadership. There were some who were not so certain, who with Fulbright thought that a review of American national security policy was long overdue, but the issue was never clearly debated during the election campaign.

The result of the 1964 presidential campaign was a foregone conclusion even before the Republican national convention nominated Goldwater. Months before, there were predictions that Johnson would win in a landslide no less impressive than Roosevelt's 1936 victory. There were complaints from some of the old Kennedy men still at the White House that Johnson had paid too little attention to organization. What there was seemed to be divided and wastefully conflicting, but of course Johnson began with tremendous assets. He was the incumbent and had proved his leadership and capabilities after being thrust into the presidency under the cruelest circumstances. His legislative record was good, and the promise of the Great Society had wide appeal. He had good speech writers, although they were often misused, and he understood consensus politics when events were conspiring to make possible a consensus much broader than that which held the old Roosevelt coalition together. The once solid South had been moving away from the party since 1948, but the Negro vote was more solidly his after the Civil Rights Act. Many Republicans and independents had been won over. The white backlash had not yet become a harsh reality of American politics. The archsegregationist Governor George Wallace of Alabama had done well in his trial runs in three state primaries but was not a presidential candidate. Johnson also insisted that he was not a labor, business, liberal, conservative, northern, or southern president but president of all the people, and before the conventions Republican businessmen, especially executives and presidents of large corporations, were crossing the party lines in droves.

The crossing was speeded by Goldwater. The primary results were inconclusive before California, but Goldwater said enough along the campaign trail to terrify many of his listeners. He was and is a likable man but with no intellectual pretensions or understanding of the requirements of a modern industrialized society. He took seriously many of the old frontier and business myths of self-sufficiency and independence from Washington, although he had worked hard in the Senate for federal handouts for his home state of Arizona. Much of what he said about the old virtues was sound, but he had an extraordinary insensitivity to the needs of the old, the sick, and the oppressed. He lectured old people on the iniquity of Social Security. He voted against the civil rights bill. He refused to dissociate himself from extreme right-wing organizations such as the John Birch Society.

Nevertheless, the road to victory had its difficult moments for Johnson. First there was the movement to make Robert Kennedy the vice-presidential candidate, which came to public view in the New Hampshire primary when a write-in campaign was launched. It was doubly presumptuous. The presidential candidate traditionally nominates his running mate, and Johnson did not officially enter the primary race. Whoever was responsible, Johnson was understandably suspicious. Kennedy's ambitions had not exactly been kept secret, and the possibility of a pro-Kennedy movement sweeping the country, spontaneously or otherwise, was real. Kennedy issued a disclaimer. He also said that the nomination should be made by the national convention, guided by the wishes of Johnson. The statement was correct in that only the convention can nominate candidates, but the suggestion that Johnson's wishes were not absolute also rankled. Governor John King of New Hampshire saved the situation by launching a Johnson write-in. The president did better than Kennedy, but another Kennedy write-in campaign was begun in Wisconsin.

To be fair to both men, the electoral outlook at that time as well as the ambitions of both men should be recalled. Even as early as March, there was no doubt that Johnson would win, and without the help of Kennedy. The urge to go it alone must have been overwhelming. With Kennedy on the ticket, there would always be lingering doubts about which of the candidates actually swung the election. The doubts would certainly have been nurtured by the Kennedy men, if not by Kennedy himself. This was a negative but powerful factor. The positive and most compelling factor was the thought of being the first elected southern president since before Reconstruction. Andrew Johnson was denied the 1868 nomination after succeeding Lincoln in 1865, and the president had always been aware of the regional mill-stone round his neck. Since acquiring a national reputation as Senate majority leader, he had also tried to appear in the guise of a westerner but was known, and knew he was known, as a southerner. The prospect of rehabilitating the South politically was rarely far from his thoughts.

Then there was the antipathy between the two men. Johnson knew, or believed, that Kennedy had little respect for him. He also knew that Kennedy wanted to be on the ticket as crown prince, and crowned in 1968. No president who had succeeded to office had been twice re-elected, and the assumption of a Kennedy restoration in 1968 was widespread. Kennedy was dominated by the firm conviction of his right to rule, to carry on what he saw as the unfinished work of his brother. To some of his followers, it was almost a divine right, and the inference that the Johnson administration was only an interregnum would have been galling even for a less sensitive and insecure man than Johnson. Refusal was inevitable, especially after the rumors that Kennedy would only accept the vice-presidential nomination on certain conditions.

This then was the situation early in the year, and Johnson's response was typical. The word was passed down the line, and a Democratic conference in the Middle West resolved that Johnson should have the right to choose his own running mate at the national convention. This compulsion to touch all bases, to leave nothing to chance, was typical of Johnson. It was similar to the Bay of Tonkin resolution, in that with the president's authority to involve the country in war in the nuclear age the question of vice-presidential nominations is best left in the gray area where contending authority—presidential, congressional, or party—is not affronted. No one seriously questioned Johnson's right to choose his own man, but the resolution floated in the Midwest did seem to flout the democratic process of the national convention. If the presidential candidate had the right to nominate, the party certainly had equal right to speak its many minds in open convention. There had been the opposition to Johnson's nomination as vice-presidential candidate behind the scenes in 1960, and Roosevelt's nominations were also questioned in 1940 and 1944. The will of the presidential candidate prevailed on each occasion, but the party had had the opportunity to speak out. Little wonder, in the spring of 1964, that other state parties refused to go along with the midwesterners.

This was especially true in states where Kennedy could expect to run well, but the polls showed that his popularity was widespread throughout the country except for the South. The Democratic national convention in Atlantic City that August was also to be a requiem for the murdered president. A commemorative film was to be shown, and in the White House at least there was some apprehension over the possibility that the movie might ignite an emotional Kennedy draft. Johnson more or less disposed of that problem by postponing the showing of the film from the first to the last day of the convention, until after the vice-presidential nomination, but the doubts, or insecurity, persisted. Eventually, on July 30, three weeks before the convention, Johnson announced on television that he would not nominate any member of his cabinet. He afterward said that none, including Kennedy, could be spared from the task of building the Great Society.

This struck many people as Byzantine in the extreme, even farcical, but it was an astute move. Kennedy, who had been told by Johnson the day before that he would not be on the ticket, was excluded from public consideration as gently as possible. The personal animosity remained private property more or less, although Kennedy had another of those last words that continued to annoy Johnson. He issued a statement saying, "It is the interest of all of us who were associated with President Kennedy to continue the efforts to advance the programs and ideals to which he devoted his life, and which President Johnson is carrying on." Thus were the president and the country reminded that the Kennedy family still saw the Johnson administration as an interregnum, and one incapable of anything much except advancing the Kennedy programs until such time as power returned to the family. Johnson should be forgiven if he swore that night.

Johnson had only himself to blame, of course. He had earlier decided to nominate Humphrey, who by any standards was an acceptable candidate. He balanced the ticket in every way. His liberalism was unquestioned, he enjoyed wide support outside the South and business circles, and his performance as floor manager of the 1964 civil rights bill demonstrated his statesmanship. He even enjoyed some support from the Kennedy followers. If he talked too much, he was almost the perfect running mate for Johnson, who knew him well. An early announcement, or at least a broad hint, would have avoided a great deal of unnecessary trouble. Unlike many other candidates for the presidential nomination, including John Kennedy, Johnson did not have to play off one faction against another by suggesting that the second nomination would go to their man. His position was much too strong. He had an opportunity to lean toward Humphrey when he called a surprise press conference just before announcing that no cabinet member would be considered. He said that his vice-presidential candidate should be a man of the people long engaged in public service. "I would like for him to be a man who is attractive and prudent and progressive. I would like for him to be one that would work in cooperation with Congress and the Cabinet and with the President."

This description, general though it was, fitted Humphrey better than any other possible candidate, but Johnson's craving for secrecy led him astray.

The secret was kept until the very last moment at the convention, and it stored up further trouble for Johnson at a time, four years later, when he would need all the help he could get. Playful in the cruelest way, he allowed Senator Eugene McCarthy of Minnesota to believe even at that late stage that he was being considered. In 1964, McCarthy was not a well-known figure outside his state and Washington, but was a Catholic, which theoretically could be helpful because Goldwater had chosen a Catholic running mate, Representative William Miller of New York. He was also a proud man, and even a political hack would have resented Johnson's cat-and-mouse-game. At Atlantic City, where the convention was held, McCarthy waited in his hotel room for a call, and three or four did indeed come from the White House. They were from members of Johnson's staff, who did nothing but talk around the subject of nomination. Quite clearly Johnson had decided against McCarthy, but was too feline to admit as much. In a white fury, McCarthy decided that he had had enough and put out a statement for the press saying that he was not available. Whether or not McCarthy brooded over this for the next four years, as some people have it, it was certainly a factor in his decision to seek the presidential nomination in 1968.

Johnson and Humphrey were nominated by acclamation and on a platform that straddled the political center. It was mild and restrained by Democratic standards and could be summed up as a three-P program: peace, prudence, and prosperity. All three had obvious attractions for the American majority, but peace was seen to be the winning issue after the missile-rattling of Goldwater. The peace plank claimed that the preservation of peace required the strength to wage war and the wisdom to avoid it. The world was closer to peace than in 1960, when freedom had been on the defensive. Kennedy and Johnson had removed any question of American power and will. In the Cuban missile crisis, the communist offensive was shattered on the rock of Kennedy's determination, and the American ability, to defend the peace. Johnson responded to another communist challenge two years later in the Gulf of Tonkin. Once again power exercised with restraint repulsed communist aggression and strengthened the cause of freedom. International communism had lost its unity and momentum. The commitment to defend freedom in South Vietnam was reaffirmed. Johnson said in his acceptance speech that the world was beginning to respond to the American belief that strength, courage, and responsibility were the keys to peace. The world knew where

America stood, so did the allies, and the adversaries had learned again.

The Republicans had held their national convention earlier, and before the Gulf of Tonkin incident, but no incident was required to spark demands for victory over communism. The platform said that the nation's leadership must be judged by the stand it took on communism, and that stand must be victory for freedom. A dynamic strategy aimed at victory reduced the risk of nuclear war. Accommodation, not opposition, tempted an aggressor into war. Not content with victory in Vietnam, the platform called for the liberation of Hungary, Poland, East Germany, Czechoslovakia, Rumania, Albania, Latvia, Lithuania, Estonia, Armenia, Ukraine, Yugoslavia and its Serbian, Croatian, and Slovene peoples, Cuba, China, and many others. Only the Soviet Union was not specifically mentioned. In his acceptance speech, Goldwater said, "Yesterday it was Korea, today it is Vietnam. We are at war in Vietnam—yet the president, who is the commander in chief of our forces, refuses to say whether or not the objective is victory."

Perhaps not too much should be made of party platforms, especially when they call for the liberation of most of the communist world. But they do represent a consensus within the leadership of each party, and there was nothing in either platform to suggest that anybody was ready to quit Vietnam. The Democratic platform in fact stated national security policy as it had evolved under Truman, Eisenhower, and Kennedy. If men such as Fulbright felt the need for a change, other honest and experienced men sincerely believed in the necessity and efficacy of the system of alliances, the containment policy, and the concept of negotiating from a position of strength. Apart from Fulbright, no politician to my knowledge publicly suggested that Vietnam was any different from Greece or Korea. The principles of the Truman-Eisenhower-Kennedy national security policy had become part of the conventional wisdom. Buttressed as they were by popular anticommunism, they were not an issue in the campaign. Indeed, what anxiety Vietnam had aroused was not articulated. One could argue, as many people did afterward, that Johnson should have been more honest. He knew that the situation was deteriorating, and the dispatch of American troops was almost inevitable, but the country was concerned more with the control of nuclear weapons than the possibility of a conventional war. For a reason that still escapes most rational men, Goldwater thought that there was electoral support for his proposal that the president should share the control of nuclear weapons with the generals. He then went on to claim, as if to prove that the proposal was not outrageous, that Johnson had authorized military commanders in South Vietnam to use tactical nuclear weapons as required.

Johnson seized his opportunity. There was no suggestion of his being ruffled by this surprise attack. In moments of excitement he might have chastised the White House staff, seized an offending reporter by his jacket lapel, or picked up a beagle by its ears, but he was rarely accused in those days of being anything but icy cool in a political scuffle. He knew that his opponent had made a ghastly mistake, and much worse than his attack on Social Security. The statement issued by the White House read in part:

The control of nuclear weapons is one of the gravest of all the responsibilities of the Commander-in-Chief, the President of the United States. Loose charges on nuclear weapons, without any shadow of justification, by any candidate for any office, let alone the Presidency, are a disservice to our national security, a disservice to peace and for that matter a great disservice to the entire free world.

Goldwater persisted and said that he regarded tactical nuclear weapons as the successors of yesterday's conventional arms. The heavyweights of the administration then weighed in. Adlai Stevenson said that he interpreted the Republican platform as regretting that world tension was relaxed and that the United States was not involved in a colder war. The secretary of state said, "This is not the time to indulge in reckless deeds or words which would cost us the confidence of both allies and other free nations and stimulate irrational action by our adversaries." The director of the Disarmament Agency, William Foster, noting that the Republican platform made little mention of disarmament, said, "It seems that the American eagle should have more arrows but his olive branch should be stripped—or perhaps I should say defoliated." And so it went on, with Goldwater's margin of defeat growing daily.

Johnson's victory was much more sweeping than the most ebullient optimist, with the possible exception of Johnson himself, had anticipated. He ran 15,951,083 votes ahead of Goldwater, the largest plurality in history. He carried forty-four states, and the electoral vote was 486 to 52. The political coloration of the country was also transformed as hundreds of Democratic candidates for lesser office rode to victory on his coattails. The Republicans lost 38 seats in the House of Representatives. With 295 Democrats and 140 Republicans returned, the Democratic majority was 155, sufficient to obliterate the old conservative coalition of Republicans and southern Democrats. The net Democratic gain in the Senate was two, enhancing the party balance, or rather imbalance, by 68 Democrats to 32 Republicans. In state legislatures, Democrats gained 452 seats in the lower and 150 in the upper houses.

Johnson publicly accepted the results, as well he could, as a mandate for national unity and for a government that served no special interest. Privately, he took it as a mandate to introduce far-reaching social legislation. This alone was justification for the simulated heat of the campaign, but alas the country paid a heavy price. There were a few anxious voices heard from the sidelines. The drone of military air transports bearing men and matériel halfway around the world could be heard by anybody who cared to listen, but Vietnam was never a campaign issue. Americans faced the next four years unprepared for what was to happen and led by a president who, because of the absence of debate, was much freer to lead his people into what was to become the most unpopular and the third largest war in their history.

1965

The inauguration has been described as a mystical marriage between the president and the nation, and on occasions it can be a national rebirth. For a few brief hours everything is magically new, and nearly everything possible. The mistakes, the possible corruptions, the silent compromises and backsliding of the past are forgotten. Almost everybody is willing to believe that a new day may have dawned and that with luck these United States might within the next four years draw a little closer to the professed high ideals that can captivate the imagination if not command the earnest endeavors of most Americans. The ceremony has taken place in war and in the depths of a terrible economic depression, when the promise of a new beginning had a special and urgent meaning.

It has been marked by splendid oratory such as Lincoln's second and FDR's first inaugural addresses, but there is more to an inauguration than speeches. The atmosphere can be a better indication of what is to come. Jackson's frontier friends wreaked as much damage on the White House as he later did among his congressional adversaries. There was no public money for Madison's inaugural celebrations, and tickets were sold at the bar of Long's Hotel. In 1961, Robert Frost read one of his poems, and somehow the stuffiness of the Eisenhower years disappeared with the reading. On January 20, 1965, the Mormon Tabernacle choir sang the "Battle Hymn of the Republic" for the first southern president since the Civil War. There were also large men in five-gallon hats, but the promise of that day was not of another period of brash frontier egalitarianism but of national reconciliation.

It was Johnson's finest hour. He had made it on his own, and with overwhelming majorities in both houses of Congress, which could make many things possible. He rose to the occasion with the confident assertion that all the ancient wrongs and new problems could be resolved if the old promises and old dreams were remembered. In almost Scriptural language, he spoke of the American covenant of justice, liberty, and union. There was the calm assumption that the pace of change, as swift as the rocket then on its way to Mars, would shake old values and uproot old ways. There was the recognition of poverty in this land of wealth, the old enemy which Johnson said he had fought for thirty years and knew would not surrender easily. "But change has given us new weapons. Before this generation of Americans is finished, this enemy will not only retreat—it will be conquered." Change, he said, had also brought new meaning to the old American mission of showing the way for the liberation of man. Americans could never again stand aside, prideful in isolation. Dangers once called foreign now lived among them. If American lives must end in barely known countries, then that was the price change demanded of conviction.

Unabashed, he spoke of the secret places of the American heart, of the faith that could not be seen or imagined but which brought victory. "For this is what America is all about. It is the uncrossed desert and the unclimbed ridge. It is the star not reached and the harvest sleeping in the unplowed land. Is our world gone? We say farewell. Is a new world coming? We welcome it—and will bend it to the hopes of man." Johnson spoke with perhaps more awareness of change than the younger man who preceded him, and with apparent confidence. In spite of those five-gallon hats and high-heeled boots, there was no

Texan bravura; only the confidence of a supreme parliamentarian who believed that everything was possible for those who reasoned together. Inevitably, he finished with a reading from the Bible. Recalling the words of Solomon when he ascended the throne of Israel on the death of David (2 Chron. 1:10), he said, "For myself, I ask only in the words of an ancient leader. 'Give me now wisdom and knowledge, that I may go out and come in before this people: for who can judge this thy people, that is so great?' "

The shadow of Kennedy's assassin still lay across the land. Armor plating and bulletproof glass separated president and people, and Secret Service agents stood guard with rifles. As usual, Johnson was impatient with security arrangements, and returning to the White House he stopped his car to greet the brass band from his old college. He walked through a protective screen of agents to shake hands with pretty drum majorettes who, like most Texans that day, more than ever, looked a little larger than life. At the reviewing stand he was back again on the job, shaking hands and otherwise pressing the flesh of the politically powerful of both parties. Not a single governor was ignored. As the companies of cadets from the military academies, American Indians, and high school bands marched by, he kissed every wife within kissing distance and collected three deliriously happy young children in his arms. It seemed that warmhearted, middle-aged America was again in charge at the White House.

Tom Wicker of the *New York Times* thought he saw a more significant change. Kennedy, he wrote, achieved great personal popularity but failed politically because he appeared to threaten stability and demean the office of the presidency by becoming a partisan. Johnson, on the other hand, had made the presidency fit not only circumstances but also his own experience and inclinations. He had been able to maintain the position of national leader in the actual conduct of his office. His leadership might not seem so bold, demanding or inspiring as Kennedy's, but it had persuaded some men to do what they ought to do without persuasion.

In retrospect Wicker seems only to have reflected the euphoria of inauguration day, but he didn't seem to then. Johnson had done well since succeeding to the presidency. He had assumed and maintained the position of national leader, and reform was in the air. Men did seem persuaded that the time had come for a great leap forward in the direction of what Johnson chose to call the Great Society. Subsequent disappointments have dulled the memory, and for that reason the promise of his first State of the Union Message is worth recalling. "The Great Society asks not only how much, but how good—not only how to create wealth but how to use it—not only how fast we are going, but where we are headed...." He proposed programs to improve and extend education, to conquer crippling and killing diseases, to make American cities better places to live in, to control and prevent crime and delinquency, to guarantee everybody the right and opportunity to vote, and to honor and support learning and the arts.

There was some hyperbole in this. Johnson always asked too much in the belief that presidential requests set national objectives. He knew that some could be achieved only after years of effort, and perhaps after his departure, but insisted that a prior display of presidential interest was an essential first step. To make promises to the electorate and send requests to Congress was to act. With that one qualification, he meant it, every word, and believed also that he had the opportunity and the authority to deliver many of his promises during one Congress. It must have been exhilarating. It was certainly dangerous. This was perhaps the moment when Johnson the Superman began to emerge. He was so described four years later, after he had been hounded from office, by a visiting British cabinet minister who knew him well. The label was more fitting than he realized because in January 1965 the balance of power in American government was about to be upset.

The founding fathers knew what they were doing when they separated the powers of government. In the age of the modern presidency, specifically beginning with Franklin Roosevelt, more power had inevitably flowed to the White House, but the checks and balances were all the more necessary, as much for the man in the White House as the country. For FDR, the Supreme Court had been a check, but by the middle sixties the outlook of the Court had changed enormously. Indeed, it had engineered its own revolution and in many ways was more radical than the executive. Before Johnson's landslide victory, a balance of sorts between the executive and the legislative branches had been maintained by checks unmentioned in the Constitution. They included committee chairmen, who could delay or bottle up legislation in committee, and the southern Democratic–conservative Republican coalition. Both could be seen as an offense to representative democracy, but nevertheless a balance between the nation's various regions was more or less maintained. In the 89th Congress, these elderly gentlemen were forced to come to terms. The country was in the mood for change, and Johnson had his consensus. He was ambitious, and determined to be remembered as a great president. He was a masterly politician.

These factors were collectively unusual, but Johnson also blurred the areas of responsibility of the presidency and Congress. He was perhaps too much a man of Congress to do otherwise, but he acted as if he were a prime minister in a parliamentary democracy where the executive is part of the legislature. A prime minister and his party swim or sink together. They have to if they are to avoid parliamentary defeat and a new election. Johnson demanded the same support, but unlike a prime minister he did not have to justify his policies and decisions in open debate. Whatever happened, he would also remain in power for four years, from noon, January 20, 1965, to noon, January 20, 1969, come what may. With private wheeling and dealing, the control of most outlets of official information, and the occasional dishonesties, Johnson also avoided the further check of public oversight. One does not have to recall Lord Acton to emphasize the corruption of superpower. The country had a taste of it in the previous year when Johnson, with consummate timing and breath-taking guile, rushed the Gulf of Tonkin resolution through Congress. With all the extra authority of his majorities, he could now persuade the 89th Congress to go along with his Great Society programs and the secret war, for that is what it amounted to early in 1965, in Vietnam. Johnson's inner circle of congressional friends included nearly all the powerful committee chairman, but not Senator William Fulbright, the chairman of the Senate Foreign Relations Committee. Most of them were men with rather conventional minds, especially in foreign affairs and defense. They were accustomed to leaving the conduct of wars to the president and the Defense Department and saw communism as an enemy to be defeated. All had close working relationships with the military and wanted more than their fair share of defense contracts for their states and districts. This presidential-congressional combination explained much of Johnson's superpower and the reluctance of Congress to speak out on Vietnam or to listen to the few members who did.

This was not altogether evident in the early months of 1965. The Republicans were demoralized after the Goldwater defeat, and the liberals, the city dwellers, the national groups, the blacks, and the aged were anxious for the promised social legislation. The economy continued to boom, and the corporate world was content. The Kennedy men were silent. The South was apprehensive of Johnson's civil rights programs but proud that one of their own had reached the top. The greatest legislative program since the New Deal was promised, and the assumption was that Johnson knew best how to deal with Congress. The Capitol was where the action was, and for the most part the country sat back and waited for the goods to be delivered.

The messages to Congress began to move before the inauguration. On January 7, he called for Medicare for the aged, improved health services for children, the disabled and the mentally retarded, more medical research, and consumer health protection. On January 12, he requested help for the public schools and special programs for low-income school districts such as preschool training for poor children, better libraries and instruction, scholarships and loans for students, aid for smaller colleges, and a university-community extension program. The following day there was a message on the reform of immigration laws, and the next another on foreign aid. On the 18th, there was a defense message, and the day after the inauguration the commerce secretary was requested to make the nation's highways more attractive. The budget was presented five days later, and was quickly followed by a message of presidential disability.

So began the first ripples of the legislative tidal wave which was expected to sweep the country into the distant land of the Great Society and Johnson into the pantheon of great presidents, but some of his personal insecurity also became evident. For instance, Johnson was in the Bethesda Naval Hospital when Winston Churchill died. He was reported to be suffering from a bronchial complaint. Whatever the reason, he was apparently unfit to go to London for the funeral but refused to send Vice-President Humphrey as his representative. He could not share the limelight with another even at a moment of international mourning for the man he professed to admire most after FDR.

This personal insecurity was later seen to be another explanation for what went wrong during his administration. I am not equipped to explore the dark alleys of psychogenesis, but in 1965, after being in the White House for more than a year and obviously relishing the power of the presidency, he was clearly suspicious of much that went with it. There was more to his dislike of ambassadors than impatience with the strange protocol of diplomacy. His preoccupation with domestic legislation was an obvious factor, but even ambassadors of small countries represented a world he knew little or nothing about. He was cautious with the more influential newspaper columnists, who were accustomed to discussing the issues with presidents on more or less equal intellectual terms. His discreet moves in Congress explained part but not all of the caution. For all his years in Washington, he was suspicious of ideas. Foreign correspondents seemed to flummox him, although he was invariably polite and often helpful. The accents may have bothered him, but one often felt an impatience or suspicion of the extra and strange dimension their backgrounds gave to events.

He was also suspicious of many of the American establish-

ment men who served in the White House and the great departments such as State and Treasury. Presidents have long been
dependent upon such men because without them they cannot
begin to shoulder the responsibilities of their office. The Brook-
ings Institution was later to publish a report on their kind entitled *The Men Who Govern*. It discovered that more than half
were easterners, that six out of ten had attended private schools
such as Groton and Choate, and that most had gone on to the
Ivy League universities. Johnson, the president, needed them.
Johnson, the product of rural public schools and the Southwest
State Teachers College, Texas, was uncomfortable in the company of most of them. This antipathy drove him closer to Congress and to those old friends with whom he had settled
countless deals over countless glasses of whisky.

The gathering tidal wave of legislation did not submerge or
diminish Johnson's intense preoccupation with Vietnam. On
February 6, the Vietcong again attacked American camps, this
time at Pleiku and Camp Holloway. Seven military advisers
were killed and a hundred wounded. McGeorge Bundy, the
presidential special assistant for national security affairs, was in
Vietnam and visited Pleiku. Horrified by what he saw—perhaps
it was the first blood he had seen—the normally imperturbable
New Englander advised retaliation. The bombers immediately
flew north, and the massive air assault against North Vietnam
was launched. Johnson also ordered the evacuation of American
dependents from Saigon, and announced the dispatch of a marine air defense battalion equipped with Hawk missiles. They
were only to defend airfields but were the first of the hundreds
of thousands of fighting troops to be sent to Vietnam. Two jumps
had been taken up the escalator in a matter of hours. The president said, "We have no choice but to clear the decks and make
absolutely clear our continued determination to back South
Vietnam in its fight to maintain its independence." McNamara
said that the Vietcong attacks were a test of will and of the
political purpose of the United States. A response was necessary
to ensure that there was no misunderstanding.

Many people thought at the time that Johnson had acted impulsively, and they pointed to the presence of Aleksei Kosygin in Hanoi as conclusive evidence. Nothing could have been further from the truth. Kosygin's visit to Hanoi had not been forgotten. A destroyer patrol in the Gulf of Tonkin was canceled and the number of aircraft carriers on station reduced to avoid incident. Some of Johnson's advisers also thought that prompt and stern action would make the Russians think twice before allying themselves with North Vietnam. Moreover, Johnson had long been preparing for war. The U.S. Pacific Command was ordered to get ready soon after the passing of the Gulf of Tonkin resolution. In the words of Admiral U. S. Grant Sharp, commander in chief Pacific (CINCPAC), "Extensive plans were made for future punitive or retaliatory strikes to be made in response to any renewed overt acts of aggression." An operation order, with the code name Flaming Dart, was developed. Pleiku only provided the opportunity to put it into action. The advice of Bundy was not much more than an elegant establishment stamp on what had long been decided. General Harold Johnson, chief of the army staff, had also just visited Vietnam. It was his first visit to Asia. He knew nothing about the local terrain and people but concurred with the findings of the 1963 and 1964 war games. It is no exaggeration to say that Johnson had declared war, albeit secretly, against North Vietnam months before he made the announcement of the first expeditionary force.

There was, of course, no reference to the Southeast Asia Treaty Organization, which was to be used as a diplomatic cover for intervention. Nor was there any further reference to Congress after the passage of the Gulf of Tonkin resolution. The reason was that Johnson and his advisers anticipated a quick and relatively painless victory. North Vietnamese air defenses were farcical, amounting to twenty early-warning radar sets with little tracking ability. There were then no surface-to-air missiles, and the air force consisted of about thirty trainers, fifty transports, and four light helicopters. Admittedly air reconnaissance had reported the arrival of Chinese MIG-15 and MIG-17 fighter aircraft at Phuc Yen airfield near Hanoi. A number of airfields were also under construction in southern China. The major base was at Ningming, some twelve miles from the North Vietnamese frontier and close to the vital railhead at Pingsiang. Clearly they were intended to provide air cover for the lines of communication to the south. Chinese fighters were also concentrated on Hainan island, but this did not disturb the Johnson administration. It had long been decided that China could not intervene. Even Chinese air cover for North Vietnamese cities was considered unlikely by the intelligence agencies as long as American aircraft did not venture too far north of the 19th Parallel.

North Vietnam was seen to be a sitting duck. Whatever its ability to fight a guerrilla war, there was nothing it could do to stop the American bombers. This was the argument of the air force, but it was a major miscalculation. In the previous November, Pham Van Dong, the Prime Minister of North Vietnam, had gone to Moscow ostensibly to celebrate the anniversary of the October Revolution. He also went to request military and technical assistance, and he arrived at the right time. Khrushchev had just been deposed, and the new Russian leaders were busy reviewing Soviet policy. They had to act. The bombing of a communist country was for them an affront, no less than for the United States if Soviet bombers had attacked a Latin American country.

Other power factors demanded action. They could not hope to retain what was left of their once monolithic power in the communist world if China was allowed to become the sole supplier of North Vietnam's war requirements. The decision was made to send them surface-to-air missiles (SAMs) and other modern weapons and equipment that China could not provide. Pham Van Dong returned to Hanoi with assurances that all requirements would be met. Thus the effect of the first American retaliatory raid was to achieve, if only temporarily, what many had regarded as impossible—a degree of Sino-Soviet unity. More important, Soviet aid was to upset all those computer calculations. Much of this was not missed by the Kremlinologists. The usual scholarly assessments were passed up to the top, but they were ignored. Or rather, the computers were reprogrammed. Nothing could convince Johnson and his advisers that anything could be done to offset the overwhelming power of the United States.

With the vital exception of military aid, the original American assessment that the Soviet Union and China would not intervene directly proved to be correct. Rusk's warning that the United States would not respect so-called Chinese sanctuaries, as it had during the Korean War, might have helped. There was Russian talk at the time of providing East German and Czechoslovak pilots for the North Vietnamese air force, but nothing came of it. China did send some 30,000 troops south but only to strengthen and protect the lines of communication between the two countries. Antiaircraft units were also sent. For the next three years American aircraft attacked Chinese troops and were fired on in return. At times it seemed that both countries were on the edge of the abyss, but Peking remained cautious, never admitting the presence of Chinese troops, and Washington never lost its nerve. But a price was paid. The two communist giants provided North Vietnam with the necessary arms, ammunition, and food, without which it could not have continued the war. One could perhaps argue that Johnson lost it when he avenged Pleiku with too little regard for the consequences.

Little or nothing of this was known to the American people, but concern over the bombing was not widespread. One must assume that the majority was outraged by the deaths of American servicemen and saw the retaliatory strikes as an eye for an eye. In Washington the newly created consensus began to show some cracks, but this did not deter Johnson. He told a group of Boy Scouts that he hoped American strength and fortitude would not be miscalculated. "We love peace. We shall do all we can in honor to preserve it for ourselves and all mankind, but we love liberty more and we shall take up any challenge, answer any threat, pay any price to make certain that freedom shall not perish from this earth."

As the old cliché has it, the president now had the bit between his teeth. He did not try hard to seek public or open congressional support. How could he, when he was determined to pursue the war with as little debate as possible? Instead of twisting congressional arms, pressing flesh, and indulging in all the other parliamentary calisthenics of which he was the undoubted master, he even refused to admit that targets in Laos had been bombed in the previous week. He avoided the press (the chummy walks around the White House garden had stopped long before) and when cornered chose to speak only of the Great Society and peace. He was now launched on what was known as controlled escalation. The objectives were said to be unchanged, a negotiated settlement or the withdrawal of North Vietnamese help to the Vietcong, but there was to be no expansion of the war. Controlled bombing was to be the instrument of persuasion.

In fact, operation Flaming Dart had already been superseded by operation Rolling Thunder. Bombing was no longer to be confined to retaliatory acts, but was intended to destroy the will and the capability of the enemy to continue the war. In a message to unit commanders, CINCPAC described Rolling Thunder as a precise application of military pressure for the specific purpose of halting aggression in South Vietnam. The first strikes were launched on March 2 and were under the strict control of the president, who even selected the targets. For the sake of appearances, they were first made dependent upon the participation of the South Vietnamese air force. In theory, the United States was still only helping South Vietnam to defend itself. Attacks were limited to primary targets. There were no alternative targets for pilots who could not reach their destinations. Unused bombs had to be dropped into the South China Sea. There were other prohibitions to ensure complete presidential control. The air force was irked by this and complained that the air crews were not being allowed to be fully effective. Certainly the communist infiltration of men and matériel to the south continued unabated. The first Russian SAMs had also been delivered, and two American F-105s were quickly shot down. In future, American pilots would no longer bomb defenseless peasants at their leisure and in absolute safety. They would have to contend with the most modern antiaircraft missiles available. The number of MIG fighters provided by the Chinese had also increased to about seventy, and reconnaissance pictures of unpacked crates indicated that more were awaiting assembly. North Vietnamese radar had been improved, and some IL-28 light bombers delivered. Johnson needed time to review the situation, and the bombing was suspended for six days. The pause was mistaken as a peace move, perhaps because of Johnson's speech at Johns Hopkins University. He said that he was prepared to hold unconditional discussions to bring about an end to the war. He would try to prevent the conflict from spreading. He proposed an economic development program for Southeast Asia, including North Vietnam.

Unhappily, neither the speech nor the bombing pause was the prelude to a diplomatic offensive. Peace was certainly not on Johnson's mind, and his impatience with peaceful foreigners was publicly revealed when Lester Pearson, the Canadian Prime Minister, suggested a complete halt to the bombing. The presidential anger was awful but delightful to observe. Afterward, in the privacy of his office, Johnson called for the list of foreign visitors expected that year. He went down the column of names with a thick pencil. Out went the president of Pakistan, and out went the prime minister of India. The pencil hovered over the name of Harold Wilson, the British prime minister. An assistant reminded Johnson that Wilson had defended his Vietnam policy at considerable political cost against the left wing of the Labour Party and that the Foreign Office was cooperating splendidly with the State Department. Britain of all countries could not be accused of irresponsible neutralism. Her troops were defending Malaysia in the Indonesian confrontation. Indeed, there were many more of them in Southeast Asia than Americans in Vietnam. Britain was also a co-chairman, with the Soviet Union, of the 1954 Geneva Conference, and had a special responsibility for the final peace settlement. The pencil still hovered until it was recalled that Wilson had essential business to transact with the International Monetary Fund in Washington. Johnson was told that the visit could not be canceled without creating an international incident, and Wilson was reluctantly allowed to come.

Michael Stewart, the British foreign secretary, had already been in Washington that spring. The visit was dramatized by the reluctant admission that nauseous gases had been used in Vietnam, and Stewart was asked about it after addressing the National Press Club. He spoke softly. The difficulties of fighting a jungle war were recognized, as was the American obligation to defend South Vietnam. Military measures had to be taken, but their effect upon world opinion must be considered along with their operational effectiveness. As the Declaration of Independence said, there must be a decent respect for the opinions of mankind. It was the only criticism Stewart allowed himself, but it was made clear that Britain, and other American allies, also hated the bombing. Johnson was reminded that he had embarked upon a war with weapons abhorrent to nations which, unlike the United States, had been exposed to the horrors of bombing.

Nevertheless, the bombing was resumed after the military review. So much for a decent respect for the opinions of mankind. Indeed, it became much more vicious. One air force officer said that it was a different ball game. Johnson still retained control of the selection of major targets, but many of the old limitations were removed. The bombing zone was extended northward to the 20th Parallel, and beyond when specific targets were called for. The prime purpose now was to demonstrate the ubiquity of American air power. Bombing was in theory confined to military targets, but the new strategy of attrition and harassment, coupled with the establishment of strike zones, in which anything suspicious could be attacked, in fact gave the air force a fairly free hand. Unused bombs were no longer dumped in the sea but dropped on any inviting target. Large cities were still off limits, but otherwise the air war was limited only by the supply of aircraft and airfields available. The last bottleneck was avoided when Thailand allowed bases to be built on its territory.

When one country bombs another, even with the best of intentions, explosions must be expected in both, and the second stage of operation Rolling Thunder had more effect at home than in Vietnam. The first student demonstration was held outside the White House, and there were teach-ins across the country. The reaction of the State Department was to send so-called truth squads to the campuses to remind students of the responsibilities of power. Truth was, of course, the first casualty of the Vietnam conflict, but conflicting reports of Rolling Thunder brought the first major complaint about the credibility gap. The Associated Press Managing Editors' Association complained of "the contradictions, the double-talk and half truths ... in Washington and Saigon." The editors did not then know the extent of the gap. Even as they sat in convention, the Pentagon was planning to take over the conduct of the war from the South Vietnamese. This was not made known, of course, and only after more talk about peace did the State Department announce that American troops might soon be engaged in offensive action against the Vietcong.

Prevarication continued, although troops were already being trained for jungle warfare in Hawaii and elsewhere. As late as June, McGeorge Bundy publicly announced that Johnson had rejected advice to extend the war. United States policy was to stay put in Vietnam and seek a peace conference. Then the following month, Johnson appeared on television and said that American military strength in Vietnam would be immediately brought up to 125,000 men, and further forces would be sent as needed. The final step had at last been announced, without reference to Congress and while the American people had been led to expect a move toward peace as well as the Great Society. Only afterward was it discovered that Johnson had committed troops in Vietnam without the formal request or permission of the Saigon government.

Some reasonable explanation had to be given why American divisions were to be sent to Vietnam and why more would be sent when requested by the commanding general, General William Westmoreland. What Johnson, Rusk, and McNamara said was supposed to define American policy, the objective and the commitment, but as we shall see, honesty did not at last prevail. The statements did, however, serve as the justification for the American involvement until events in Vietnam and at home finally forced Johnson to bring about negotiations by stopping the bombing. They are summarized here.

Speaking at his press conference on July 28, when the dispatch of fighting troops was announced, Johnson said that three times in his lifetime, in two world wars and Korea, Americans had gone to far lands to fight for freedom. They had learned that retreat did not bring safety and weakness did not bring peace, and this was the lesson that was to take them to Vietnam. He admitted that some South Vietnamese had grievances and had joined in the attack against the Saigon government, but this did not mask the central factor that this was war. "It is guided by North Vietnam and spurred by communist China. Its goal is to conquer the South, to defeat American power, and to extend the Asiatic dominion of communism." Great stakes were in the balance. The United States was the vital shield for noncommunist states in the area against the growing might and grasping ambition of Asian communism. If driven from the field, no nation would ever again have the same confidence in American promise and protection. The forces of independence would be weakened, and an Asia so threatened by communist domination would imperil the security of the United States. Surrender would not bring peace. The lesson of Hitler and Munich was that success only fed the appetite of aggression. "Moreover, we are in Vietnam to fulfill one of the most solemn pledges of the American nation. Three presidents—President Eisenhower, President Kennedy and your present president—over eleven years, have committed themselves and have promised to help defend this small and valiant nation.... We cannot now dishonor our word or abandon our commitment or leave those who believed us and who trusted us to the terror and repression and murder that would follow. This, then, my fellow Americans, is why we are in Vietnam."

Johnson said that the draft would be increased but that the reserves would not be called up, and went on to define the objective. "We do not seek the destruction of any government, nor do we covet a foot of any territory. But we insist, and we will always insist, that the people of South Vietnam shall have the right of choice, the right to shape their own destiny in free elections in the South, or throughout all Vietnam under international supervision. And they shall not have any government imposed upon them by force and terror so long as we can prevent it. This was the purpose of the 1954 [Geneva] agreements which the communists have so cruelly shattered. If the machinery of those agreements was tragically weak, its purposes still guide our action."

Then the president added a personal note that reminded his listeners of the anguish of his decision. For all the wheeling and dealing, the deviousness and reluctance to play square with the nation, Johnson already thought he knew the costs of his decision. For a brief moment he was also honest with himself. "I do not find it easy to send the flower of our youth, our finest young men, into battle. I have spoken to you today of the divisions and the forces and the battalions and the units. But I know them all, every one. I have seen them in a thousand streets, in a hundred towns, in every state in this Union—working and laughing, building, and filled with hope and life. I think that I know, too, how their mothers weep and how their families sorrow. This is the most agonizing and the most painful duty of your president.

"There is something else, too. When I was young, poverty was so common that we didn't know it had a name. Education was something you had to fight for. And water was life itself. I have now been in public service thirty-five years, more than three decades, and in each of those thirty-five years I have seen good men, and wise leaders, struggle to bring the blessings of this land to all of our people. Now I am the president. It is now my opportunity to help every child get an education, to help every Negro and every American citizen have an equal opportunity, to help every family get a decent home and to help bring healing to the sick and dignity to the old. As I have said before, that is what I have lived for. That is what I have wanted all my life. And I do not want to see all those hopes and all those dreams of so many people for so many years now drowned in the wasteful ravages of war. I am going to do all I can to see that that never happens. But I also know, as a realistic public servant, that as long as there are men who hate and destroy we must have the courage to resist, or we will see it all, all that we have built, all that we hope to build, all of our dreams for freedom—all swept away on the floods of conquest. So this too shall not happen; we will stand in Vietnam."

Dean Rusk, the secretary of state, testified before the House Foreign Affairs Committee on August 3. He said that the war in Vietnam was a test of a technique of aggression, what the communists, in their upside-down language, called wars of national liberation. The term described the communist effort, short of large-scale war, to destroy by force any noncommunist government. The communists knew that thermonuclear war would be ruinous and that large-scale invasions, such as in Korea, were risky. They had therefore resorted to semiconcealed aggression through the infiltration of arms and trained military personnel across national frontiers. The assault on South Vietnam was, beyond question, an aggression, organized and directed by North Vietnam with the backing of China. That the dividing line between North and South Vietnam was intended to be temporary did not make the attack any less of an aggression. The United States was committed to oppose aggression, through the United Nations Charter and many alliances. American power and readiness to assist others to resist aggression, and the integrity of the American commitment, were the bulwarks of peace in the world.

"The primary responsibility for defeating the Vietcong will remain, however, with the South Vietnamese. They have some 545,000 men in military and paramilitary forces. . . . The primary missions of the American ground forces are to secure the airbases used by the South Vietnamese and ourselves and to provide a strategic reserve, thus releasing South Vietnamese troops for offensive actions against the Vietcong. In securing the airbases and related military installations, American forces are pushing out into the countryside to prevent build-ups for surprise attacks. And they may be used in emergencies to help the South Vietnamese in combat. But the main task of rooting out the Vietcong will continue to be the responsibility of the South Vietnamese."

On the following day, Robert McNamara, the defense secretary, spoke before the Senate Appropriations Defense Subcommittee. He said that the situation had deteriorated rapidly since the overthrow of the Diem government. Throughout 1964 the communists had greatly increased the scope and tempo of their subversive efforts, and the flow of men and supplies had increased. The ratio of South Vietnamese to Vietcong strength had seriously declined to about three to one. This was far too low a ratio for a guerrilla war even if it had been offset by the greater mobility and fire power provided by the United States. The full weight of the communist attack had yet to be felt. More American combat troops would be needed, but "the principal role of U.S. ground combat forces will be to supplement this [central] reserve in support of the front line forces of the South Vietnamese army. The indigenous paramilitary forces will deal with the pacification of areas cleared of organized Vietcong and North Vietnamese units, a role more appropriate for them than for our forces. What we are seeking through the planned military build-up is to block the Vietcong offensive, to give the people of South Vietnam and their armed forces some relief from unrelenting communist pressures—to give them time to strengthen their government, to re-establish law and order, and to improve their economic life which has been seriously disrupted by Vietcong harassment and attack. . . .

"Fortunately, we have greatly increased the strength and readiness of our military establishment since 1961, particularly in the kinds of forces which we now require in Southeast Asia. The active army has been expanded from eleven to sixteen combat-ready divisions. Twenty thousand men have been added to the Marine Corps to allow them to fill out their combat structure and at the same time facilitate the mobilization of the Marine Corps Reserve. The tactical fighter squadrons of the air force have been increased by 51 percent. Our airlift capability has more than doubled. Special Forces trained to deal with insurgency threats have been multiplied eleven-fold."

These statements reveal a good deal of the thinking of Johnson and senior advisers at the time. They were convinced of the righteousness of their cause. There can be no doubt about that. They and the preceding administration had also got ready for this moment. Vietnam was probably the first war in American history in which sufficient forces were ready, equipped, and trained to do battle. McNamara remarked that fortunately the military establishment had been greatly increased in strength and readiness, but the fact of the matter was that, first under Kennedy and then Johnson, the civilian leadership of the Defense Department had been actively preparing for such a war. This high state of readiness helped to explain the unspoken assumption that American troops would quickly dispose of ragged Asian guerrillas—certainly by the 1966 midterm elections. The march toward the Great Society would be interrupted, but only briefly. Otherwise the country would not be much incommoded. No reserves would be called up. No plans were made to increase taxation to pay for the war. To some extent, their confidence was well founded.

A majority of Americans, reluctantly or otherwise, were ready to accept the presidential decision that war was necessary. Convinced that the Russians and Chinese would not intervene, Johnson and his advisers believed that the war would remain small and manageable. The number of men available for the draft was so high that there would be no need to call up the reserves. Indeed, service in Vietnam was limited to one year, including an extended leave in nearby countries. At home the economic boom continued, promising increased revenue without higher taxes. The funding of the Great Society was a relatively slow business, and cutbacks would not be necessary except in some antipoverty programs. Some Americans who saw their country as the successor of Britain as a world policeman recalled that during her imperial period Britain had fought many such peripheral wars without taxing the economy and without a military draft.

Nevertheless, there were reasons for less confidence. Apart from the French experience, which was rarely if ever mentioned in Washington at the time, the commitment was both strange and dangerous. It was not a straightforward matter of going to the defense of a plucky little country invaded by an outside aggressor, such as the German invasions of Belgium in 1914 and of Poland in 1939, which brought about the First and Second World Wars. Prior to the American bombings, the conflict was undoubtedly a civil war, in that only southerners were fighting southerners. Even when he testified before the Senate Subcommittee in August, McNamara could only report that from one to three North Vietnamese regiments appeared to be moving southward. Yet they could hardly be said to be foreigners. All were Vietnamese. Moreover, no viable government ruled in Saigon after the overthrow of the Diem regime. The United States treated with a bewildering succession of political generals who strutted briefly on the world stage with no pretense of a popular following. Worse, as McNamara intimated, South Vietnam no longer existed as a recognizable state. The war in fact had been lost. Thus Johnson proposed not only to reverse the decision of the battlefield but also to recreate a state.

The reasons given were hardly persuasive. There was no evidence that China was in any way responsible for the civil war, beyond providing arms, as did the United States to its own client states. It was difficult to see how American security was threatened. The integrity of American commitments was certainly one of the bulwarks of world peace, but there was no commitment in Vietnam until Johnson chose to make one. To be fair, he had been gravely compromised by Kennedy, who in 1961 had chosen to send military advisers, but the relevant official documents written after the 1954 Geneva conference did not commit the United States to defend South Vietnam.

For instance, Eisenhower offered aid to Diem in a letter dated October 1, 1954, but added the following qualifications:

The purpose of this offer is to assist the government of Vietnam in developing and maintaining a strong, viable state, capable of resisting attempted subversion or aggression through military means. The government of the United States expects that this aid will be met by performance on the part of the government of Vietnam in undertaking needed reforms. It hopes that such aid, combined with your own continuing efforts, will contribute effectively towards an independent Vietnam endowed with a strong government. Such a government would, I hope, be so responsive to the nationalist aspirations of its people, so enlightened in purpose and effective in performance, that it will be respected both at home and abroad and discourage any who might wish to impose a foreign ideology on your free people.

In a second letter, dated October 26, 1960, Eisenhower promised continuing assistance but prefaced it thus: "The main responsibility for guarding that independence will always, as it has in the past, belong to the Vietnamese people and their government."

Kennedy went far beyond Eisenhower. Apart from sending military advisers, he wrote to Diem on December 14, 1961, referring to the Geneva accords. He went on, "The United States, although not a party to the accords, declared that it 'would view any renewal of the aggression in violation of the agreements with grave concern and as seriously threatening international peace and security.' We continue to maintain that view." Many of his admirers have said that Kennedy, had he lived, would have avoided deeper involvement in Vietnam. No one can say. Walt Rostow, who served both Kennedy and Johnson, afterward said that Kennedy would have been forced to pursue the same escalating course. He said that Kennedy was very tough and would not have accepted defeat. He might have moved in earlier than Johnson did.

Rostow may not be the best witness, but if Kennedy was the cooler, more thoughtful man, he had accepted the new concepts of wars of national liberation and had prepared to fight them. He gave Khrushchev an avenue of retreat during the

Cuban missile crisis, but I am not so certain that he would have retreated in Vietnam. He had the opportunity in 1961 and 1963 and refused it. Johnson also had the opportunity, but he was caught in a greater trap than was Kennedy. In 1963 his first purpose was to demonstrate continuity at home and abroad. Nineteen sixty-four was an election year, and by the beginning of 1965 South Vietnam was about to disintegrate completely. It would have taken more than moral courage to withdraw. The American tradition of victory was too strong, no more for a Texan than for an Irish-American from Massachusetts. And yet even on that grim day in July, the Johnson administration refused to be honest with the American people. Both Rusk and McNamara said that the prime responsibility for fighting the war would remain with the South Vietnamese, although both knew that they were then hardly capable of fighting a platoon action successfully.

General Westmoreland had earlier reported from Saigon that government institutions had deteriorated and in some instances had disappeared altogether. Local government officials had come to terms with the Vietcong. The effectiveness of the army had decreased markedly and was compounded by desertions. The army seldom chose to close with the enemy, and patrolling had virtually ceased. In comparison, the military and political organization of the Vietcong had assumed the scope and strength of a regular government. In one province, forty-six of its forty-eight villages were administered by the Vietcong. The first Vietcong division had been organized and committed to combat, and most of its forces were moving from guerrilla warfare to a more conventionally organized offensive. By late summer of 1964 they posed an immediate threat to Saigon. In December they had seized the village of Binh Gia and virtually destroyed two South Vietnamese battalions. The battle, said General Westmoreland, was a major event for both sides. For the enemy, it marked the beginning of the classic and final mobile phase of the war. For the South Vietnamese government, it meant the beginning of an intensive military challenge which the government could not meet within its own resources.

Collapse was inevitable by the late spring of 1965, when General Westmoreland recommended the large-scale commitment of American combat troops. His reasons were given afterward: "The South Vietnamese army was losing almost one infantry battalion a week to enemy action. Additionally, the enemy was gaining control of at least one district capital town each week. It was my estimate that the government of Vietnam could not survive this mounting enemy military and political offensive for more than six months unless the United States chose to increase its military commitment."*

These were the troops who were supposed to retain the prime responsibility for fighting the war.

Nineteen sixty-five was an extraordinary year by any standard. While Johnson was misleading the country into war, the unmanned Ranger 8 space capsule televised to earth 7,126 pictures of the moon's surface. They persuaded most scientists that astronauts could be landed without disappearing into a bottomless pit of cosmic dust. Major Edward White became the first American to walk in space, and in July Mariner 4 successfully beamed back over a distance of 135 million miles the first closeup pictures of Mars. Not perhaps since Galileo first pointed his telescope at the moon had man taken so gigantic a step into the heavens. The following month Gemini 5 orbited earth for eight days, and by the end of the year Gemini 6 and 7 rendezvoused in space.

There was also considerable progress in Congress. Both houses acted with dispatch on bills, including some which had spent years gathering dust in the pigeonholes of committee chairmen or had previously foundered on the submerged rocks of the southern Democrat–conservative Republican coalition. Elderly legislators bustled about like so many youngsters. Others tugged deferentially at their forelocks before hurrying back from the White House to attend hearings and urge all undue speed. Johnson's reputation for getting things done was en-

*Report on the War in Vietnam (Washington: Government Printing Office 1969).

hanced beyond the wildest expectations as the legislative foundations for a quiet domestic revolution were laid. Some congressmen complained that things were moving too fast, but their air of resignation indicated that the tide of reform was too strong to resist. Senator Sam Ervin of North Carolina, for instance, said that he was prepared to be legislatively lynched but hoped to make the process as painless as possible. A group of Republicans raised their voices in the wilderness to protest against the manner in which the House version of the education bill was urged on the Senate. They appealed to the Constitution, which vests legislative power in Congress, and said, "Now, by decree of the President of the United States, the Senate is to be shorn of its equal share of that power. This important and complex piece of legislation on which your committee heard more than 90 witnesses, whose testimony filled six volumes and more than 3,200 pages, is to pass this body without a dot or comma changed: this by fiat of the chief executive."

They were crying in the wind. The Democratic majorities were decisive, Johnson's leadership incomparable, and his consensus too broad. One of the more noteworthy products of this trinity of strengths was the Elementary-Secondary Education Act mentioned above. Earlier attempts to help the schools had failed because the constitutional separation of state and church was seen to deny aid to parochial schools. During the Kennedy administration, the Roman Catholic hierarchy successfully lobbied against an aid bill excluding their schools as discriminatory legislation. Johnson avoided a frontal attack and proposed that assistance should be made available to children, especially in poor areas, and not to schools. The two largest lobbies, the National Education Association and the National Catholic Welfare Conference, were quietly approached and eventually brought into the national consensus. The bill was drafted in such a way as to attract the maximum number of votes in Congress, and in April it was enacted by the House without major amendment. The Senate voted on the House version with no change.

This tactic of debating and passing a bill in one house and then persuading the other to vote on it without amendment, which the Republican senators complained about, was brilliantly executed by Johnson. Each house normally holds separate committee hearings, drafts, amends, and votes on its own version, and the differences between the two are finally resolved in conference. This is time-consuming, especially when the process is repeated twice, once for authorization and once for appropriations. Opportunities are also created for the opposition to resist, amend, or kill legislation. Much of this was avoided by persuading the House or Senate to vote on the other's version. Thus the Senate accepted the House education bill after its own Appalachia bill whizzed unchanged through the House. Such cooperation was not always achieved, but the legislative pace, often hectic, overwhelmed a number of other barriers. Johnson was helped by Lawrence O'Brien, the postmaster general, who at the time spoke of building a bridge between the president and congressional leadership within, he hastened to add, the requirements of the Constitution.

In an interview with *U.S. News and World Report,* he said,

We started immediately to arrange for regular meetings, regular contact with our leaders on Capitol Hill on a week-to-week basis. We provided for a series of meetings, social gatherings, informal meetings of one sort or another that would bring the President in direct contact with the members. We tried to forge this and expand it and utilize people in the departments and agencies. We met regularly, for example, with some 40 key congressional-relations people. They represent every department and agency of the executive branch. They report to us in writing every Monday noon. These executive-branch people detail their activities with Congress over the previous week, we review these reports. We prepare, in turn, a report for the President for his night reading on Monday night—and we prepare a suggested agenda for the President when he meets with the congressional leadership on Tuesday morning.

Thus did Johnson exercise his extraordinary leadership and the authority of the national consensus which he had built. Yet he could not have achieved so much had not social legislation been long overdue. For instance, the Kennedy faction claimed the Medicare bill as their own because John Kennedy had introduced one version. When it was finally enacted, Johnson indulged in some delicious theatrical symbolism by flying to Independence, Missouri, to sign it into law in the presence of former President Truman, who had introduced the original version some twenty years before. Two decades were a long time, especially when medical costs had skyrocketed and other democracies had established far more comprehensive national health services. Johnson was further helped by the many young liberal Democrats who had come into office on his coattails. They even succeeded in expanding his requests for education, regional development, and antipoverty programs. Many did not survive the 1966 midterm elections, another price Johnson was to pay for Vietnam, but for a brief period he enjoyed the benefit and made the most of an almost unprecedented conjunction of forces eager for reform.

The first session of the 89th Congress, with the second of the 88th, will probably be his monument, and some of the major victories are worth listing. They were: the Appalachia Development Act, which was to revitalize one of the most depressed areas in the nation; the Education Act referred to above; the Constitutional Amendment Act, subsequently ratified as the Twenty-Fifth Amendment, which ensured presidential continuity by providing for the vice-president to become acting president if the president was unable to perform his duties, and also for the appointment of a vice-president; and the Medicare Act, which established a health-care insurance program under Social Security for persons aged sixty-five and over, larger Social Security pensions, and expansion of the Kerr-Mills program of medical assistance to the indigent-aged and child-welfare program. Many saw it as the thin end of the wedge for a more comprehensive national health service on the European model.

The Voting Rights Act was the second important civil rights act in two years and went significantly beyond the administration's bill. The law suspended literacy tests and provided for the federal registration of voters wherever necessary. The conference committee failed to resolve differences over the abolition of the poll tax, but the final version directed the attorney general to take action against its enforcement. The Department of Housing and Urban Development Act created a new cabinet post and a new federal department for the purpose of improving metropolitan areas. The Immigration Act liberalized the existing immigration laws, and eliminated the national origins quota system over a designated period. The Highway Beautification Act sought to improve the appearance and landscaping of interstate highways and was enacted only after an intense struggle between Johnson, representing his wife, and congressmen acting for the billboard lobby. The result could only be considered a draw.

In retrospect, the proposed constitutional amendment was probably the most important bill enacted by the 89th Congress because it helped to ensure presidential continuity. Certainly it came as a profound relief after the horror of November 22, 1963. As tragic as was Kennedy's death, what would have happened if he had survived the assassination attempt but with his brain irreparably damaged? The other legislative victories probably do not now sound quite so resounding. People are quick to accept the results of such advances as normal. Some of the acts were also too hastily drafted or were subsequently inadequately funded. Then the United States is also a union, and the federal government must invariably work through the state governments. A bill can be only an approximation of the original intention, and its application an approximation of an approximation. Nevertheless, Johnson carried on the good work begun during the New Deal, and the country will eventually be a better place to live in because of his efforts. By legislative standards, 1965 was certainly a vintage year. Together with 1964, it bore favorable comparison with the first two years of the Roosevelt New Deal. More impressive in retrospect, there were events apart from Vietnam that would have distracted most presidents, but Johnson proceeded single-mindedly and ruthlessly with his legislative program as if nothing untoward had occurred.

The first were the bloody happenings in Selma, Alabama, where a racial confrontation ended with the murder of a white woman, a civil rights worker, shot to death by a member of the Ku Klux Klan. Selma was in a way a historic turning point, and a turn for the worse. While there were to be other demonstrations in the South, Selma was the last of a series led by Dr. Martin Luther King, Jr. which could still persuade an anxious country that the Negro civil rights movement would and could remain essentially noviolent. As with most events of this kind, the tide of history had already turned. It had begun to turn when there was racial conflict in New York and other northern cities and in Mississippi in the previous summer.

The leadership of the civil rights movement had until then been peaceful and evolutionary. It had always been multiracial, a coalition of black gradualists and white liberals dedicated to the proposition of integration, but there was no single leadership. King was only the president of the Southern Christian Leadership Conference, a group based in Atlanta to mobilize the movement in the South. King achieved national prominence by organizing the Montgomery bus boycott, and was subsequently awarded the Nobel Peace prize. He was often compared with Gandhi, who successfully practiced Satyagraha, or nonviolence, against the British raj in India. He had borrowed from Gandhi but was essentially American, the son of a reasonably well-to-do family educated in the North but still a recognizable southern Negro preacher, who ultimately depended upon a God-fearing, or God-loving, flock. He was a superb speaker, but in the North, where the old relationship between preacher and congregation rarely existed, he was less successful.

King captured the imagination of the world, and its headlines, but much of the Negro progress over the decades was directly attributable to the National Association for the Advancement of Colored People. By far the largest and oldest of the various Negro groups, in 1965 it had a membership of 400,000 and had already celebrated its fiftieth anniversary. Its faith was in education, organization, and due process of the law, and it will long be remembered for its campaign against school segregation. A NAACP lawyer, Thurgood Marshall, pleaded the cause of school integration before the Supreme Court and was upheld in the historic decision of 1954. Marshall afterward became the first Negro to be appointed to the court. Roy Wilkins, the executive secretary of the NAACP, was a cultivated man who carried on the fight at many levels, including the White House, where he was a frequent caller. There were other organizations, such as the National Urban League and the Congress of Racial Equality. The latter was similar to the Southern Christian Leadership Conference in that it was more activist and practiced nonviolence at the barricades.

They were joined by the common goal of seeking by peaceful means an honorable place for the Negro in American society but they did not directly represent the masses of the northern ghetto. In 1930, long before King led his bus boycott, Elijah Muhammad, the Messenger of the Temple of Islam, had founded the Black Muslims in Detroit. This was a separatist movement in the tradition of Garvey which preached hatred of whites. The most favored of his followers, known as the Fruit of Islam, dropped their surnames and used the letter X as a rejection of the past, when many Negroes had taken the name of their slaveowner. For all the talk about Islam, the organization at times looked more like a black Mafia, and the many murders suggested that internal discipline was severe. Nevertheless, a splinter movement, the Organization of Afro-American Unity, was formed by Malcolm X, who was subsequently murdered. Malcolm X was an extraordinary man who taught self-discipline and got rid of the rhetoric of Elijah's Islam. Neither organization was numerically big, but their influence in the northern black ghettos, especially Chicago and New York, was much greater than was supposed at the time. Certainly they were responsible for the new spirit of revolt in the ghettos and the search for a black identity. This received more impetus when the Student Non-Violent Coordinating Committee changed course.

Snick, as it was usually called, began as a genuine student movement with religious roots. Many of its early members had come from southern Negro theological colleges. They were idealistic, activist, and brave. I had watched them often in the early sixties, and they had commanded the highest admiration.

Their religiousness was evident when they came to Washington in 1964 to attend a youth convention. While the young whites argued about participatory democracy and against Vietnam, they held prayer meetings and observed periods of silence. They were from another country, a very harsh place where stoicism was one of the few defenses against white prejudice and violence.

The change came that year when thousands of young white students went South to work for voter registration and generally help the civil rights movement. Some were beaten, a few killed, but the summer appeared to be a splendid promise of youthful idealism rising triumphant above racial animosity. I am not sure what happened. If God works in mysterious ways His wonders to perform, the forces against good can be equally difficult to detect and define. Perhaps the young Snick workers had been exposed too long to violence, and certainly when the change came there were more militant leaders ready to take charge. There was the assumption that these poor, relatively unsophisticated young southern Negroes were overwhelmed by the bright volunteers from Berkeley, Harvard, and a hundred other northern campuses. For many of them, it was the first time they had met the new generation of the affluent North. Perhaps they did not like what they saw or heard. In any event, their thing was no longer their own, but had suddenly been taken up by strangers, friendly, but nevertheless white strangers who had no concept of life in the South but had taken charge. Whatever the reason, Snick went separatist, and the new leaders preached violence and subsequently black power. Another fragile link between the races had snapped.

Separatism afterward swept through the northern ghettos, where the foundations had been laid by the Black Muslims. A black majority almost certainly held to the hope of being absorbed into the mainstream of American life, but rejection of white standards made violence respectable for others. Tens of thousands of youngsters, many from broken homes and all of them creatures of the ghetto streets, were ready for violence. It erupted suddenly in Watts, and after three days and nights of rioting more than thirty were killed and hundreds injured.

The eruption came as a terrible surprise for Johnson. There was unemployment and injustice in Watts, but generally speaking its inhabitants enjoyed a much higher standard of living than most black slum dwellers. As one of the presidential special assistants said at the time, the objective of the antipoverty programs was to raise the living standards of Negroes to those of Watts, and the killings seemed to suggest that material improvement was not the only answer to the growing racial antagonisms. Apart from federal aid programs, there was little Johnson could do directly. The state and city governments had prime responsibility, but final responsibility rested with the individual American. The president could divert some resources to hard-pressed state and city governments and set a personal example. Johnson did not have the personal magnetism of John Kennedy or Franklin Roosevelt, and I doubt if they could have done much. Johnson was in fact the first president to have accepted the fact that something had to be done to help Negroes take their place in American society. He was absolutely sincere, as were most members of his cabinet.

All things considered, I doubt that in 1965 the country could reasonably have expected a better administration for the task of reconciliation, but the terrible past was catching up with the American present and at the worst possible time. The United States began to move into a period of what was euphemistically described as hot summers. The Mississippi experience, with its rejection of white volunteers, was also to exacerbate the alienation of the younger generation and contribute to campus disorders. Thus Johnson, who had done more for Negroes and education than any president, was to see most of his high hopes disappear, if only temporarily, in violence.

As if that were not enough, American army troops and marines were landed at Santo Domingo in May to protect foreign nationals and to save the Dominican Republic from communism. Admittedly the Central Intelligence Agency could only identify fifty-three communists trained in the Soviet Union,

China, or Cuba, and the suspicion was that Johnson had recklessly responded to a situation misreported by the American ambassador there. Certainly the troops were landed without reference to the Organization of American States. Chile, Mexico, and Venezuela accused the United States of violating the OAS charter and the inter-American tradition of noninterference. If there was such a tradition, the origin must have been too recent for most Americans to know about it. When the excitement eased a little, critics were made aware that the president had the support of the country. He was even commended by Walter Lippmann, who devoted a column to explaining that the intervention was a welcome return to classical diplomacy. "It is normal, not abnormal, for a great power to insist that within its sphere of influence no other great power shall exercise hostile military and political force. . . ."

The Monroe Doctrine had, of course, long influenced American thinking about Latin America, but Johnson told congressmen at the time that he had intervened in the Dominican Republic, as in Vietnam, to stop wars of national liberation. The extension of the Monroe Doctrine, or the Johnson Doctrine, still had a rational appeal to most Americans, but their allies were apprehensive. To them, it seemed that Johnson was prepared to act almost anywhere in the world to maintain the status quo and regardless of alliances and the United Nations. The prospect was unnerving, especially after James Reston suggested in the *New York Times* that there was a need for allied action because the Johnson Doctrine would require more marines than the president had under his command. The thought of British, French, and West German troops serving like so many Hessians under American command did not please London, Paris, or Bonn, but these observations by two of the country's most distinguished journalists were a better indication of the American mood than the occasional protests against Vietnam. Indeed, Santo Domingo helped to justify that war.

Most Americans shared Johnson's conviction that a show of force would soon put an end to hostilities in Vietnam and that Hanoi would come to terms or quietly withdraw its troops. This expectation of early negotiations was to plague the administration later, but in 1965 Johnson listened to a hint from the Soviet Embassy that serious negotiations could begin if the bombing of North Vietnam was stopped. The Canadians were represented on the International Control Commission, one of the remnants of the 1954 Geneva accords. They therefore had access to Hanoi and began secret soundings. Diplomatic pressures increased. Wilson, the British prime minister, came to Washington again in early December and refused to condone the bombing of North Vietnamese cities, although Johnson supported the oil embargo against Rhodesia. He had jumped into the role of peacemaker, and somewhat reluctantly Johnson allowed himself to be persuaded. The first intimation of the American peace offensive was given by Rusk to foreign correspondents. The North Vietnamese had their four-point program, but the Secretary of State went back to Woodrow Wilson and similarly listed fourteen points.

It was a bit of a hodgepodge, but the relevant points were that the United States was ready for unconditional negotiations or, if Hanoi preferred, informal unconditional discussions. The 1954 and 1962 Geneva accords were accepted as a basis for negotiation, but the other side's four-point program could also be discussed. The bombing would be stopped if Hanoi was prepared to take similar reciprocal action. The bombing had in fact already stopped, and a number of special envoys were immediately dispatched around the globe. The American eagle flew into the new year with more than its usual solitary olive branch.

1966

Nineteen sixty-six was a midterm election year, a fact that had not been overlooked by Johnson when he agreed to the peace initiative and carried it out with a display of Johnsonian showmanship that must have impressed Hollywood. Averell Harriman, his special envoy, suddenly appeared in Warsaw looking every inch the honest but tough Ave who knew how to deal with communists. Vice-President Humphrey joined in the pursuit, and Arthur Goldberg, then United States permanent representative at the United Nations, added to the excitement when he arrived at the Vatican. They went on to girdle the earth, proclaiming that peace was the foremost American objective and requesting all and sundry to help bring it about. At first sight, their perambulations were rather baffling. There was no shortage of foreign peacemakers, everybody seemed to be getting into the act, but no one had any influence in Hanoi. Nevertheless, the bombing was stopped. The envoys did demonstrate the American willingness to negotiate. That said, Johnson also had secondary objectives. In the event of failure, he could demonstrate that the United States had no option but to fight. If the war was to go on through the summer, he had to prevent it from becoming an election issue. Still dreaming dreams of more legislative victories, he was determined to nurse his consensus.

At first it did not seem difficult. There was widespread disappointment when the bombing pause ended on the thirty-seventh day, but he had stopped the bombing for a longer period than the Russians or his advisers had proposed. Hanoi's intransigence had been proved. A large majority of Americans still supported the basic policy of resisting communist aggression. Life was also very good for them.

Affluence was unprecedented. The country was one huge cornucopia of every imaginable variety of consumer product, and the hucksters did not have to shout too much to attract the customers. The main problem in the big cities was still to provide parking space while they inspected the new light Scotch whiskies, sniffed the imported cheeses and—in Washington, at least—lined up for the frozen French bread flown in daily from Paris. There were more cars and color television sets than customers, and not because money was short. Taxes had not been raised, and unemployment continued to fall. The party talk was of coming vacations, of trips to Europe, to Latin America, and even to the Far East. The Taj Mahal and Tahiti beckoned from the pages of *The New Yorker*. Anxious to keep the dollars at home, at least until American business had invested them in Europe, Johnson called on his countrymen to see America first. Tens of thousands were saving to fly to Miami, but relative penury rather than patriotism explained this unfashionable summer choice.

The sale of small boats had boomed so much that nautical congestion was almost as bad as downtown traffic, and the pollution of coastal waters became a national problem. Higher mortgage rates (6 to 6½ percent) had affected housebuilding, but more families were putting in swimming pools and patios with barbecue pits. Gas barbecues were advertised to go with the old-fashioned gas lamps already installed on a million or more suburban lawns, which were tended with expensive care. Central air conditioning was going into many modest homes. Air-conditioned cars were a must in many areas, and those whose credit had been strained by payments on university fees, the fiberglass cabin cruiser, or the new kitchen were said to drive with their windows up. They would rather sweat than admit the shame of not being with it.

There were tears, alas. If the casualty rate in Vietnam was still politically bearable, a small fraction of the carnage on the roads, such comparisons or military and political calculations were of small comfort for the next of kin. But there was affluence also in death. The dreaded announcement was no longer delivered by Western Union messenger. An officer called at the afflicted homes to break the news. Americans who had no direct involvement in the war, and they remained a majority, were aware of the tears, of course, but the plain fact was that in the midst of war they had never had it so good and most were determined to enjoy themselves. I remember remarking upon the mood to a presidential assistant, who was surprised only by my surprise. He said, "Surely it was like that in England when British troops were fighting in Kandahar." The reference to that Afghanistan campaign, which ended in a disastrous British retreat, was unfortunate but apt. In 1966, the United States was spending about $12 billion on the war. The mind boggled at such a sum, but it was less than 2 percent of the gross national product, or proportionately no more than Britain had spent on her colonial wars. Moreover, the American economy continued to perform its usual miracles. Johnson reported to the nation that "despite the fact that we deployed a military force of more than 100,000 men within 120 days and sent them halfway round the world, we have been able to keep that force constantly supplied and equipped so that at all times they have been capable of bringing their full power against the aggressor.... No required air sorties have been canceled. As a matter of fact, the air support given our forces is without parallel in our history." Even the production of ammunition outpaced the conspicuous consumption of the army in Vietnam, and McNamara said that a substantial reduction of planned rates of production was desirable.

The most lavishly equipped army the world had ever seen

(the airmobile division had 450 helicopters) had been supplied with everything it wanted without financial or economic controls. The strength of the economy was such that government revenue had again exceeded the estimates of the Budget Bureau. Some stresses and strains were apparent. The cost of living rose, but the inflationary pressures would then have been welcomed in Western Europe as evidence of price stability. Affluence was not yet the birthright of every American family, and the poor were beginning to suffer from the postponement or reduction of some antipoverty programs. The country could clearly afford both guns and butter, and some argued that it could afford to produce and share more butter with the poor. They called for a tax increase to take out what heat there was in the economy and finance the Great Society programs as originally planned. But such an increase would not have been popular with the business world and middle-class majority, and Johnson wanted to make the war as painless as possible. The boat could not be rocked.

His was a sophisticated policy and not nearly as cynical as it may sound given Johnson's belief in the righteousness of the war and the American capability of winning it. After his landslide victory in 1964 he had to expect some Democratic losses in the coming elections, but he would need all the votes he could get in the new 90th Congress if the old conservative coalition was not to starve the Great Society programs of funds. In retrospect it can be argued that a more responsible president would have requested a tax increase when the troops were first committed, but the arguments against were not all political. It would not have been deflationary if the money had been spent on the antipoverty programs, and there were those who argued that inflation would create more jobs than any federal program. This was proved correct: unemployment fell from 5 percent in 1965 to about 3.6 percent in 1968 in spite of the continued population increase.

In retrospect, the policy was perhaps too sophisticated, both for Americans and the North Vietnamese. Most people associate war with at least some austerity at home, with shortages of consumer goods and higher taxes. Such inconveniences have proved to be great civilian morale builders. The housewife who is denied her favorite cut of meat and the secretary who cannot get enough nylons can be persuaded that they are doing their bit for the war effort. Instead, there was unprecedented abundance, and if this helped to keep the war at a distance the eventual shock was to be all the more damaging for Johnson when the war was seen to be unwinnable. The strategy of the carrot and the stick, of offering peace to the North Vietnamese one day and bombing hell out of them the next, was also confusing for ordinary Americans and dangerous for the two governments locked in what was seen to be a contest of wills. Senator Fulbright decided that only psychologists could explain the dangers, and he invited Professor Charles Osgood, of the University of Illinois, to testify before the Senate Foreign Relations Committee.

Osgood doubted that the strategy of intensifying the level of attack while holding out an olive branch was psychologically feasible because the reactions to both were incompatible. He seriously questioned if escalation and de-escalation could go together. There was the trouble of knowing when to get off the escalator. The opponent was always expected to get off first. Then there was the difficulty of communicating intentions to the enemy. The messages never got through with equal clarity when the promise of de-escalation was made with each escalating step. It was easier for North Vietnam to believe American aggressive statements because threats and not promises were expected from the enemy. As a consequence, there was a constant bias of credibility which favored further escalation.

Osgood went further. He said that if the United States was experimenting with calculated escalation as a strategy for dealing with wars of national liberation then it was in danger of swallowing a baited hook. For twenty years this nation had been building up the mightiest military force ever seen, yet it had been sitting on those arms, and for some people this was a frustrating and downright humiliating posture. The strategy of calculated escalation offered a rationalization for the use of force and gave it a hard, scholarly legitimacy. The temptation to use this military power was the bait.

Real escalators can run down just as easily as up, but psychological escalators tend to keep on going up. Each increase in tension makes more difficult the accurate communication and understanding necessary for de-escalation. Internally, especially in a democracy, it also becomes extremely difficult politically to back down. Externally, escalation hardens rather than softens the enemy's resolve. Psychologically one can become glued to an escalator only too easily, and this was the hook.

The professor was to be proved impressively prophetic, but the day had not yet dawned when psychologists were admitted to the National Security Council. The intellectual arrogance of men such as McNamara, who had created this mighty military force and devised the basic strategy of the graduated deterrent, was impervious to such warnings and criticism. A statistician and former chairman of the Ford Motor Company, McNamara had won the admiration of liberals by asserting civilian control over the military. That was the claim, but it did not bear close examination. In fact, he had bought them off. As defense secretary in the Kennedy administration, McNamara had discovered that there was no missile gap in spite of what Kennedy had charged during the presidential election campaign. Nevertheless, he went on to order hundreds of Minutemen intercontinental ballistic missiles and flotillas of Polaris submarines. Nor was the army forgotten. A new generation of troop-carrying aircraft was pressed upon it. The Special Forces were expanded, and infantry tactics revolutionized by equipping divisions with helicopters. It was the largest jump in the postwar arms race with the Soviet Union, and it is worthwhile recalling that there were no outraged objections from the liberal community.

Indeed, McNamara was seen to be representative of all that was best in the new generation of modern American technological man. The management tools he brought to the Pentagon, such as systems and cost analyses, were welcomed as a new form of rationalism, an extension by computer of the best of the

Age of Enlightenment in which the Republic had been founded. Certainly he used them to steamroller the presumed obstructionism and rural obscurantism of elderly southern senators such as Senator John McClellan, who was chairman of a committee investigating the TFX aircraft. Subsequently known as the F-111, it was the brainchild of McNamara, who had a passion for standardization. He had even tried to standardize the belt buckles of the armed services, oblivious of the fact that morale and *esprit de corps* could depend upon such little traditional differences. In the case of the TFX, he also overruled various experts who had concluded that one aircraft could not serve the purposes of the army and navy. Years afterward, and several crashes and hundreds of millions of dollars later, it was reluctantly agreed that this was the case. It was also revealed that the project had not been exposed to systems analysis.

Such was the arrogance of old New Frontiersmen who had remained to advise Johnson, and their blind faith in computer logic further misled the president when they applied to guerrilla warfare a strategy devised, but still untested, for a nuclear confrontation. The danger was pointed out by another professor in the *Bulletin of the Atomic Scientists.* William Polk, of the University of Chicago, said that the mechanistic approach associated with the RAND Corporation had spread from military planning to politicomilitary affairs. The approach was characterized by the so-called war-games theory. The professor, who had earlier served on the policy planning council at the State Department, said that in war games foreign problems were reduced to scenarios. Anatagonists were pitted against each other in a confrontation, and logical responses to given moves were analyzed and escalated to a showdown. The perception of international politics was thus changed. Confrontation was implicit, as was the existence of two opposing teams with some irritating interruptions by bit players such as Britain and France. The real stuff of international relations, the peculiarities of the several players, was washed out. "A sort of world-man, who logically and coolly understand and rightly play the game, was posited. That this school of thought deeply affected our thinking on the Berlin and Cuba crises is evident."

The new generation of nuclear theorists devised the methodology to equip the president with the means and discipline to control and use nuclear weapons. It was unthinkingly extended to politicomilitary affairs after the realization that the nuclear balance might be disturbed by the so-called wars of national liberation. Nuclear war can, of course, only be waged by commanders on what amounts to a games board. The strength and the location of the enemy's missiles are known, and the unknown factors of conventional war, such as leadership and the courage of troops, are absent. Given electronic efficiency, the only questionable factor is the courage of the president and his closest advisers to exchange, say, New York for Leningrad; hence the so-called games to prepare them for the superhuman authority to destroy much of the world. The games of the superpowers, however, are ill suited for dealing with the pygmies of this world. In examining the consequences in Vietnam, Professor Polk said that its extension outside the framework of the cold war into counterinsurgency so simplified policies as to mislead. Related to problems such as Vietnam were enormously complex political, psychological, and economic forces. To attempt to deal with them as mere ploys on a world game board was inappropriate and likely to be unsuccessful. No American politician faced with local forces and attitudes would attempt to bypass them with broad and vague issues, or cope with them by the use of devices such as strategic hamlets, helicopters, and defoliation.

Professor Polk did not exaggerate the position, as anyone living in Washington at the time could attest after listening to the theorists or to senior officials jokingly play one of these games after dinner. It was evident in the strategy for Vietnam with its steady escalation, and the attempts to rationalize political policy. The intellectual dishonesties were stupendous but essential. The games-theory approach could not be applied to such a complex drama as a civil war with a history going back beyond the 1954 Geneva conference to a long nationalist struggle against colonialism. The methodology demanded simplifica-

tion if only because the intricacies of Buddhist politics could not
be programmed for the computers. Therefore Vietnam had to
be a confrontation between aggressive communism and free-
dom-loving countries led by the United States.

The average American did not read the *Bulletin of the
Atomic Scientists* and at the beginning of 1966 was no more
than perplexed or uneasy about the war. On the whole, Congress reflected the unease but went along with the administration. This would not have been dangerous if American military
power, as was first supposed, could frighten Hanoi into submis-
sion. But Johnson and his advisers gradually realized that the
war would not be over by the midterm election in November,
and in trying to insulate the electorate from the war he committed a grave political blunder. It might almost be characterized
as a crime. People do not live by bread alone, or by air-conditioned cars and large steaks broiled on gas barbecues in trim
suburban gardens. Small but vocal groups in Congress began to
realize that they were committed to an open-ended war on the
Asian mainland without a public debate such as had been held
before the involvement in Europe. In the immediate years after
the Second World War, the North Atlantic Treaty had been
argued before congressional committees and thus had been
widely understood and accepted. This political process, in the
best American tradition, had permitted the safe reversal of the
foreign and defense policies that had been pursued for more
than 150 years.

It was magnificent, and good politics. The Truman administration had also sought the help of Republicans, notably Senator
Vandenberg. Johnson was only a young congressman at the
time but he ought to have remembered how the administration
had kept in close touch with the Senate Foreign Relations Committee. He probably did remember. He was above all a man of
Congress, but presumably the need seen to fight a secret war
influenced his judgment. The committee chairman, William
Fulbright, was, of course, opposed to the war. Irritated by the
lack of comprehension, Johnson had already invited him to the

White House to explain his position. They were together for about two hours, in which time the chairman had a hard time getting a few words in edgeways. Johnson only wanted to justify himself and his policy. Fulbright was not persuaded, and soon after the bombing pause the Senate Foreign Relations Committee held six days of open hearings. They were supposed to be on an administration request for more foreign aid, although little was heard about that prosaic subject.

Vietnam dominated the hearings, but if anybody hoped for a repetition of the NATO hearings they were disappointed. Instead, Johnson chose to regard them as a confrontation and wheeled up his big guns to demolish the opposition as he used B-52 bombers against jungle hideouts in Vietnam. They included Rusk, McNamara, and General Maxwell Taylor. Fulbright called General James Gavin, U.S. Army retired, who had previously written an article for *Harper's Magazine* in which he advocated limiting American military operations to coastal enclaves. George Kennan, the former ambassador who had devised the containment policy from which Vietnam was unexpectedly spawned, was also called. The confrontation took place before television cameras, which probably persuaded the administration witnesses to defend the official policy at all costs. The spirit of the advise-and-consent clause, admittedly often ignored by past presidents, evaporated under the klieg lights. Compromise was impossible and was never to return while Johnson remained in office. The consequences were not immediate, but the divisions that seemed to threaten national unity within two years were first glimpsed during those hearings.

Gavin and Kennan were not particularly good witnesses. The first was hardly a national figure, and his enclave theory had all the dangers of a static strategy. Any military man could think of a dozen respectable reasons to reject it. Kennan was a public man respected in most of the world's foreign ministries, but he appeared fussy and didactic. Fulbright was also inhibited by the fact that he had been the floor manager for the Gulf of Tonkin resolution. He said, "At the time of the 1964 resolution I really had no realization of what we were about to get into, or how it was about to escalate." It sounded a poor excuse from a senator so long suspicious of the direction of national security policy.

Secretary of State Rusk pressed the point home. He said that every action taken was justified in acts of Congress, treaties, resolutions, and other actions on record. Special mention was, of course, made of the 1964 resolution. The SEATO treaty was identified as the fundamental obligation guiding American action in South Vietnam, and Rusk said that its far-reaching implications were well understood by the committee and the Senate at the time of ratification. He defended American unilateral action by saying that the treaty did not require collective decision or action. He insisted that the United States was obliged to act, regardless of other treaty members, if it determined that an armed attack had occurred. This in fact was not the case. The SEATO treaty contains no automatic trigger clause as do the NATO and Rio treaties, but the claim passed unnoticed presumably because Fulbright had not done his homework.

General Taylor, who had been ambassador and proconsul in Saigon, said that the United States intended to show that wars of national liberation were doomed to failure. He did not believe in the domino theory, but he was concerned with the probable worldwide effects of such a communist victory in Vietnam. The defense secretary insisted on testifying in closed session, but his formal statement was subsequently released. Far from being a civil war, he said, the conflict was a direct and flagrant aggression by the North against a treaty ally. He could not say how long the war would last; peace depended ultimately on Hanoi's estimate of American determination. Nor did he know how many troops would be needed, but he believed that there was a ceiling above which the Vietcong and North Vietnam could not provide and supply additional troops. The enclave strategy was dismissed because it would sacrifice the greatest American advantages of mobility and fire power. Vietnam was not an open-ended commitment, and at no time since the Second World War, indeed never before in history, had the

United States been in a better economic position to fulfill its commitments abroad. "Far from overextending ourselves, we have actually strengthened our military position. It is essential that this point be clearly understood . . . so that there may be no miscalculation as to our capabilities to meet our commitments anywhere in the world." He lied. Plans had already been completed to withdraw 15,000 specialist troops from Germany.

At the same time, there were desultory debates on the floor of the Senate, in which criticism was about equally divided between those who wanted to diminish the American commitment and others who demanded instant victory. Johnson received some powerful support from leaders of both parties, but to remove the limelight from adverse attacks the president, on February 4, made the surprise announcement that he would fly to Honolulu to meet the leaders of the Saigon government. There were three days of talks, followed by a communiqué and what was described as the Declaration of Honolulu. It seemed innocuous enough. There was agreement to continue the diplomatic search for peace and to combat inflation in South Vietnam. Johnson promised full support for an intensified program of rural construction, and better agricultural, health and education, and refugee help programs. But once again Johnson was being carried along by events—and almost helplessly, because of the burden of irrelevant concepts of global war and peace which had ignored the realities of Vietnam. On his return, he said in Los Angeles that the war must be won on two fronts. One was military. The other was the struggle against social injustice, hunger, disease, ignorance, and political apathy and indifference.

Except for the last political enemies, there was nothing apparently new in this view of the war. It had been standard doctrine since Britain successfully defeated the attempted communist terrorist takeover in Malaya. For years there had been talk of fighting for the hearts and minds of the people. The British strategy of resettling in defended villages those Malayan Chinese who had supported the communists, willingly or otherwise, and providing them with employment and essential services, had been admired and in theory applied. So-called strategic hamlets had been built in Diem's time, but with miserable results. There were many reasons for this failure, but paramount in American eyes was the fact that in Vietnam the United States did not exercise the direct control enjoyed by the British in Malaya. The hidden significance of the Declaration of Honolulu was that for most purposes the United States was to assume that kind of control. To repeat a phrase afterward used by Richard Rovere, Johnson had placed both feet in the Big Muddy. Without reference to Congress and the American people, the president had assumed full responsibility not only for fighting the military war but also for running another country.

The decision was not taken lightly. There were very few neocolonialists in Washington, although Fulbright was not convinced that the dreams of Manifest Destiny of the previous century had been completely expunged from some officials' imagination. Perhaps, but the majority had been too often reminded of the nationalistic susceptibilities of the South Vietnamese. They would much rather have worked through the junta in Saigon and what was left of the local administrative machine, but not much was left. Apart from the assassination of so many district officials by the Vietcong, many senior men had been deposed by upstart colonels. Nepotism and jealousies beyond the comprehension of westerners accounted for further losses. The complexity of administration during a full-scale war, involving the movement and care of hundreds of thousands of refugees and the running of villages threatened or infiltrated by the Vietcong, was also seen to be beyond any small and backward country such as Vietnam. This was arguable. More to the point was the hard fact that the junta in Saigon was not a government more or less representative and responsive to the wishes of the people. Wishful thinking in Washington and the need to provide some reason for intervention other than global concepts of war and peace had had it otherwise, but the reality could no longer be ignored. To maintain the pretense, the administration of Vietnam as well as the war had to be "Americanized."

It was an ugly word for what was to become an uglier development. Ironically, one of the men who helped unwittingly in this development was the model for Colonel Hilandale, the unusual hero of *The Ugly American*. Major-General Edward Lansdale had been an adviser to the late Ramón Magsaysay during the Philippines insurrection and to the Diem regime in South Vietnam. He was subsequently posted back to Saigon as a special adviser to the American ambassador. He was one of the first Americans to see that the war could not be won by military means, that the Vietcong and the Vietminh before them had a revolutionary idea that could not be bombed out of existence. "You don't win guerrilla wars by bombing and napalming people and then have all their relatives and tribesmen turn against you." He argued that a better revolutionary idea, such as the Declaration of Independence, was necessary. The United States had contributed money, equipment, technical advice, and men, and in spite of a natural inhibition it could not escape the political and ideological responsibilities.

Lansdale recognized that many Americans believed that no nation could endow another with the will to be free and that they should not interfere in the domestic affairs of another country. Nevertheless, he looked to the example of the Philippines and Malaya. There was also the successful Allied tutelage of postwar Germany and Japan. Such comparisons were, of course, dangerous. There was much to build on in Germany and Japan which did not exist in Vietnam. One obvious instance: West Germany regained its sovereignty with one of the world's most modern trade-union movements, but unions had been accepted there when American labor leaders were still fighting for the right to organize. As for the Philippines and Malaya, their insurrections were led and fought by tiny minorities. Certainly they had not captured the nationalist movement as had the communists in Vietnam.

The general was an intelligent man who did not have to be reminded of this, but the situation was desperate. Withdrawal could not then be contemplated and something had to be done. The slow process of building up a political structure and identity was begun, but otherwise Lansdale must have been appalled by the general official approach that made success all the more difficult by putting Americans in charge. In effect, two parallel administrations came into being, one under the Saigon junta and the other under the American ambassador. The second was, of course, better equipped to work with the American armed forces and became dominant in the country areas. While the outward forms were observed, and the trappings of authority retained for the South Vietnamese, they were in fact shunted aside. The great shortage of local and administrative talent made this necessary to some extent, but there were few comparable training programs such as Britain introduced during the Malayan insurrection. Then recruits for government jobs as well as military officers were taken to Britain for training. Even a special teachers' college was established at home to ensure that the schools would be adequately staffed.

Foreign countries without an established colonial service cannot hope to administer another. That was the fundamental difference between the British performance in Malaya and the American efforts in Vietnam. This became apparent when the Buddhists, who claimed a majority of the South Vietnamese as co-religionists, launched their agitation against the Saigon junta and fighting broke out in Danang. Some troops went over to the rebels, who demanded early elections, and Johnson was faced with a civil war within the larger civil war he had refused to recognize. The Buddhists were unarmed and proved easier to deal with than the Vietcong, although their dissatisfaction boded ill for the future. Who were the plucky little people America was supposed to be defending from communist imperialism? It seemed at the time that they were reduced to the junta and the bulk of the army, and Johnson understandably got jumpy when his private forebodings were voiced by many Americans. In a fit of temper or frustration, he flew to Chicago and in an emotional speech dismissed his critics as "nervous Nellies." He said that there were always some who broke ranks under strain and turned on their leaders, but the good sense of Americans would prevail. This was proved a week later, if good sense could be equated with support for his policies in Vietnam. The public-opinion polls still gave him a greater number favoring his policies over those who either wanted to retreat from Vietnam or "go in and win."

In early spring, J. Edgar Hoover, the director of the FBI, uncovered a new threat to the Republic. Writing in the bureau's *Law Enforcement Bulletin,* he said, "The American college student today is being subjected to a bewildering and dangerous conspiracy perhaps unlike any special challenge ever before encountered by our youth. On many campuses he faces a turbulence built on unrestrained individualism, repulsive dress and speech, outright obscenity, disdain for moral and spiritual values, and disrespect for law and order. This movement, commonly referred to as the New Left, is complex in its deceitful absurdity. . . . The Communist Party, U.S.A., as well as other subversive groups, is jubilant over these new rebellious activities."

Hoover was a little late, although his colorful language made up for tardiness. The collective wisdom had long been shocked, and many parents were understandably distraught. They had read of the Free Sex Movement at the University of California, whose members were said to meet naked. The widespread use of drugs by students was even more disturbing. Nevertheless, there was a smack of McCarthyism in the indiscriminate charges. Clearly there was a student—and an adult—revolt of sorts against conventional American social and sexual values, but the New Left was essentially a political movement. Whatever its members did after hours, the New Left was not a group of drug addicts practicing free love. Most found participatory democracy more exciting. Nor was it led by communists. Indeed, the movement was utterly indifferent to the established revolutionary ideologies. There was not much organization. Trotskyists, or Trots, as they were known, had tried to take over, but they had been rejected along with the Democratic and Republican parties, consensus politics, and most established political institutions. If labels must be used, the large majority could best be described as romantic anarchists.

The origins of the New Left were obscure. Unlike in Europe, there was no tradition of political activism at American universities, or of violence apart from spring panty raids and the cruelties of fraternity initiation ceremonies. This quietism had become absolute during the McCarthy period and the intellectual torpor of the Eisenhower years. There was an earlier but broader movement in Britain, where the label "New Left" was first heard. The Campaign for Nuclear Disarmament—an early example of modern participatory democracy—had created a large movement outside the structure of the British political parties. In the United States, the New Left first became prominent at the University of Wisconsin, an historical irony in that Wisconsin was a pioneer in involving academics in government. The early stirrings were slow. The nearest thing to a manifesto was produced in 1962, when the Students for a Democratic Society, the more militant group of the New Left, met in convention at Port Huron, Michigan. It began,

We are people of this generation, bred in at least modest comfort, housed in universities, looking uncomfortably to the world we inherit. Our work is guided by the sense that we may be the last generation in the experiment with living. But we are a minority—the vast majority of our people regard the temporary equilibriums of our society and the world as eternally functional parts. In this is perhaps the outstanding paradox: we ourselves are imbued with urgency, yet the message of our society is that there is no viable alternative to the present . . . that our times have witnessed the exhaustion not only of Utopias, but of any new departures as well. . . .

This was pretty portentous stuff, and to be expected from young men housed in universities with little or no experience of the world. Nevertheless, the pessimism was a reflection of what was going on outside. For the intellectual community, and indeed for well-to-do families who had enjoyed affluence for more than one generation, discontent was more than a distaste for the modern consumer society, for built-in obsolescence and the vulgarity of the hucksters. A new and higher plateau had been reached, and there seemed to be nowhere else to go. This was recognized by Dr. Grayson Kirk in a commencement address at Columbia. Kirk was subsequently to be a victim of student violence, but in suggesting then that the American Dream was over he did indicate that the New Left was symptomatic of a national malaise. As Kirk saw it, the country had rounded a corner in its history and had found none of the legible signposts that had guided earlier generations. Many of the old beliefs no longer seemed to fit the conditions of modern life. The future no longer seemed to be so sure, and Americans appeared to be unsure of themselves, of their course, and of their prospects. "We have become uncomfortably conscious of the fact that, though our history is, on balance, a success story without parallel, we continue to have a multitude of ugly and difficult problems that cause much of the world to look upon us with a judgment that is far from that which we would wish them to have."

Between Port Huron and that commencement address came the Free Speech Movement at the University of California at Berkeley, participation in the southern civil rights movement, and rejection by black separatists. The latter caused confusion within the New Left, but did not stop its influence from spreading to more campuses. Johnson was genuinely puzzled. He had considerable sympathy for youngsters, although it was often dipped in cloying sentimentality. His *Weltanschauung* was firmly based on the assumption that education was the elixir of life, that all problems would be resolved when everybody had a university education. His education laws were intended to be his memorial, and now he was being kicked in the teeth by the beneficiaries of his vision. He could not understand it. Students were not then directly affected by Vietnam. Unlike most Negroes and poor whites, they could avoid the draft. In few other countries had students been so privileged, even unfairly privileged. European students were required to do their military service before going on to university. They had to take their chance in the ranks with the poor and the stupid.

The United States, moreover, had devoted a larger share of its resources to higher education than any other country, and the prospects for graduates were glittering. Johnson looked about him in the White House, which still had some self-conscious products of the better universities left over from the Kennedy administration. Hardly anything was done in Washington without calling in experts from Harvard, MIT, and other campuses with special centers of learning. Academics were retained as consultants with fat fees which helped to raise their incomes to the level of successful business executives. Almost any of their pet projects could expect to receive federal support. But power was more alluring than money. Presidential special assistants, the whiz kids in the Pentagon, and the intellectuals brooding in the think tanks such as RAND and the Hudson Institute had more direct influence over national security and other policies than Congress. The academic community had replaced the press as the fourth estate.

This new status, which for most purposes made the community an informal coequal branch of government, was also apparent in industry. The nuclear-power and arms industries had perforce depended largely upon university laboratories since the days of the Manhattan Project, and this dependence was maintained and extended by the missile and space programs and modern progress generally. Recruiting officers of the large corporations competed for the cream of graduating classes at the campus gate. The future was assured for any bright student. More and more stayed on as postgraduates, earning draft postponements and safe in the knowledge that opportunity was awaiting them in government, industry, research, or education, which had become one of the largest industries in the country.

In fact, most of the more earnest dissidents of the New Left were repelled by this prospect. Some argued that the function of the university was not to become part of any establishment. They were appalled by the advice given by their academic superiors, which had helped to shape Vietnam policy. Others were angered by the consequences for many campuses of academic cooperation with government and industry. Too many professors were so engaged in special projects that they had little or no time for their primary task of teaching. The projects also tended to change the direction and quality of university life, and the secrecy which shrouded so many of the defense projects offended the ancient ideals of learning. There were other complaints stemming mainly from the impersonality of large universities, or multiversities. Classes were enormous. Even without their preoccupations beyond the campus, most professors could not possibly give students the personal attention that had been traditional in higher education.

Here, of course, American idealism and ambition were largely at fault. No other country had accepted the proposition that every child was entitled to go to a university, to sixteen or more years of education. The tradition went back more than a hundred years to the founding of the land-grant colleges, but since 1950 the student population had risen from 2.7 million to 5.5 million. The American concept of a university had perhaps also been taken too far. To the British tradition of undergraduate instruction and the German emphasis on research and specialized training for graduate students had been added the essentially American notion of serving the community. Again the intention was noble, but by 1966 some undergraduates were beginning to realize that a price had been paid and thought they were paying too much of it.

The response of the New Left, still a tiny minority, was hardly a surprise for anybody who had bothered to read their little magazines. Mainly they were contemptuous of established political parties and institutions and believed that salvation could be found only in participatory democracy. Definitions were not always clear, but causes were obviously more attractive than programs. Vietnam and the draft were of course heaven-sent (or hell-sent) opportunities. Johnson's refusal to take Congress into his confidence and the reluctance or inability of Congress to assert itself in fact excluded much criticism from the established political process. In the event of a prolonged war the question of public support could be decided in the streets. The New Left was well aware of this, and it was in the streets that the militant students had one of their early successes in reaching the outside world. They found some unexpected allies. Traditional pacifists such as the Friends were already joined in silent protest. Increasing numbers of clergymen, who had been first aroused by the civil rights movement, added respectability to the agitation. There was no formal alliance, but none was needed. Members of professional and upper-middle-class families, the backbone of any established order, were sympathetic if apprehensive. The nucleus of the antiwar movement began to grow. In turn, patriotic and right-wing groups were aroused by this dissent. The process of polarizing American opinion was thus begun.

For a foreign observer, it was possible to feel sorry for Johnson as well as the United States. To a large extent he was a victim of circumstances beyond his control. Elsewhere I suggested that the long history of the United States divides into three eras.* The first began with independence, or more specifically with the ratification of the Constitution after the failure of confederation. The Civil War ushered in the second, and the third began in 1932 when Franklin Roosevelt was elected president at a time when a once-confident America seemed in danger of collapse. Roosevelt did more than save the country from economic and social chaos. The Roosevelt coalition of labor, intellectuals, ethnic groups, and the South transformed the Democratic party into an instrument of change and reform. The country regained a sense of purpose and, despite Republican hatred, achieved a new unity, especially by accommodating the relatively unassimilated ethnic groups. Roosevelt also assembled an administrative machine essential for a modern industrial democracy in a revolutionary period of technological change and rising expectations. It was capable of mobilizing the country for the Second World War and providing world leadership.

When I arrived in Washington just before the inauguration of John Kennedy, the mood of the city could only be described as one of euphoria. The Rooseveltian inheritance was about to be passed to a new generation of young Americans, and the country, already powerful and great, was promised an even brighter future. It was not to be, at least not within that decade. More than Camelot came to an end with Kennedy's death. As I in-

*The New American Commonwealth (New York: Harper & Row, 1968).

117

dicated in the first chapter of this book, a new era of technological and social change was under way before the fatal shots were fired in Dallas. Almost inevitably, the country was confronted with the friction, conflict, and disturbance of vast fundamental movements.

I am not suggesting that the New Left were the instigators of change or that the new era was theirs. At best they were only a symptom of change and further proof that the Rooseveltian era was passing. To divide history into eras is, of course, arbitrary. There is a strong argument that the conflict of the sixties was no more than the consequence of a change begun during the Roosevelt administration and that the old ways would endure. FDR was a hero for Johnson, who saw the Great Society legislation as the completion of the New Deal, but there were no nuclear bombs or computers in the thirties or much else of the technological developments that were transforming America. Then the Negroes were quiescent, and the Puritan ethic was still dominant. The urban population was already a majority, but popular attitudes still reflected a simpler rural past. The thought of the federal government intervening to save the cities from decay would have horrified most people. The habit of international authority had not been assumed, and again the majority would have been horrified by the prospect. Lastly, the thirties were years of hope, of new initiatives. Most of the initiatives had run their course by the sixties. Much had been achieved, but each step forward had opened vistas of new problems crying for attention. The United States had also turned its back on the examples of social reform prevalent in northern Europe, and the intellectual isolationism was to say the least stultifying. In 1962 the *Wall Street Journal* said, "National politics today is pretty much a vacuum or at least a desert. It is arid of ideas."

More specifically, one could say in 1966 that the liberal intellectuals, who had for so long provided Democratic presidents with ideas, did not seem to realize that the old answers were often irrelevant. Surveying the period, admittedly with hindsight, one can now see that they were captives rather than heirs of the past. Apparently oblivious of the lessons of Korea, at home as well as on the battlefield, they became increasingly hard-nosed and adventuresome and landed the country in Vietnam. They chose the very moment when Senator Fulbright and others were preaching the necessity of change. At home, their record was not much better, especially in the so-called war against poverty. Many of the programs could be traced directly to New Deal thinking and were at best outmoded. Their one innovation demonstrated that they did not understand that times had changed. I refer to the principle of maximum feasible participation of the poor—mainly Negro—in the community action programs.

The principle is of special interest because it revealed once again the fundamental adversary stance of the intellectuals. One might say that the war-game theory, already transposed with disastrous results from nuclear strategy to guerrilla warfare, was applied on the home front. A confrontation between the haves and have-nots was deliberately engineered. This was done at a time when the country was already in a turmoil, as much over Negro demands and violence as the Vietnam War. The ghetto areas of a hundred and more cities had gone up in flames, white vigilantes were patrolling the streets, decent people were apprehensive over the swift pace of change, and even liberal and moderate men in Congress felt that the time had come to digest other wedges of legislation before venturing further into the unknown. There was, of course, the realization that in its swift progress the United States had detoured and even created problems such as hard-core poverty, overcrowded schools, and dreadful slums. Many agreed that something had to be done for the poor, especially the Negro poor. But the Office of Economic Opportunity was not content with trying to reduce poverty. The director, Sargent Shriver, declared that the community action programs, built around the principle of maximum feasible participation of the poor, were to be the corporations of a new social revolution.

Maximum feasible participation meant many things. The theory was that the poor, in participating in programs designed to help them, would develop self-respect and self-reliance. The argument was persuasive, and in some areas it worked. Cambridge, Massachusetts, and Denver, Colorado, are two much quoted examples, but neither city is typical. The men who promoted the idea acted in the old Roosevelt tradition, in that they hoped to create a new constituency with complete loyalty to the Democratic party. This was a typical Rooseveltian tactic, but apart from the fact that there was a war on, the intellectuals were oblivious of or arrogantly ignored the mood of the majority. The city halls were the first to be frightened because they could see the loss of patronage and power to new and contending constituencies, but the local political bosses were not the only frightened people. Too many working-class folk and groups on the lower rung of the ethnic ladder already felt the hot breath of Negroes pressing behind them. It was all very well for the liberals of Cambridge and Washington to talk about fair opportunity and integration, but the blacks were not moving into their neighborhoods. Their children's schools were not crowded with young blacks bussed in from the ghettos. Shriver's revolution threatened the values of little mortgaged houses and the education of children—indeed, much that tens of millions of Americans lived for. Moreover, these people did not share the liberals' feeling of guilt toward the Negro, as Eric Hoffer made clear.

This longshoreman-turned-philosopher wrote,

The simple fact is that the people I have lived and worked with all my life, and who make up about 60 percent of the population outside the South, have not the least feeling of guilt towards the Negro. The majority of us started to work for a living in our teens, and we have been poor all our lives. Most of us had only a rudimentary education. Our white skin brought us no privileges and no favors. For more than twenty years I worked in the fields of California with Negroes, and now and then for Negro contractors. On the San Francisco waterfront, where I spent the next twenty years, there are as many black longshoremen as white. My kind of people does not feel that the world owes us anything, or that we owe anybody—white, black, or yellow—a damn thing. We believe that the Negro should have every right we

120

have: the right to vote, the right to join any union open to us, the right to live, work, study, and play anywhere he pleases. But he can have no special claims on us, and no valid grievances against us. He has certainly not done our work for us.

There was much unfairness as well as rude truth in this, but Hoffer spoke for millions who felt that they were being pushed too far. The bitterness and confusion that followed further polarized American opinion. The threatened ethnic proletariat began to view the blacks, the antiwar demonstrators, the New Left, and the establishment liberals as enemies. Apparently deserted by their own party, many looked to George Wallace, the former governor of Alabama, for leadership. Tensions increased and so did violence as defensive group attitudes became more inflamed. One of the primary causes of violence in the United States had long been group competition. The National Commission on the Causes and Prevention of Violence was later to confirm this with impressive historical evidence, but the liberal intellectuals ought to have known this at the time. Nevertheless, they chose to create a new competing constituency in an atmosphere already poisoned by racial prejudice and strife.

Back in August 1964, when Johnson signed the Economic Opportunity Act in the rose garden of the White House, he said, "On this occasion the American people and our American system are making history.... Today for the first time in the history of the human race, a great nation is to make, and is willing to make, a commitment to eradicate poverty among its people." This was absolute nonsense. Northern European countries had made that commitment years before, and some had already succeeded, but this gaffe did not explain the complete silence of the White House in the summer of 1966. Johnson was increasingly preoccupied with the Vietnam War, but he had read the adverse political signs and had quickly lost interest in the antipoverty program. He still hoped to maintain some semblance of a consensus with which to meet the midterm elections, and there was no point in exacerbating the situation. A

majority of Americans were worried about the war and domestic violence, but he thought that they were still undecided or
too confused—indeed, too patriotic—to upset the electoral balance in November. Prosperity was still sweet. For all its weaknesses and contradictions, the strategy devised at the beginning
of the year could still pay off.

He knew that there would be some losses. There always were
after landslide victories. As early as spring, Johnson forecast in
private conversation that the Democrats would lose at least
forty seats in the House of Representatives. He anticipated
more defeats in contests for the state houses and legislatures,
where Americans could register internal discontent without ap-
pearing to vote against the war. He had enough fortitude and
political experience to accept these defeats, although it would
mark the end of his remarkable domination of Congress. He at
least pretended to dignified resignation. The mounting costs of
the war made immediate progress toward the Great Society
almost impossible, but he thought that the war would be over
before the 1968 presidential election. Then he would have another four years to do all that was to be done. This was the
general direction of his thoughts as expressed in private conversation.

The spring and summer of 1966 in fact were to prove to be
the last period during his administration when he could face the
future with some of the old confidence. His public dealings with
the press were thereafter steadily reduced, but he still privately
received correspondents, singly or in small groups. Personal
insecurity was evident from time to time, and one could not be
certain whether he was trying to persuade listeners of the greatness of his cause or practicing a form of group therapy. His
callers would never know how long the sessions would last, the
usual twenty to thirty minutes of brisk questions and answers or
an hour and more of brooding soliloquy. More than once I was
reminded of a Shakespearean actor playing Hamlet or Henry V.
The extraordinary thing was that this was no actor mouthing
well-known lines but the most powerful man in the western
world talking about great questions of state and exposing, or

pretending to expose, his innermost thoughts and anxieties. I can remember being invited with a few others for 6:30 one evening and not being released until after nine. McNamara telephoned about eight to remind him that he was expected for dinner. Johnson told him to have another martini and tell Mrs. McNamara that he was delayed but would be happy with a can of Campbell's soup, and the soliloquy went on for another hour to the dismay of cabinet officers waiting outside—and presumably of Mrs. McNamara. He would often repeat himself, produce public-opinion polls from his back pocket, and send powerful special assistants scurrying for secret documents. A senior official bound for Saigon, where he was to take charge of the pacification program, was required to spend his last minutes in Washington explaining to a few of us what he hoped to achieve. Certainly his wife could not have been amused. Johnson was nearly always very polite in the old-fashioned and rather attractive way of the South. His voice was low-keyed, changing as an actor's would, when he quietly expressed immense determination to save the world from communism or near to weeping when he spoke of the courage and sufferings of the troops and their families. For all the lurking memories of Olivier, Richardson, and Burton, I would nearly always go away convinced of his sincerity. Looking back, there was no question of it. Of course there were the appeals, sometimes crude and obvious, for support or sympathy, but he was the President of the United States. He was deeply aware of the power and the glory of the office and was enlarged and perhaps ennobled by it. This belief in the power of the office and in the country's intrinsic strengths had persuaded him in the past that the war would end in time to establish himself in the presidential pantheon alongside FDR, but he was now no less aware of the potential for tragedy and ignominy.

Johnson could also be very funny. His was an earthy humor, bawdy but not obscene. There was the occasional coarseness. He once compared the Vietcong to a young man trying to seduce a girl. He was the girl, but reversed the role to demonstrate what he meant. "You can remember," he said, "putting your hand on a girl's knee and sliding it up her thigh until she told you to stop." The thought of him protecting his virginity thus· was ridiculously funny, until his powerful fingers first clenched .my knee and then my thigh. I cannot recall the thoughts that passed through my mind but was immensely relieved when his fist relaxed. Nevertheless, the jokes could provide some insight into his character and ambition. I often thought that he should reveal some of this in public. He was much too controlled for his own good when on the platform or before the television cameras. He appeared to be mealymouthed and not altogether honest, but presumably he thought that Americans expected their presidents to be polished.

Then there was the memory of President Kennedy's grace, wit, and sophistication. Considerable as they were in life, they had grown immeasurably in memory, and before the summer was out Johnson was again beginning to be disturbed by Senator Robert Kennedy. Not much had been heard of him since his election in 1964, but the third Kennedy brother had already completed his fascinating metamorphosis. He had entered public life as a rich and rather conventional Catholic anticommunist and had worked for Senator Joseph McCarthy. Service under his brother as attorney general had taken him to left of center, but after Dallas and the long period of terrible personal grief he had begun to move farther to the left. His raw political power was still firmly based on connections with shabby machine politicians. He delivered the eulogy at the funeral of Congressman Charles Buckley, the boss of the Bronx Democratic machine, although elsewhere grief was mixed with profound relief. Nevertheless, he was a compassionate man. As he was moved by poverty and oppression and pushed by young assistants, his position became more radical.

Kennedy was said to represent the new politics. There did not seem to be much that was different from the old politics of the Roosevelt coalition, except for an impatience with its internal contradictions, but from the White House it looked as if he was establishing an independent power base within the Democratic party, but left of center, from which he could challenge Johnson. Old enmities stirred. There was no thought that the challenge would come in 1968. Indeed, politicians of both parties were convinced that Johnson would be unbeatable. Certainly there seemed little to worry about. Kennedy had not been in the forefront of senatorial oppostion to the direction of the war in Vietnam, perhaps because he had been inhibited by memories of the decisive role he played as his brother's adviser in getting the country involved. When he did speak out, he was clumsy and clearly diffident.

He began by suggesting a coalition government for South Vietnam in which the National Liberation Front would be represented. Senator George Aiken, the Republican from Vermont, asked why he did not proffer similar advice when his brother was in the White House. Vice-President Humphrey said, or was required to say, that it was like putting a fox in a chicken coop. A few days later, Kennedy said that the administration was demanding impossible conditions for peace negotiations. This was, of course, denied by the White House. Bill Moyers, the press secretary, said that the administration wanted free elections and would abide by the results. Kennedy decided to back down a little, protesting that he did not mean that communists should be members of an interim government but that it should not be ruled out.

The first public exchange was indecisive and of little importance except that willingly or otherwise Humphrey, the true liberal, was pushed to the right and established as a firm defender of the policy in Vietnam. Thereafter he was unable to move away from what was to become an unpopular position until it was much too late in the 1968 presidential election campaign. But nobody then saw the vice-president as a presidential candidate, and he could hardly dissociate himself from the president as the British prime minister dissociated his country from the bombing of Hanoi and Haiphong in June. These raids created an international furor, but McNamara claimed that the raids had destroyed half the enemy's stocks of fuel oil. North Vietnam would only be able to continue the war for a few more weeks. The optimism of the defense secretary was no longer convincing, and Kennedy jumped into the fray again by rejecting the argument that increased bombing would bring the communists to the negotiating table. The danger, he said, of a conflict or confrontation with China outweighed any military advantages.

There was in fact little danger of another conflict with China, as Kennedy must have known. McNamara was after all a close personal friend, and his conviction that China would not intervene was based on more than optimism. They must have discussed it together. Of course, the bombing of Hanoi and Haiphong neither brought North Vietnam to the conference table nor China into the war. Instead the queer chemistry of interaction between events and men seemed to harden, at least briefly, the popular resolve to end the war quickly, and increase impatience with foreign and domestic doves. This became quickly evident, as far as Johnson was concerned, in his annoyance with Harold Wilson, the British prime minister. The new sneer word was "spectator." Only countries that had joined in the battle had the right to criticism or comment.

One foreign agent in the chemistry was the late Harold Holt, the Australian prime minister. Visiting Washington before the Commonwealth Prime Ministers' Conference in London, he could find nothing wrong with American foreign policy and was convinced that Vietnam was a critical battle for the future of mankind. Western European countries were condemned for refusing to join the United States and Australia in the good fight against Asian communism. He finished a speech at the National Press Club with the rallying cry "All the way with LBJ." Johnson intensified the bombing and the new mood. On June 30, in Des Moines, Iowa, he said that the North Vietnamese leaders could not escape paying for aggression and they would pay a very high price. He threatened them with massive retaliation, and McNamara said that the limit of American air power over North Vietnam had not been reached. The Pentagon was reported to be planning the systematic destruction of Haiphong and the mining of its harbor approaches. A Soviet freighter standing in the roads was bombed, and Moscow protested sharply. Its note was rejected by Washington as false, but the air force discovered that one of its bombers had hit the ship and the flight commander had destroyed the film in the plane's cameras. Cooler heads prevailed, but Johnson briefly gloried in the role of the confident leader of a fighting nation sure of ultimate victory. He was roundly applauded.

Dovish talk was hardly popular in this atmosphere. The country had quite suddenly become not so much warlike as resentful, and the impatience which had been growing throughout the year came to the surface. Not all of it was over the war. A number of peace candidates were defeated in primary elections, which also revealed a white backlash against Negro demands and violence more than a longing for peace. Many such voters believed that an early victory could be won if the war was fought with more resolution. George Ball, the under-secretary of state who had become the most persistent critic of the war within the administration, announced his resignation. A civil rights bill with a controversial open-housing provision was stopped by a filibuster. The cloture vote was 52 to 41, ten less than the required two-thirds majority. George Wallace, the former Governor of Alabama, said that he was seriously thinking of running for the presidency in 1968. Southern Democrats in the House of Representatives launched their campaign to unseat Adam Clayton Powell, the Harlem congressman.

Johnson nevertheless decided to play both sides of the street, and Dean Rusk said that he was unique among national leaders in his refusal to foster a war psychology. The secretary was probably right, but apart from the occasional outbursts Johnson could hardly give stirring patriotic speeches without rocking the boat. He announced in late August that another peace offer had been made to North Vietnam. The United States would halt the bombing if Hanoi sent no more troops south. In October, he went to Manila to discuss with the allies another peace offer. It was a response to Hanoi's four-point peace program. These were: withdrawal of all American military personnel, equipment, and bases from South Vietnam; the two Vietnams must not enter into foreign military alliances pending final reunification; the internal affairs of South Vietnam must be settled in accordance with the program of the National Liberation Front; and peaceful reunification was to be achieved by the Vietnamese people without foreign interference. The allied position agreed upon at Manila was labeled "essential elements of peace." These were: an end to aggression; the preservation of South Vietnam's territorial integrity; reunification according to the principles of the 1954 Geneva accords; and the reciprocal withdrawal of all foreign forces within six months after the cease-fire. The last element was intended to dramatize the sincerity of earlier statements that the United States was not interested in permanent bases, but the American position remained essentially unchanged. This was reinforced when Johnson flew to Cam Ranh Bay in South Vietnam and to a group of officers said, "Come home with that coonskin on the wall." The frontier phrase hardly suggested that he was prepared to meet Hanoi even halfway.

In flying around Asia, the president had once again used his extraconstitutional power of pre-empting the headlines. Kennedy retreated into relative silence, but his popularity remained high, and not only among young people, Negroes, and other traditional Kennedy followers. The polarization of public opinion was now well advanced. Apprehension as well as impatience was increasingly apparent. The savagery of the war was sickening for many. There was a fear that the global proportions of the national security policy were too much and that the humanistic qualities of the American people would be destroyed. Kennedy obviously sensed the beginnings of a new constituency as he moved about the country speaking for liberal congressmen seeking re-election. These travels attracted attention, and in October he felt compelled to announce that he would not be a candidate for the presidency or the vice-presidency in 1968. He was to deny presidential ambition repeatedly until the final announcement of his candidacy in 1968, but this was probably the last time even the most naïve believed him. Soon the rivalry between the senator and the president

128

broke into print, and from then on the two men were to be mortal enemies.

I can recall reporting at the time that a great drama was slowly unfolding, the like of which, perhaps, had not been seen since medieval times. Two great American political princes were struggling for power, and many Americans seemed to feel that it must end in tragedy for one of them. Both vehemently denied the struggle, but they could convince nobody. It mesmerized Washington, where even the war was occasionally forgotten although it was part of the drama. The drama had already been presented in the form of a play, *MacBird*, by Barbara Garson. It portrayed Johnson as Macbeth, President Kennedy as Duncan, and Senator Robert Kennedy as the conspirator who regained the throne of his dead brother. It was a cruel and irresponsible work, but together with some foul rumors, and prepublication excerpts from William Manchester's book *The Death of a President*, it persuaded the White House that Kennedy was determined to destroy Johnson. *U.S. News and World Report* reported as follows:

The most reprehensible rumor, in the view of the President's friends, is to the effect that Lyndon Johnson—then Vice-President—lured John F. Kennedy into coming to Texas in the autumn of 1963 and was, therefore, in some manner responsible for his death.... One Kennedy aide (on the flight back from Dallas) barked, "Well, they have gotten in, but we will get back in again.". . . One of President Johnson's associates has said bluntly, "The entire post-assassination series of events has been a calculated, contrived, emotional build-up, not for the sake of paying honest respect to, and showing genuine grief for, John F. Kennedy, but to enhance the image of the Kennedy family and the Kennedy name. The Kennedys have the attitude that this is not an honor that the American people conferred on Jack Kennedy, but that the Kennedy family as a whole achieved a position of power in American society—and the important thing is to retain that position for which the family fought so long ago starting with Joe Kennedy [the late President's father]. With the Kennedys the White House is still their house—and Jacqueline Kennedy is the widowed queen in exile, awaiting a return of the dynasty to the throne."

No Hail, No Farewell

U.S. News and World Report is a magazine of unquestioned respectability, and certainly not given to wild reporting and the retailing of cheap gossip. If the quotes were startling, people in Washington could have provided a dozen more. For instance, one of the monkeys in Kennedy's private menagerie was said to be called LBJ. The significance of this challenge can best be appreciated by accepting, if only for a moment, the comparison of the modern American presidency with a medieval monarchy. Powerful American politicians are not merely members of political parties, and subject to their discipline; they also wield power in their own right, are surrounded by courts or entourages as so many great territorial magnates, and can be afforded similar respect. Some are scions of dynasties, and none was then more powerful than the Kennedy family. Its followers were everywhere, and the court was compared with a government-in-exile. There was even a Kennedy coat of arms. Kennedy was only the junior senator from New York, and with an indifferent voting record, but he was seen to have a claim to the throne as his murdered brother's heir. The Kennedy legend was not only an instrument in the power struggle but proof of his legitimate claim.

Johnson was no less exposed than a medieval monarch who could not control his magnates. An electoral mandate is the modern equivalent of the divine right of kings to rule, but, as in the past, it is not much use if he cannot maintain the essential balance. For the first time, as the old year closed, he was seen to be in danger of losing that balance. He could not look to the congressional or national party for help. He had their formal allegiance, but the Democrats were losing their unity. They were becoming Johnson men or Kennedy men, or followers of a lesser man who could afford to wait until the victor emerged. The weakness of Johnson's position was still due only in part to his preoccupation with the war in Vietnam. The main cause was that the Kennedy family was beginning openly to challenge his succession. The refusal, in 1964, of the senator as vice-presidential candidate, or crown prince, had not been forgiven. Johnson's subsequent victory was dismissed by the Kennedy followers as the popular rejection of the then contender to the throne, Senator Barry Goldwater. To that extent, Johnson's succession was seen to be temporary, despite his benign rule at home.

In this winter of discontent, Johnson took little part in the election campaign. He was due to appear in twenty cities in fifteen states during the last week, but he called reporters into the Cabinet Room and casually announced that he was to undergo abdominal and throat surgery. The incision made during his gall bladder operation in the previous year needed attention, and a small polyp would be removed from his throat. One could only admire the man. The operations were not urgent, but he had calmly anticipated the election results, and had decided that he could not improve them. With the country involved in the elections he might as well go to hospital.

The Republicans recovered from their shaming 1964 defeat by capturing eight more governorships, three seats in the Senate, and forty-seven in the House of Representatives. The Democrats still controlled both houses. Their losses were more than Johnson had estimated earlier, but not many more. He had lost his dominating position in Congress, but the national consensus had survived, or so most people concluded. It was a little smaller, and perhaps strained, but no one could say that the American people had voted, at one stage removed, against the Vietnam War. Indeed, rather than electing opponents to the war, the electorate chose new representatives more in favor of a larger military effort than their predecessors. Men such as Senator Charles Percy won only after moderating their dovish position. Down at the ranch on November 10, the president met reporters and had all the conventional things to say about the swinging of pendulums and the glory of the two-party system. He refused to anticipate future difficulties. "As I said to Mrs. Johnson last night, it just looks like we will have to get by with 248 [in the House], which will be some 63 margin, and in the Senate almost two to one. I hope what we propose will be sufficiently meritorious to command a majority vote."

The next day, at another press conference, he was talking

about creative federalism and the need for closer cooperation
with state and local governments. Averell Harriman, who had
visited eleven countries as a special ambassador after the Manila
Conference, was invited to talk about the prospects for peace.
He reported on the peace initiatives of many countries, especially Britain, which had a special responsibility as one of the
co-chairmen of the Geneva Conference. Everybody wanted
peace, except China and North Vietnam, and this consensus
was encouraging. Most countries understood the reasons why
Johnson could not take unilateral action and wanted the North
Vietnamese to take some reciprocal steps. There was no indication that they would, but again he was encouraged by the willingness of the Soviet Union and Eastern European countries to
make representations in Hanoi. Thirdhand conversations suggested that the North Vietnamese were willing to talk provided
the United States did certain things, but no specific discussion
was going on.

There were many more press conferences before the end of
the year, largely because Johnson was anxious to announce new
programs and discuss the budget. Asked about Vietnam, he said
that the military operations continued to be successful. Allied
forces held the initiative, and losses were light. McNamara anticipated a leveling off in the rate of the build-up and expendi-
tures. The two men were back on the job of lulling the country,
but figures released by the Defense Department at the end of
the year indicated that they could not long avoid the coming
storm. Since the end of 1964 the number of American troops in
Vietnam had increased from 23,000 to 389,000, and the dead
from 239 to 6,644.

1967

Nineteen sixty-seven was to have been the Year of the Offensive, according to General William Westmoreland, the American commander in South Vietnam. The logic as he saw it was indisputable. Nineteen sixty-four had been the Year of Crisis, 1965 the Year of Military Commitment, and 1966 the Year of Development, and now the time had come to take the offensive and win the war. He had built up a superb supply-and-support organization capable of sustaining 1,200,000 troops. Every month some 550,000 tons of general supplies and 86,000 tons of ammunition were flowing through great new ports such as Cam Ranh Bay and Newport on the Saigon River. Twenty-eight tactical fighter squadrons were flying from fields in South Vietnam, Thailand, and aircraft carriers stationed in the Gulf of Tonkin. The capacity of the giant B-52 bombers operating from distant island bases was stepped up to 1,200 sorties a year. The number of American troops was increased to 486,000 and the actual fighting strength to 278 battalions. There were more than 3,000 helicopters. The thought that ill-equipped Asian soldiers with no aircraft or tanks could withstand such an onslaught was seen to be ridiculous, no less in the

133

White House than in the Headquarters of the U.S. Military Assistance Command, Vietnam.

Large-scale military operations, such as Cedar Falls and Junction City, were mounted. The pacification program was placed under military control because, in the words of the general, pacification and war were essentially inseparable. In Saigon there were more elections, and a new constitution was ratified. There seemed to be movement on every front, and Westmoreland refined his original concept of a three-phase war. He now saw four phases, two of which had already been completed. In the third phase the United States was to transfer more of the war effort to the South Vietnamese forces, increasingly capable and better armed. The fourth and decisive phase would see the American presence become superfluous. Infiltration from the north would slacken, and as the local communist infrastructure was destroyed South Vietnam, led by a stable and popular government, would carry its own war to a successful conclusion. The end of that phase was to coincide with the 1968 presidential election.

This was the master plan devised by a very capable field commander. Johnson had every reason to believe that it would be carried out on schedule. One can usefully wonder what success would have brought him. For a start, I would have written something like this.

"Johnson emerged as a very considerable president who had won a war and made Asia safe for democracy, while maintaining at home an unprecedented level of prosperity and social reform. The concepts behind the national security policy were triumphantly vindicated. The national confidence rose to a new level. Much of the violence in the cities was expected to be avoided now that he could direct his remarkable energy and talents to resolving domestic problems. His political enemies, the Kennedys and the liberals, were confounded. He was nominated by acclamation at the Democratic National Convention, and won another splendid victory at the polls. His place in the presidential pantheon, somewhere between Andrew Jackson and Franklin Roosevelt, was assured. He expected to be better placed, between Washington and Roosevelt, but few Americans questioned his elevated place in the history of the Republic."

It was not to be. All of this came to nothing because of a major miscalculation over the enemy coupled with understandable confidence in American strength. The analysts and military men in the White House and the State and Defense departments thought that they understood the strategy of the enemy. They had all read their Mao and Giap. The universities had added to the knowledge of Vietnam and Asian nationalism and communism. Not an ideological or biographical stone had been left unturned. A few officials were not overly optimistic about the chances of maintaining the schedule, but all agreed that American air power, mobility, and sheer force of arms made another Dienbienphu impossible. North Vietnam could not therefore win the war in Washington as it had won the earlier struggle against the French in Paris. All that had to be done, now that the tide of battle had turned and a magnificent army stood poised in the field, was to take the offensive. Hence the Year of the Offensive.

The basic miscalculation became evident before the summer was out. The big operations were not decisive because there were just not enough troops available. The extra factors of fire power and mobility could not match the advantages of a guerrilla force operating largely in a jungle terrain and among its own people. Westmoreland afterward said, "I knew that it was necessary to strike out against the very formidable forces assembling in the border sanctuaries and remote base areas in order to prevent them from planning and executing deliberate attacks against the populated areas and against government centers. At the same time, I was aware of the necessity to protect the pacification effort, whose success or failure would, in the long run, determine the fate of South Vietnam." In April he was obliged to move troops from offensive strikes and clearing operations in the south to protect populated areas elsewhere. In the north the marines, who had initiated an intelligent combined military-pacification program of their own, were precipitately moved to the demilitarized zone that divides Vietnam. The

North Vietnamese had launched a sharp offensive across the zone, and Washington cried unfair. It was hard to know why, but so it went on. Westmoreland was nearly always caught off balance.

The military also complained that the enemy had the unfair advantage of being able to retreat across the demilitarized zone or the Cambodian frontier to rest and regroup, but this factor had been known from the beginning. There could be no question of hot pursuit, except for an occasional small action. The decision was made in the beginning that a limited war had to be fought if a larger conflict with China and the Soviet Union was to be avoided. This did not prevent the bombing of the Ho Chi Minh trail in Laos or clandestine operations in Cambodia, but they were to no avail. The basic fact remained that nearly half a million American troops, the South Vietnamese army, and contingents from Australia, New Zealand, South Korea, and Thailand were not enough to defeat a revolutionary force led by one of the greatest guerrilla generals in history. Westmoreland believed, of course, that his legendary opponent, General Vo Nguyen Giap, shared his own dilemma in not having a decisive superiority. He was correct, up to a point. The evidence suggests that Giap had underestimated American air power, mobility, and fire power. He can be excused. Nothing like it had ever been assembled on any battlefield, especially one traditonally given to small-unit action and political penetration. Again and again his forces were badly mauled when he tried to move in the classical progression of such wars from guerrilla forays to battalion-size engagements. But he had time, almost limitless time, while Johnson had to reckon with the natural impatience of the American people. The war had to be over before the 1968 elections.

There were other miscalculations. For Westmoreland, the war became one of cruel attrition, of wearing down the enemy until he could no longer fight. If the size of Vietnam and the political climate at home prevented the deployment of much larger numbers of troops, manpower was seen to be a favorable factor for the Americans. North Vietnam was a small country with only

17 million people, and had been at war on and off for many years, but Westmoreland was assured of a continuing stream of fresh soldiers. He could even afford to rotate his troops every twelve months, a questionable luxury never before enjoyed by a general. The fact remained that Giap was not hard pressed. Only a small proportion of the North Vietnamese army were committed in the south at any one time. Much of the fighting was still done by the Vietcong. In his own crude way, Giap could also afford to rotate his troops.

The air war against North Vietnam, the Rolling Thunder operation, was intensified. The Hanoi-Haiphong area was repeatedly bombed, but this was another miscalculation. The economy of a relatively primitive country such as North Vietnam could not be easily destroyed by bombing. Indeed, conventional bombing had yet to be proved a decisive weapon. The blitz did not defeat Britain in the Second World War. Allied bombing did not destroy the German economy. Germany was producing more aircraft in the last months of the war than at the beginning. Some of Johnson's advisers had served in the Allied Bombing Survey—Rostow was one of them—and they ought to have remembered. Giap was to be denied a second Dienbienphu, but as the Year of the Offensive proved indecisive, and the killing and destruction continued, American civilian morale did begin to buckle. This was the final miscalculation.

It is difficult to pinpoint the moment of change. The chemistry of morale or national will is mysterious. If one had to attempt an equation for 1967 several factors would have to be included. Everybody had agreed that the war was not a major issue in the midterm elections. Vice-President Humphrey afterward said in private conversation that it had settled like a layer of dust, shrouding the administration's achievements but not of itself politically decisive. Nevertheless the elections did mark a change. The Democrats might have anticipated the loss of many congressional seats, but when it came the loss increased their pessimism. The old conservative coalition of Republicans and southern Democrats once again became effective. They were to succeed that year in defeating thirty-eight bills sponsored by

the administration, and the prospect was chilling. Even before
the new year was rung in, there was a growing disposition to
criticize Johnson. He had an early taste of it from the state
governors of his own party.

The year also began badly. China had just held its fifth nuclear test, and there was gloomy talk of her developing a delivery system within a few years. Three astronauts died in a fire
while testing the new Apollo spaceship, and early reports suggested that complacency was the main cause. Bobby Baker,
Johnson's former Senate assistant, was brought to trial on
charges of fraud and tax evasion. *Ramparts* magazine revealed
that the National Student Association had secretly worked for
the Central Intelligence Agency. Old memories of the Kennedy
assassination were reawakened by an investigation flamboy-
antly launched by Jim Garrison, the district attorney of New
Orleans. Congressman Adam Clayton Powell was unseated, and
Negroes and others suspected racial prejudice. Johnson was also
obliged to propose a tax surcharge to help meet the cost of the
war and reduce inflation.

A tax increase, whether or not it is called a surcharge, is never
popular, and there was more behind Johnson's proposal than
emerged in his budget proposals. He was not to blame for all
that had gone before. When planning the budget, all American
presidents have the difficult and often impossible task of an-
ticipating what may be required eighteen months hence. The
budgetary year runs from July 1 to June 30 of the following year,
but the president must make his request in January, which
means that most of his decisions must be made or approached
in December of the preceding year. In December 1965,
McNamara had estimated that the cost of the Vietnam war for
the 1966 fiscal year would be $10 billion. It was to cost at least
twice as much, but the leading exponent of cost analysis was led
astray by the prevailing belief in American omnipotence. He
could just not believe that the war would last much beyond June
1967, the end of the fiscal year. Thus his estimates had assumed
a rundown in defense procurement and troop levels in Vietnam.
These proved to be illusory, and clearly a tax increase was

required if rampant inflation was to be avoided in future, but in 1966 Johnson had been inhibited by political considerations. As mentioned in the last chapter, he did not want to rock the boat, and there was the counterargument that a little inflation would do more to reduce unemployment, especially for Negroes, than any antipoverty program. Congress would also have insisted upon cutting such domestic programs if requested to raise taxation. Johnson did in fact inquire among congressmen and businessmen about the advisability of raising taxes, but without mentioning the war. They had rejected the notion.

The failure to take fiscal action at the appropriate time, and the subsequent delays, were to lead to a roaring inflation from 1968 onward. Some Americans realized this in early 1967, but more were dismayed by the astronomical costs of the war. They had risen that year to an estimated $21.9 billion, or twice as much as the combined costs of the strategic nuclear offensive weapons systems and civil defense. On January 24, the administration requested $12.3 billion in supplemental appropriations to finance the war until June 30. Most of the money was to be appropriated under existing authorizations, but new authorization for $4.467 billion was required. Authorization was prompt. Congress provided a further $81 million for good measure, but a Vietnam declaration was attached to the bill, which Johnson signed into law on March 16. It was the first congressional policy statement on the war since the 1964 Gulf of Tonkin Resolution, and it indicated the anguished mood of Congress. All necessary support for the fighting men was promised, but the declaration also promised support for the president and other men of good will in their efforts to prevent an expansion of the war and bring about a negotiated settlement. It called for the Geneva Conference to be reconvened. The tone was polite. There was no suggestion of incipient revolt, but the message was unmistakable. There was no heart for the war; hence the longing for a negotiated settlement.

McNamara, long known for his optimistic and misleading reports on the course of the war, had also made a surprising statement when giving testimony in support of the supplemental request. Asked about the effect of the bombing, he said, "I don't believe that the bombing up to the present has significantly reduced, nor any bombing that I could contemplate in the future would significantly reduce, the actual flow of men and matériel to the south." This conclusion was denied by General Earle Wheeler, the chairman of the Joint Chiefs of Staff, but its effect was probably more damaging than any of the bombs dropped on the 39,550 targets attacked in North Vietnam in the previous year.

Few decent men had liked the idea of bombing a small and relatively defenseless country, in spite of the reports of the killings in the south by Vietcong goon squads. The argument that there was little difference between destroying a target from the air and attacking one with ground weapons was logical but still not convincing. Some consciences had been assuaged by the assumption that bombing was inevitable in modern war, or by the thought that it could save American lives. Then there had been assurances that only military targets were attacked, and talk of modern bombsights and navigational aids suggested that bombing was similar to a clean surgical operation. Jargon such as "taking out a target" had given the impression that a power plant or munitions factory could be destroyed without injuring the surrounding population. Harrison Salisbury's reports from Hanoi in the *New York Times* of civilian casualties and the bombing of civilian targets had reawakened much of the old uneasiness. The admission of the defense secretary that the bombing had not stopped the flow of men from the north was just too much.

Disgust not only fueled the peace movement. Many among the majority which still supported their president and believed that communist expansion must be stopped became convinced that Johnson had listened too much to the generals and that they were fighting the wrong kind of war. There were reports that peace signals from Hanoi had been ignored. The idea became widespread that North Vietnam was prepared to negotiate a compromise settlement if only the bombing was stopped. It was fed by further reports, from London and other Western

European capitals, of intense diplomatic activity. There was a further explosion when Kennedy returned from a trip to Europe pursued by rumors that a French official had passed on to him a significant peace feeler from Hanoi. The rumors were without foundation. The Senator's French was not good, and he had apparently misunderstood what had been said. Nevertheless, he was invited by Johnson to report on his trip. The White House subsequently denied that there was an intemperate exchange, but it was a tense meeting and Kennedy was supposed to have called Johnson a son of a bitch. Whatever he said, the last tenuous links between the two snapped. They were not to meet again until the following year when Kennedy tried to usurp the powers of the presidency just before announcing his candidacy for the Democratic presidential nomination. There was now open war between the two men, and Kennedy did not drop the idea that peace could be negotiated if only Johnson would stop being beastly to the North Vietnamese.

Kennedy pressed home the attack on and off the Senate floor. There had just been a Tet truce, and resumption of the bombing had been delayed while Kosygin was in London, but Johnson was urged to stop the bombing and to offer to negotiate within the week. In a television program Kennedy said that the bombing could be resumed if a basis for negotiations was not found. In the *New York Times* James Reston dismissed this as opportunistic. Certainly there was no evidence that Hanoi was prepared to negotiate within the context suggested by Kennedy. Every indication was to the contrary. To Hanoi's four-point peace program, which was unacceptable to most Americans, a fifth point had been added by Pham Van Dong, the North Vietnamese prime minister, in an interview with Salisbury. He said that the United States must, unconditionally and for good, put an end to the bombing and all hostile activity against North Vietnam. Nor was there any lack of communication with Hanoi. If the reports of diplomatic activity abroad were misleading, they did indicate an informal communications network with the United Nations, London, Warsaw, Delhi, Paris, and Algiers as the main relay centers. There was a lot of talk about signals, oblique and esoteric, but it was nonsense for the most part.

American and North Vietnamese representatives even met in Moscow, but without success. Hanoi remained adamant in its demands. There must be an unconditional cessation of the bombing, and the talks that would follow must accept its four-point program as the agenda. The first was unacceptable to the administration, which wanted reciprocal de-escalation. It dismissed the four-point program, especially the third point, as a demand for abject surrender. It could be argued, as I did at the time, that Johnson was too inflexible, but few Americans then would have willingly agreed that the internal affairs of South Vietnam must be settled in accordance with the program of the National Liberation Front. It was not considered, but the idea grew that if only the bombing was stopped some movement toward an acceptable solution would begin. Subsequent events showed that this was much too optimistic, and in early 1967 Johnson and many Americans had yet to be convinced that further military action could not improve his bargaining position. That the idea flourished can only be explained by the fact that Giap was beginning to win his war in Washington, New York, and a hundred other American cities. The vast majority had not accepted defeat, but having lost heart in the war they were looking for an easy way out.

The mood was contagious, and restriction of the bombing was proposed on more than one occasion within the administration. McNamara proposed that the bombing should be restricted to below the 20th Parallel after he had admitted the relative ineffectiveness of the bombing campaign. The idea, which Johnson was to accept in the following year, had considerable merit. Much of the populated areas of North Vietnam, including Hanoi and Haiphong, would have escaped the bombing. This would have calmed some of the agitation at home and would have been a de-escalatory move. Moreover, the narrow strip of land south of the 20th Parallel was the best tactical target area. Most of the regular North Vietnamese army was deployed in echelon between the demilitarized zone and the 20th Parallel. All the infiltration routes to the south, including those which went through Laos, were funneled through this panhandle. Rusk took up the idea in the summer, somewhat tentatively, but Johnson would not hear of it. He still assumed that the sheer force of American arms would force Hanoi to yield before the next election. The Joint Chiefs of Staff were optimistic, and in spite of public anguish there was still considerable support for the bombing in and out of Congress.

Johnson was also losing faith in McNamara, whose admission had been publicly damaging and personally hurtful. He depended more on the defense secretary than he probably cared to admit, although his public commendations had been effusive. Vietnam had always been McNamara's war, and Johnson had admired his ruthlessness. He had ridden roughshod over all the opposition, and his calm assumption of infallibility had been of great comfort to Johnson. When McNamara's plans went awry, and he proved to be as fallible as other humans, he seemed to suffer a partial moral collapse.

He did not desert Johnson. He was a decent and honorable man. He went on with his grandiose schemes, such as the McNamara line. The bombing having failed, he devised a kind of electronic Maginot Line just below the demilitarized zone. It was equipped with sensors that were supposed to detect infiltrators. It was no more successful than the bombing. He still defended official policy but with little enthusiasm. Johnson realized eventually that the fight had gone out of his defense secretary. With a kindness not often attributed to him, he arranged at the end of the year for McNamara to become president of the World Bank. He left after the 1968 Tet offensive.

With hindsight, one can see that the delay in departure was a tragedy. Discouraged though he was, McNamara continued to escalate the war. He frequently went to Vietnam, not to review the situation, as was supposed, but to meet halfway the generals' continuing demands for more men. Even after the 1968 Tet offensive, which led finally to the bombing halt and Johnson's withdrawal from the presidential campaign, he was still prepared to provide some of the 206,000 troops wanted by the generals. Thus until the end he could see no alternative to further escalation. Had he gone earlier, say in the summer of 1967, his successor, Clark Clifford, might have changed the course of the war, as he was to do, but with too little time for it to be effective for Johnson, in the following year. Instead, throughout that decisive year, McNamara remained in office, in effect cushioning Johnson from the demands of the military, but lending his still considerable prestige to the forces of escalation.

McNamara was part of a larger tragedy. Johnson had many advisers, official and private, in spite of reports of his increasing isolation. They included Dean Acheson, Averell Harriman, McGeorge Bundy, and Clark Clifford, then still a Washington corporation lawyer. They were the cream of the American establishment. These and other advisers were experienced and courageous, and there were men of similar caliber within the administration. Cyrus Vance and Paul Nitze in the Pentagon, William Bundy in the State Department, and Arthur Goldberg at the United Nations were typical. No country could hope to have finer men at the top. Collectively, they represented a sum of knowledge, experience, and shrewdness probably without parallel at the time. All were available, and all were sought out from time to time. If most of them still had faith in the force of American arms, and supported the principles which led to intervention in the first place, a few were beginning to have doubts about the wisdom of continuing the existing policy.

Some of this apprehension was communicated to Johnson, but his closest advisers were McNamara, Rusk, and Rostow. The first two were statutory members of the National Security Council, and Rostow was in charge of its apparatus. One or the other saw the president every day, and they all joined him for the Tuesday luncheon in the White House, when national security was discussed. Again all three were honorable men of considerable experience, but their intimacy and influence with Johnson was the larger tragedy.

Rostow, the special assistant for national security affairs, was the least of the three in rank but closer to Johnson to the extent that his office was in the basement of the White House. He was known as Washington's foremost hawk, and the label fitted as well as most. He was an academic economist and a prolific writer. He had served Kennedy, first as deputy to McGeorge Bundy and then as the chairman of the Policy Planning Council in the State Department. He had immense energy—he played tennis most mornings before his killing twelve-hour days—and not a negative reflex in his entire nervous system. He was an ideologue with more than his fair share of charm. Nothing could deter him, or shake his confidence—in himself, in his country, and in ultimate victory in Vietnam. To the very end, he believed that the war was being won. When the 1968 Tet offensive finally crushed Johnson, I can remember Rostow, in his basement office, showing me aerial pictures of the bombing of Khesanh as proof of the North Vietnamese defeat. One of Rostow's main functions was to organize the flood of paper that came into the White House. It was a task of the utmost importance. Special assistants such as he must protect the president, not only from that flood but also by making available all the relevant information and proposals in such a form that the president can make informed choices between strategies to be followed and force levels to be set. There were some who believed that Rostow purposely misled Johnson by providing him only with selective reports supporting his own view of what was happening and what had to be done. I do not believe this, but no man with such positive views and self-confidence should have been given such a delicate job.

Rusk was probably the most attractive of the three. Unlike most luminaries of the American establishment, the secretary of state had no money other than his salary. As the son of a poor dirt farmer, his background was similar to Johnson's, but he had the good manners of the true southerner and none of the racial prejudice. He was one of the first members of Kennedy's cabinet to speak out against racial injustice. He had a nice sense of humor and appreciated the jokes that make Englishmen giggle, perhaps because he had been a Rhodes scholar. He had as great a capacity for drink as for hard work and was blessed with a wife who seemed not to object to missing weekend excursions and vacations. She cheerfully took on most of the dreary social chores of the secretary while Rusk remained at his desk at Foggy Bottom. I do not suppose that they had more than one vacation together in all the eight years Rusk spent at the State Department.

With the Achesons, Bruces, Harrimans, and McCloys, who came to influence American foreign policy during and after the Second World War, Rusk unquestioningly accepted the responsibilities of superpower. He assumed that they would always be demanding and costly, but was convinced that the American people were good and brave enough to bear them. I can remember listening to him when his many friends in the Washington press corps gave him a dinner on the occasion of his fifth year in office. His belief in his country, its people, and its destiny was unassailable. He spoke with a passion that lifted patriotism to one of the virtues. Little of this was generally known because of his refusal to seek popularity. He also had a very narrow view of his office. Not for him the independent freewheeling of the late John Foster Dulles. Instead, he saw himself as the president's first adviser on foreign affairs. He was a staff officer, a very superior one, but nothing more. Once policy was agreed upon, his first and only duty was loyalty to the president.

Within this limitation, Rusk saw the improvement of East-West relations as his prime responsibility. He had also been an advocate of the Anglo-American special relationship. At first the thought of intervention in Vietnam had appalled him. He had not been a party to the early moves, such as sending military advisers, which made intervention inevitable. Kennedy had been impatient with the formalities of the official decision-making process. He had preferred to seek the counsel of his intimates, and Rusk had not been one of them. But there was no looking back once the decision had been made. Rusk did not quit when the going got rough, as did most of the Kennedy liberals who were more responsible for the war, and take refuge in a university or foundation. Nothing could make him flinch from his duty. He just increased his work load. He never lost his cool until the end, and then only briefly and privately. As Johnson would have said, he was a man to go to the well with.

Rusk was a fine man with many admirable qualities, but in the political conditions of 1967 they led him, again to use Johnsonese, to hunker down. Apart from his acceptance of what he saw as America's destiny, he was not inflexible by nature, but Johnson needed his loyalty, consistence, and fortitude. The combination of these qualities, fine as they were, did not make him the secretary of state who might have saved the president from himself. More was needed than loyalty and a narrow view of his job.

Thus Johnson was dependent upon men convinced of American omnipotence and of the American destiny to man the defenses, alone if necessary, against communist imperialism. Inevitably they saw themselves in a Churchillian role, and this heroic view was another part of the tragedy in that it misunderstood or failed to perceive American and international apprehension.

The situation reflected what I had long believed to be a weakness of the American form of government. Members of the cabinet are appointed. They are accountable only to the president, and few have the connections or antennae of the politician. This can be compensated for in normal times, and of course the president is generally alert and responsive to the political moods of the country. But Johnson had also hunkered down. McNamara had no political sense whatsoever, and Rostow was essentially a technician. Rusk had always been good with Congress but by then had refused to testify to its committees whenever possible. He spent too much time in his office, but apart from Johnson's occasional press conferences he was then the man who mainly had to deal with the rising discontent in the country. He did his duty with the usual patience, fortitude, and good humor, but he was dealing with an extraordinary phenomenon. There had been war-weariness before in American history, especially during the Civil War, but this was different. Johnson, the man he tried to defend, still had to contend with a factor that had never bothered his predecessors. Television, which had helped to establish the Kennedy legend, was bringing the war into the living rooms of millions of American homes. Wives and mothers were said to see their husbands and sons killed or wounded as they sat with their families after supper. There was no escape from the war with instant photographic reportage on television screens three or four times a day.

There was certainly no longer any question of trying to insulate the country from the war, but, alas, Johnson had done the job too well. For the most part Americans were unprepared for what they saw, and they would not listen to Rusk. The clamor to get out or to negotiate an easy peace in turn hardened Johnson's resolve. He was afraid that this was the beginning of a new isolationist movement and privately noted that most of the congressmen who opposed the war also wanted to reduce American garrisons in Europe. The very natural point that more attention and money could be devoted to domestic affairs only strengthened this conviction. Above all he was not convinced that North Vietnam would negotiate an acceptable peace once the bombing was stopped. There was the responsibility for the lives of American soldiers. He had Rusk repeat, until his listeners became word-perfect, that de-escalation must be reciprocal because the most exhaustive inquiries had established that Hanoi would not negotiate. Unfortunately, at the time he was correct, as the better informed of his detractors should have known. War-weariness was an essential ingredient in the Giap recipe for a successful war of national liberation and he would not stop the war to negotiate until it became a decisive factor. The demands for negotiations indicated that more than pacifists and student activists had had enough. They increased as the year wore on, and with them the suspicion that Johnson, for all his talk about peace, was not interested in negotiations. Reports of foreign diplomatic initiatives also suggested that Hanoi was willing, but too proud to admit it. Many were convinced that all Johnson had to do was to make the first approach and talks could begin.

A great deal has been written about opportunities missed or spurned. Not all the relevant information is available. Most of the men closely connected with these moves did not know all that occurred. Even William Bundy, who, as assistant secretary of state for Far Eastern affairs, was the general coordinator, was not certain that all information passed over his desk. Nevertheless, sufficient is known to suggest that North Vietnamese intransigence—or rather faith in ultimate victory—was a constant factor throughout that period. Certainly the available evidence suggests that would-be mediators, most of them foreign, were more enthralled by the mechanics of communication with Hanoi than with the response that filtered down their tenuous channels.

U Thant, the secretary-general of the United Nations, was one of them. Although North Vietnam had refused the invitation to appear at the UN, he believed that talks were possible if only the Americans would stop the bombing. He was not an ideal mediator. His disgust over the bombing and his coolness to the United States, which many saw as anti-Americanism, did not suggest the neutrality required. The late Adlai Stevenson, then the American permanent representative at the United Nations, was hardly a hawk, but he did not press the secretary-general's case. The Russians, who were beginning to be helpful, said that Thant had misunderstood a remark of a member of their UN delegation. The Canadians then had a go. They were represented on the International Control Commission and therefore had access to Hanoi. They reported that the North Vietnamese still insisted that the National Liberation Front was the sole representative of the South Vietnamese people. The Poles, who were also represented on the ICC, launched another probe known in the State Department files as "Marigold." With the help of the Italian ambassador in Saigon, one of their young diplomats, who flew regularly to Hanoi, made some soundings and reported to the American ambassador in Saigon. Henry Cabot Lodge was interested; with most of his countrymen he still believed in American omnipotence and assumed that Hanoi had had enough of the war. The Pole eventually reported that Hanoi was willing to attend a meeting in Warsaw. Unfortunately the outskirts of Hanoi were bombed before the meeting could take place, and that was the end of that.

There was also Britain, which, with the Soviet Union, was a co-chairman of the 1954 Geneva Conference, and both were assumed to retain some residual authority. The Russians would not act in that capacity, but the war was unpopular in Britain, and Prime Minister Harold Wilson became an active mediator. British diplomacy, perhaps because it had few other things to do, became intense. It culminated in February 1967, when the visit of the Soviet prime minister coincided with the Tet holiday in Vietnam. Wilson's thinking is still obscure, but it seems to have been obscure from the beginning. The venture was certainly shaky, because Wilson assumed that he could persuade Johnson to accept a new formula and that Kosygin could persuade Ho Chi Minh to accept it. As a matter of fact, Johnson had made a direct approach, his fifth according to the State Department, to Ho only a few days before, and was rebuffed while Kosygin was still in London. The war was resumed.

The peacemaking efforts went on, and their failure redounded on Johnson. The collapse of "Marigold" was especially damaging when news of it leaked out. The offending bombing raid looked bad. Those who wanted to think the worst of Johnson, and they were increasing, saw it as a deliberate attempt to prevent talks. This was almost certainly not the case. Johnson assumed, in the absence of a definite offer from Hanoi, that there would be preliminary discussions while the fighting continued. There was no connection with the bombing raid. All targets in the Hanoi area had been put on a restricted list on August 24, and there was bad flying weather over North Vietnam throughout September. Some of the Hanoi targets were removed from the list on October 23, but again there were adverse weather conditions throughout November. The air force took advantage of the first clear skies to bomb the Hanoi targets on December 4. It did not know about the meeting which was to have been held in Warsaw two days later. The worst that could be said about the incident was that one half of the administration did not know what the other half was doing. The few officials who did know had forgotten that the targets had been removed from the restricted list. This was not unusual, especially when secret diplomacy or clandestine activity was involved. For instance, the U-2 incident led to Khrushchev's withdrawing from the Paris summit conference.

There was no evidence, apart from the report of the young Polish diplomat, that the North Vietnamese were prepared to meet the Americans in Warsaw or anywhere else, except on their own terms. Subsequent information suggests that the entire affair was a hoax, to the extent that the Pole acted without assurances from Hanoi. In fairness to Johnson, and at the cost of some repetition, the entire situation must be looked at objectively—not only what is known of the peace efforts but American and North Vietnamese objectives and the military assessments at the time. The first thing that must be said is that nations go to war for something more than a cessation of the fighting. Johnson and Rusk could have had the kind of peace pursued by U Thant, Wilson, and others, and more peace of mind at home, if they had not intervened in the first place. They intervened because, rightly or wrongly, they saw some clearly defined intermediate objectives to be reached if peace was to be finally resurrected and ultimately preserved. Since the last great war to end wars, the United States had gone to war and intervened in foreign disputes, such as Greece, Korea, Lebanon, and the Dominican Republic, for peace. The paradox was painful for Americans as well as their friends and allies. But for Johnson and Rusk it was a real paradox, absurd and seemingly self-contradictory but nevertheless true.

Europeans winced when Rusk compared Vietnam with the German reoccupation of the Rhineland or Munich, but it illustrated the first principle of American national security policy. This was that the balance of power, both military and ideological, must not be violently disturbed. If militant communism was dead, as one academic on temporary duty with the Policy Planning Council was preaching at the time, it was perhaps because that balance had not been much disturbed since the fall of Nationalist China. Rusk believed this and thought that the alarm bells were ringing again in Vietnam. That was the main significance of the war for the secretary of state.

There was also no reason for Rusk to believe that the North Vietnamese would let Johnson off the hook which they had forged during years of war much more painful for them than for Americans. For President Ho Chi Minh and Giap there was the bitter memory of the 1954 Geneva agreement. They had then believed that the temporary division of Vietnam would not last long after the French had left because the south would quickly collapse from its own disunity and ineptitude. Countries such as Britain and India, without whose skillful diplomacy the agreement would have been impossible, had assumed the inevitability of reunification under Hanoi, with or without elections. They were realistic enough to face the fact that revolutionary nationalist forces could not be contained for long, and argued that almost any kind of government could assume power in Saigon without endangering world peace. They saw no reason to assume that a united Vietnam under communist nationalist rule could upset the balance of power in Asia. Alas, they reckoned without Dulles and his anticommunist crusade. American support and interference, often clandestine and in direct violation of the Geneva agreement, brought the processes of history to an unnatural halt.

Those processes were resumed when North Vietnam began to help the Vietcong when Kennedy was elected. An easy victory was denied to them when Johnson intervened with American troops in 1965, and in 1967 Hanoi could not risk another Geneva. American determination had weakened but it would have quickly revived with a cease-fire. American policy was still intended to bring about a return to the status quo ante, and in any language that meant defeat for North Vietnam. There was also the ideological struggle, which was waged both in Hanoi and Washington with all the intensity of medieval theology and the righteousness of a religious war. For Hanoi, the inevitable victory of a war of national liberation was an article of faith as well as a national objective. For Washington, the necessity to defeat such a war was no less than a God-given truth. The frequent public references to this ideological position proved costly for Johnson. It was resented by many Americans, because it was seen to cast the United States into the role of world policeman. Appalled by the prospect of having to fight one Vietnam war after another, they joined the ideological struggle. As so often in unstructured debates, much was forgotten or ignored. National security policy was attacked, but the determination of North Vietnam to negotiate only on its own terms was conveniently ignored. The demand for negotiations continued, and with it the growing suspicion that the poor little peaceloving North Vietnamese were being spurned by that Texas cowboy in the White House.

Johnson was not the gun-toting oaf he was said to be. Given the over-all situation as sketched above, and his belief in the eventual victory of American arms, the policy of reciprocal de-escalation was a respectable one. It was all very well for the hopeful to talk of smoke signals coming from Hanoi, but they were hard to see. There was the suspicion that the talk of possible negotiations was fed by North Vietnam. I shared it after spending fruitless hours trying to track down reports of such possibilities sent by the French news agency, the only international agency represented there. Its correspondent was not playing the communist game—I have the highest respect for Agence France Presse—but the expectation of negotiations might have made him read more into official statements than was there. Johnson and Rusk were also bored with the many mediators and had decided that the Russians were the only people who could bring influence to bear on Hanoi.

They were right, but the Russians were in a difficult position. They regarded the bombing of North Vietnam almost as a personal affront because of their claim to lead the communist world. Support for the principle of wars of national liberation was still official policy, and with good reason from their viewpoint. For them, it was no more than the principle of self-determination formulated by Woodrow Wilson and accepted by most of his successors, including Kennedy and Johnson. The Sino-Soviet dispute also prevented them from playing too positive a role in ending the war. They certainly could not stop military aid to

Hanoi. But they were alarmed by the war. It had gone on too long, and the very indecisiveness was dangerous. The United States was still escalating. Then the heavy casualties suffered by the North Vietnamese tended to reduce the ideological significance of the war. Other Giaps would think twice before launching another. Within strictly defined limits they were willing to help Johnson, but in fact their influence was not decisive in Hanoi. Khrushchev had written off Southeast Asia as of small importance for Soviet national interests and was prepared to see North Vietnam become part of the Chinese sphere of influence. This was reversed after he was deposed, but making friends and influencing North Vietnamese was not easy. They were xenophobic, distrustful of large powers, and too confident of success.

Rusk understood this. He had spent nearly seven years getting to know the Russians and patiently establishing that the two superpowers, while pursuing what they regarded as their national interests, did have areas of common interest. He had coined the term "parallelism," which neatly summed up the fact that in many instances they could work toward peace, not in active cooperation, but along self-serving, parallel courses. If history is just, he will be remembered for this patient diplomacy which made the partial nuclear test-ban treaty, the nuclear nonproliferation treaty, and much else possible. For all his shortcomings, he could be remembered as one of the more superior secretaries of state of this century.

Rusk also knew that the Russians had much better information of what was going on in Hanoi, as well as more influence, than the British, Canadians, Hungarians, Italians, and Poles. They had warned him that U Thant had misunderstood the Russian position. During the "Marigold" operation, they had reminded him that Eastern Europeans had little or no influence. The fact that the Polish representative on the International Control Commission could fly between Saigon and Hanoi did not give him the access to the central committee of the Laodong party enjoyed by the Russian ambassador. For all the excitement generated by Wilson during Kosygin's visit to London, the British initiative was a bit of a joke. Johnson and Rusk knew perfectly well what the Russians thought and what they could and could not do. Moreover, they were not prepared to permit the British prime minister to dictate American policy. There was no opportunity for so-called honest brokers, and after the Kosygin visit Johnson doubted Wilson's honesty.

The significance of this Soviet-American relationship seemed to escape public notice. Perhaps it is just as well. Many Americans, nurtured on cold-war rhetoric, would not have been happy. On the surface at least, the relationship could have appeared dangerous. In spite of their protestations to the contrary, Russian interests might have been better served by prolonging the war. They clearly thought that at the beginning. Their reports that the various peace moves were profitless would have served that purpose. But Johnson and Rusk were not naïve. The secretary had a firm grasp of the realities of superpower and a robust skepticism. He was also advised by Mr. Llewellyn Thompson, surely the best-informed and most levelheaded ambassador ever to have served in Moscow. He was in his second tour and had been adviser on Soviet affairs to both Kennedy and Johnson.

Much had also happened since the Cuban missile crisis and the test-ban treaty. They were then engaged in negotiating the nonproliferation treaty. The old fiction of the Big Four—Britain, France, the Soviet Union, and the United States—ordering the affairs of the world had long been remaindered. The bipolar world of the fifties and early sixties was also changing. Even the authority of the two superpowers over client and smaller states was diminishing. The United States had not much more authority over the Saigon government than the Russians had in Hanoi, but they shared the vital responsibility of avoiding nuclear war. Again within strict limits, they had to trust each other, and as this extraordinary relationship developed Rusk and Dobrynin, the Soviet ambassador in Washington, became more intimate.

I can remember seeing them at the White House during the annual diplomatic reception that year. A hundred and more ambassadors, some representing America's closest allies, stood about drinking champagne and talking to one another while for more than an hour Rusk and Dobrynin sat on a sofa in the Red Room in close conversation and apparently oblivious of some remarkably undiplomatic stares. This relationship paid off when peace talks were finally begun in Paris. The Soviet Union smoothed the way in October 1968, when they got over the difficulty of the seating arrangements, and in January of the following year. It was not much perhaps, but they did help to make the talks possible and to keep them going. More important, throughout those dangerous years the two superpowers managed to isolate the war. There was little or no trouble in old danger spots such as Berlin, and the slow but steady pace toward accommodation was maintained.

Nineteen sixty-seven was not the most frantic of the Johnson years, but he had more than Vietnam to worry about. The constructive side of his nature was very much in evidence, especially in foreign affairs. One member of his national security staff saw little difference between his basic domestic and foreign policies in that Johnson wanted to build a global Great Society. It was a shrewd observation. Johnson was generally impatient with the niceties of diplomacy. He accepted existing trucial arrangements, such as NATO, as a politician would accept a coalition of local and state political forces. He regarded other heads of government as fellow politicians, to be helped whenever necessary as he had helped senators when he was the Senate majority leader. This had its drawbacks when, acting as if he were still in the Senate, he tried to call in a few political IOUs. The refusal of the Western European allies to become involved in Vietnam genuinely hurt and bewildered him, but with the possible exception of Harold Wilson he was willing to accept that they too had problems.

This approach was at best refreshing and on the whole benign and useful. He refused to go along, at least publicly, with the shrill condemnation of President Charles de Gaulle of France. If the European enthusiasts in the State Department and grand old men such as Dean Acheson, who ought to have known better, had had their way he would have contested de

Gaulle's demand for the withdrawal of American troops from France. The legalisms of the draft notes drawn up for him to sign delighted diplomats of the old school, but he would have none of them. Naturally he regretted the French withdrawal from NATO, and the removal of American troops from France was shaming and costly. Nevertheless, he recognized an adamant statesman when he saw one, and his own tactical helplessness. Accordingly, striking the right note of regret, he withdrew gracefully. In so doing, the essential unity of NATO was preserved, and a sensitive situation was not exacerbated. Perhaps one of his successors will collect that IOU in Paris as a consequence of this shrewd statesmanship.

Johnson was also impatient of the many doctrines and concepts into which American national security policy is made to fit. I doubt if he ever accepted the ideology built around wars of national liberation. They were just wars to him. In the early days of his administration, NATO was almost rent apart by the struggle for a multilateral nuclear force. One American assumption was that the West Germans should be closely associated with nuclear weapons if they were not to demand possession at some future date. Whatever the merits of the argument, the project created enormous tensions within the alliance throughout the last year of the Kennedy administration. Soon after his succession, Johnson said stop. Overnight the special MLF office in the State Department literally disappeared without trace. It was rather like being in the Ministry of Truth in Orwell's *1984*. I tried to reach a senior member of the office a few days after it had disappeared without notice, and the telephone operator swore that the number had never been listed. Nothing more was heard of the destroyer, manned by a polyglot NATO crew and flying the special blue-and-white MLF flag. For all anybody knows, it may still be riding the high seas like the *Flying Dutchman* with German sailors morosely eating American rations and the Englishmen complaining about the absence of rum.

Johnson did not like communists, and I am sure that he despised neutrals, but he was willing to get along with anybody for the sake of quiet life. He could never understand why foreigners did not try to emulate the American way of life, but he was forbearing with those who were foolish or downright willfully obstinate in their refusal to try. India was the obvious example.

During his administration that poor country was threatened with widespread famine as a result of the poorest monsoon rains in a century. Millions were on the edge of death from starvation and disease. Wheat was quickly sent, but there were still desperate shortages in 1967. In February Johnson announced in a special message to Congress an immediate and interim allocation of 2 million tons of grain. An additional commitment of 3 million tons was also requested. The World Bank estimated that India needed 10 million tons that year to avoid famine and eventually the United States contributed 6.6 million tons in 1967. Altogether it provided nearly 15 million tons. The American example also persuaded other countries, notably the Soviet Union, to help. The major American role played in this international effort was more than plain charity. Apart from the human suffering, Indian democracy could hardly have survived without Johnson's initiative. The collapse of orderly representative government in the second-most-populous country in the world would have been a disaster of the first magnitude.

Johnson was not content with providing food, which ran down his country's once-enormous surpluses. Being a rancher, he had a better appreciation of the world food situation than his more recent predecessors. The United States and Canada were together the world's one remaining food basket. Regions which had previously exported food, such as Latin America, were becoming importers. Communism had failed to work on Russian and Chinese farms. Western Europe and Japan remained large importers, and Australasia produced only a small surplus. The economists in the Department of Agriculture, led by Lester Brown, calculated that the foreseeable North American grain surplus of 40 million tons a year was all that stood between an expanding world and starvation. This Malthusian forecast, with its prospect of famine and war, was not exaggerated. Johnson therefore made it a condition of his food shipments that India must stop dreaming of becoming a great industrial power before the end of the century and devote more of its resources to agriculture. He also encouraged birth control and the development of better seed, the so-called miracle seeds. At the time of writing the green revolution was getting under way, and the experts were reasonably certain that the Victorian shadow of Malthus had once again receded.

I would like to think that Johnson will be remembered for this. The sheer physical problem of shipping all those millions of tons nearly halfway around the world in freighters with an average capacity of about 10,000 tons required an American solution. No other country would have contemplated such an immense operation, but it was Johnson's comprehension of the situation and his political leadership that made it possible. If his place in American history is still uncertain, he surely deserves a place in the Hindu pantheon.

He was no less prescient and active in the field of disarmament. In March *U.S. News and World Report* asked, "What's really going on between the U.S. and Russia?" In its usual thorough way, the magazine explored all that had been said or done and concluded that it was peace. Johnson had emerged as the apostle of peace in spite of the war he was waging half a world away. Vietnam was in fact an earnest of the superpowers' intentions. American aircraft were being shot down by Russian surface-to-air missiles, but they refused to get excited about it. While both were reluctantly doing what they saw to be their duty, as superpowers they took the greatest possible care to avoid a superpower confrontation that could have destroyed hopes of a larger peace and pressed on with disarmament measures. Some Americans just could not see Johnson holding an olive branch. Vietnam got in the way. Nevertheless, the search for accommodation and relaxation of tension went on endlessly. The reason was plain, and disarmament efforts went on before and after Johnson's succession to the presidency. The power to destroy the world is a gift so awful that those who possess it must seek alternatives to nuclear war.

In the United States the full weight of nuclear decision rests upon the president. Everything has been done to guard against mistakes. A complex system has been devised to ensure that he alone can give the coded orders. Wherever the president goes he is accompanied by a man carrying these codes. That man sits outside the presidential bedroom every night. One can suppose that the presidential responsibility is not so dreadful because the basic logic of nuclear deterrence is that the orders will not be given. The logic is persuasive, but only because some kind of nuclear exchange—to use the customary delicate euphemism —in defense of national interests must be conceivable. This brings us back to presidential responsibility. It is inescapable, and the doctrine of controlled response assumes that the President can bring himself to engage in calculated mass murder. The doctrine is a controlled and damage-limiting alternative to the spasm response, or instant massive retaliation, but the presidential burden is made infinitely greater. No man has ever been expected to order the incineration of one city for another, as if he were playing a ruthless game of chess.

This is the fundamental weakness of the war-games theory when applied to nuclear weapons. In spite of the new disciplines, exercises, and rehearsals, the prime factor is presidential will. It is not something that can be quantified and run through a computer. Nobody can really know how the president would behave if the crunch came, perhaps not even the president himself. What is known is that every president of the nuclear age has sought relief in accommodation with the other superpower and in the search for arms control and eventual disarmament. When released from the messianic ardor of his departed secretary of state, Eisenhower embarked on world tours in search of peace. Kennedy established the Arms Control and Disarmament Agency and negotiated the test-ban treaty, and in between these two notable events took the world to the nuclear brink over Cuba. I, for one, am not convinced that this spectacular example of nuclear gamesmanship was the only way to remind Khrushchev of his superpower responsibility to maintain the nuclear balance. Nevertheless, it was such a dreadful experience for both sides that the movement toward accommodation was demonstrably accelerated.

Johnson maintained the momentum. He made the nonproliferation treaty possible when he scuttled the MLF, and negotiations proceeded. In his 1967 State of the Union message there
was an indication that he would propose a moratorium on the
development of antiballistic missiles. His budgetary requests
included the sum of $375 million to begin work on the Nike X
missile defense system, but only if negotiations failed. Approaches to the Russians had been made in the previous year
but with no success. They had built a limited ABM system near
Moscow and were thought to be working on another. Soon after
the message, Llewellyn Thompson was instructed to make further exploratory approaches. They coincided with the beginnings of a public debate at home. McNamara, in testimony
before congressional committees, insisted that the American
answer to a Russian ABM system must lie in more destructive
power of American offensive missiles. It was arguable. Although
ABM development was another step forward in the arms race,
at least in budgetary terms, the weapon was strictly defensive.
The Russians have traditionally attached more importance to
defense than to offense. They also had the Chinese to worry
about. The Sino-Soviet dispute threatened to become more than
ideological once China had a nuclear delivery system. Both
Moscow and Washington were unconvinced that Peking understood the new nuclear disciplines.

Moreover, in his efforts to increase American offensive nuclear capability to balance the Russian ABMs, McNamara had
taken another and more serious step in the arms race. He had
proposed, and Johnson had accepted, the development of the
Poseidon missile with a multiple warhead. When adapted to the
Minuteman missile this multiple independently targeted re-
entry vehicle (MIRV), was designed to increase the American
offensive capability up to a factor of ten. More than that, it made
arms control all the more difficult. Each side knew how many
missiles the other had, because of spy satellites, but they would
soon not know how many warheads they carried. Nevertheless,
the slow diplomacy of Rusk continued, as did the outstanding
work of William Foster, the director of the disarmament agency.

161

It was very complicated for the Americans. Unlike the Russians, they had to carry their allies with them. The West Germans were especially difficult over the nonproliferation treaty, but the Americans persisted, and their efforts eventually crowned Johnson with another notable success. In March, he also announced that Kosygin had agreed to discuss limitation of ABMs. There was good reason to believe that the Russian had not made up his mind finally, but Johnson was determined to maintain the pressure.

In April he went to Western Europe, but only to attend the funeral of Konrad Adenauer, the West German chancellor. There was no talk of grand designs, and very soon the situation in the Middle East deteriorated, and Johnson's peacemaking efforts were concentrated on Cairo and Jerusalem. There was a quick flight to Ottawa for discussions with Lester Pearson, the Canadian prime minister, and Harold Wilson flew from London to Washington. The two discussed joint action by the maritime nations to ensure the free passage of the Strait of Tiran, as Anthony Eden and Eisenhower had once discussed joint action for keeping open the Suez Canal. Into this rather uninspired diplomacy Abba Eban, the Israeli foreign minister, dropped a bombshell. He arrived in May and told a horrified Johnson that there was a secret American commitment guaranteeing free access of shipping through the Strait of Tiran to Aqaba. Eban produced copies of documents so secret that that they were not in the State Department's files.

The first commitment was made by Eisenhower's secretary of state, the late John Foster Dulles, after the 1956 war in an effort to persuade the Israelis to withdraw from Sinai, and especially Sharm el Sheikh. He had assisted in the writing of Israel's final statement in the United Nations debate in 1957. It said that interference in shipping in the Strait of Tiran would be regarded as an act of war. I understood at the time that Eban produced a copy of the statement with corrections written in Dulles' hand. He also produced a personal letter from Eisenhower to Ben-Gurion, thanking the then Israeli prime minister for agreeing to the arrangement and strongly emphasizing the

American commitment. Johnson was naturally appalled, and without corroborative documents in the White House and State Department files fobbed off Eban while a search was made. He knew that presidential papers are not the property of the state but the personal papers of the president concerned. Since FDR, presidents had followed the custom of putting their papers in special libraries, and that Friday night Tom Hughes, of the State Department, was sent to Gettysburg to go through the Eisenhower papers. He returned the following day, exhausted but with the evidence. Without the benefit of a treaty, and senatorial advice and consent, the United States was fully committed to keeping the Strait of Tiran open and morally committed to go to Israel's help in the event of war.

That was one hook Johnson was let off. Israel waged a preemptive war, and in six days once again seized the Sinai peninsula and cleared the strait. Johnson was awakened on Monday, June 5, at 4:30 A.M. by Rostow and told that hostilities had begun. He hurried down to the situation room in the basement of the White House, which connected him to every American military headquarters and embassy around the world, to the underground silos of the Minuteman intercontinental ballistic missiles, to the Polaris submarines on underwater patrol, and to the hot line to Moscow. It was through this center that Kennedy had confronted Khrushchev in the Cuban missile crisis, and Johnson had landed thousands of marines and troops in Santo Domingo within a few hours. Among its maps, telephones, teleprinters, and consoles, Johnson met Rusk, who had been at his desk in the State Department since before 4:00 A.M., and McNamara. They had to look in several directions at once, to Jerusalem and Cairo, to Moscow and London, and to the UN. Then the hot line rang. It is in fact a teleprinter, but for the first time since the line was installed after the Cuban missile crisis, the leaders of the two superpowers used it in a moment of supreme crisis.

Kosygin called first. He sought assurances that the United States would not intervene, and they were given when the Russian gave similar assurances of nonbelligerency. Relief was

short-lived. The American spy ship *Liberty* was attacked by
Israeli planes and torpedo boats, and American carrier-borne
aircraft flew to her assistance. Many members of her crew were
killed or wounded, which demonstrated in a brutally tragic
fashion that the United States and Israel were not in secret
alliance, but the presence of so many American aircraft near the
battlefield could have been misunderstood at the time. It was
Johnson's turn to call Kosygin and assure him that they were not
flying in support of Israeli ground forces. The United States was,
of course, emotionally committed to the survival of Israel, without the benefit of treaty or those secret assurances from Eisenhower and Dulles. Some collusion between the two countries
was evident soon afterward at the United Nations. Washington
began to press Jerusalem to accept the cease-fire resolution only
when the victory of Israeli arms was assured. Arthur Goldberg,
the American permanent representative, was heard to say after
one negotiating session with his Russian opposite number:
"Take your time." Russian efforts to include a demand for troop
withdrawals in the resolution were defeated. Heavy American
pressure to stop the fighting was not applied before the following Friday, when Israelis began to move into Syria. Each of the
superpowers continued to pursue what was regarded as their
national interest in the Middle East, but as long as one or the
other did not actually intervene the larger peace was maintained.

The six-day war demonstrated that Johnson understood the
superpower game and was capable of playing it with determination and caution. I can remember watching him that first
morning as he emerged from the situation room after hours of
great tension. He looked tired and gray in the lovely early sun
but was splendidly composed. For a few minutes he stood chat-
ting with Rusk and McNamara, then patted the secretary of
state on the arm, as if to comfort him, and walked back into the
White House. Washington was alive with rumors that day, dangerous rumors because the tide of battle in distant Sinai was still
not known. Johnson had it announced that all aircraft of the
Sixth Fleet were several hundreds of miles from the area of

conflict. This was a slight exaggeration, but after his diplomatic failure to pin down Israeli troops in their foxholes he had to ensure that only they and the Arabs would be involved.

Kosygin went to New York for the UN General Assembly, and Johnson was determined to meet him. Presumably he believed that he could reason with the Russian and operate in the old congressional manner. The two men who had probably avoided a large war by laconic messages on the hot line certainly deserved to meet, but there was another reason for the Americans. They believed that Moscow's collective leadership was ill suited for the quick decisions of crisis management. The hot line had worked earlier that month, but there was no reason to believe that it would always be successful. Johnson wanted to make sure that Kosygin understood American objectives, but he was not prepared to go to the United Nations, which he regarded as a propaganda circus. Kosygin was unwilling to go to Washington, presumably because of criticism in such distant places as Peking and Cairo. A place somewhere in between the UN Headquarters and Washington had to be found.

All week American and Russian diplomats conferred, and on the Friday Johnson gave a luncheon in the White House for some NATO ministers, including George Brown, the British foreign secretary. Brown apparently had had too much to drink flying down from New York, and his raucous laughter could be heard upstairs in the president's private quarters as we gathered in the East Room below. His booming geniality was better suited for a pub in Belper, his constituency, but few cared. By that time most of the guests knew that the diplomats were drawing lines and circles on a map of New Jersey. Apart from equidistances, security was involved, and Kosygin refused to meet at a military base. That afternoon, a few hours before the two men actually met, it was agreed that the campus of a state college in Glassboro was suitable for the summit meeting.

The Secret Service worked fast. The president of the college and his wife were ejected from their house. Much of their furniture went with them, and carpenters worked through the night to make a table big enough for the representatives of the two

165

superpowers. It was terribly hot, and the house was not air-conditioned. Twenty-two window-type air conditioners were installed. Their power lines draped the house like so many party streamers, giving it a festive look. It was hardly the Palace of Versailles, or Blair House, but Johnson did not mind. There was a minor crisis when the bewildered wife of the college president staged a minor revolt. Standing at the kitchen door, she said, "They can invite Mr. Johnson and Mr. Kosygin into my house, they can move my furniture about, but they are not coming into my kitchen." The Secret Service, as resourceful as ever, arranged for the food to be cooked in Washington and flown to Glassboro.

Summit conferences have lost the popularity they once enjoyed. Experience has proved what successive secretaries of state have said for many years: No meeting of heads of government can be successful unless the meeting has been planned well in advance and the principals are already approaching agreement. A brief meeting cannot change the position or policy of a government, but Glassboro was not intended to. Johnson most wanted to explain his own position, especially on the Middle East, Southeast Asia, nuclear nonproliferation, and antiballistic missiles. He suggested the informal agenda, and Kosygin was willing to go along. As expected, nothing spectacular was achieved, although Glassboro undoubtedly marked another advance toward the nonproliferation treaty. There were assurances from Kosygin that the Soviet Union recognized Israel's right to exist. The meeting also paved the way for later Soviet-American efforts to resolve the Middle East crisis. This was sufficient for most of the Americans. Only McNamara failed to understand the limitations of a summit conference. He spoke passionately against the iniquity of developing antiballistic missiles, apparently unable to grasp that the Russians had their own experts and ideas of nuclear deterrence.

Johnson was more sophisticated. After the second and final day, he said, "When nations have deeply different positions, as we do on these issues, they do not come to agreement merely by improving their understanding of each other's views. But such improvement helps. Sometimes in such discussions one can find elements—beginnings—hopeful fractions—of common ground, even within a general disagreement." They agreed to keep in touch. This was about the sum of the first summit conference in six years. It was not much to report at the time, but the patient Rusk was satisfied.

Glassboro did Johnson a lot of good politically. His rating in the public-opinion polls rose appreciably because of the euphoria that invariably attends such meetings, but it did not last long. American casualties in Vietnam had also risen, and there was another hot summer. Indeed, the civil commotions began quite early on southern campuses, and these were followed by riots in cities as far apart as Tampa, Cincinnati, and Atlanta. These were little more than worrying for Americans grown accustomed to violence, but less than three weeks after the summit meeting Newark exploded. The violence flared for five days, and by the time the National Guard eventually withdrew twenty-three persons had been killed. Six were women, and two were children. Soon afterward Detroit went up in flames, and forty-three persons were killed before order was finally reimposed by federal troops.

For foreign reporters who covered these two major race riots it seemed that the past was catching up with the United States. Newark is a sleazy town, to an outsider no more than another forgotten urban slum in the industrial sprawl of greater New York. The flight of whites to distant suburbs had abandoned much of the city to blacks. More than half of the population was Negro and one in ten Puerto Rican and Cuban, but the whites retained political control. There was not enough money for schools, or schools for children. About 20,000 of the 78,000 children were on double sessions. Half the black population had had less than an eighth-grade education, and one in eight was unemployed. Proportionately Newark's police force was the largest in the nation, and its crime rate was among the highest. The exploitation of the poor was worse than usual because of Mafia control. Much of the housing was substandard. Under such conditions, black militancy was inevitable.

In comparison, Detroit was prosperous, but the profits of the automobile industry had not been shared with the city, again because of the white flight to the suburbs. There was not enough money to provide adequate street lighting and garbage collection. The schoolteachers and policemen were poorly paid. The big corporations were indifferent to this public squalor and to the high state of tension in the poorer parts of the city. Detroit also had a long and ugly history of racial strife. In 1934 widespread rioting led to the death of thirty-four persons, and a judge said that there was open warfare between the Negroes and the police department. More than three decades later the city government was utterly unprepared for the riots. The police were untrained, and when the test came many of them went berserk. The National Guard was no better. A tank sprayed an apartment building with .50-caliber machinegun bullets. Another machinegunner opened fire at a window behind which a young Negro had lighted a cigarette. His four-year-old niece was killed, and the bullets severed his wife's arm. Governor George Romney of Michigan flew over the city and afterward said, "It looked like the city had been bombed on the west side, and there was an area two and a half miles by three and a half miles with major fires, with entire blocks in flames."

A police raid on a blind pig ignited the flame in Detroit. It was the arrest of a black cab driver in Newark, but the tinder, of course, was years of neglect and official indifference. This was more or less known at the time. The circumstances of the earlier riots had been well reported. Commissions, politicians, social scientists, and columnists had had their say, but Newark and Detroit did not so much increase national concern as worsen race relations. Newark was seen as a portent of the new black militancy. Reports of a carefree nihilism in Detroit, of widespread looting, and young people dancing among the flames conjured up in some white imaginations a nightmare of black irresponsibility. The crack of white backlash was heard across the country. The rioting also made the Vietnam war more unpopular.

Johnson could not do much except to appoint the Kerner Commission to investigate civil disorders. The creation of yet another commission was ill received by both races, and there was further irritation. Crime and violence in the streets continued to increase. Suburbanites armed themselves as if they were living alone on a dangerous frontier. Fewer people ventured out at night. This and much more was seen as evidence of a sick and disoriented society, and the ability of the federal government to do anything about it was in question. Official programs appeared to be increasingly inadequate, and apparently unrecognized in Washington. For instance, Orville Freeman, the secretary of agriculture, had boasted of the success of food stamps, a program designed to make cheap food available to the poor. "It has charted a new course in the wise and prudent use of this country's abundance of food.... It has improved the diets and health of our low-income families," he told a congressional subcommittee. Alas, the Citizens Crusade Against Poverty issued a report establishing that many states and counties refused to participate in the food programs. Seventeen of the twenty counties investigated in South Carolina had no food-distribution program. In Connecticut, the second richest state in the Union, 236,220 people were officially classified as poor, but only 4,945 were receiving free or cheap food under federal programs.

Proof of widespread malnutrition, hunger, and even starvation was the last straw for many Americans, especially when McNamara announced that work was to begin on an antiballistic missile defense system. The decision was defensible in cold-war terms. Every effort had been made to persuade the Russians to accept a moratorium, but they had refused. The assumption in Washington was that Moscow was alarmed by Chinese nuclear progress. Moreover, Russia had traditionally pursued a defensive military strategy. Its ABM system was said to be incapable of resisting a large-scale nuclear attack, but it was a movement in a direction that could eventually influence the nuclear balance between the superpowers. Reluctantly, the decision was made in Washington to begin the construction of a thin

ABM system at an estimated cost of $5 billion. For many Americans the decision, made at a time when so much needed to be done at home, was further proof of the wrongness of the Johnson administration and the power of the military-industrial complex.

The war in Vietnam was going badly. McNamara had just returned from his ninth visit to Saigon, where General Westmoreland had requested more reinforcements. The code name for the visit was "High Noon." It sounded like a bad Texas joke. Johnson afterward announced that at least another 45,000 men would be sent to Vietnam and requested a temporary 10 percent surcharge on income and corporation taxes. What was left of the spirit of Glassboro evaporated overnight. The national distemper rose appreciably. Impatience, shame, disgust, racial hatred, and a sense of helplessness were some of the symptoms. The nation appeared to be dividing and turning upon itself. It was not easy to decide who was against what. The one certainty was that the national consensus had been shattered. Those who were outraged or frightened by Negro violence appeared to support the war. Most of the pacifists appeared to sympathize with the blacks, but there was no common cause between them. There were also elements of a classical class struggle. Class is not supposed to exist in the United States of course, but apart from race and the war the educated young were in revolt against bourgeois values and the working class was defending them. In the Democratic party, the struggle was between the limousine liberals and Camelot Democrats on one side and the six-pack (of beer) Democrats on the other. These divisions were to deepen in the coming months, and the confusions increase, but for the first time one could sense that Johnson was losing control of the situation. There was also the first hint of the possibility, so often dismissed as ridiculous, that the Vietnam War could be lost in the United States as the first phase was lost in France thirteen years before. There were other portents of possible defeat which any student of crisis and revolution could recognize. One was what might be described as the desertion of the intellectuals. The other, perhaps the more serious, was the growing loss of confidence within the American establishment.

The latter began to fear that if these divisions continued the country and its institutions could not survive without permanent damage. The presidential election was more than a year away, and the campaign would only produce further tension because there was no doubt at the time that Johnson would run for re-election.

Almost to a man, the establishment saw Vietnam as the most dangerous irritant, and in the American way they established yet another citizens' committee, this one dedicated to peace with freedom in Vietnam. Two former presidents, Truman and Eisenhower, were founding members, as were former secretaries of state James Byrnes and Dean Acheson. Other grand old men such as General Omar Bradley and Paul Douglas also emerged from the shadows. They announced themselves as supporters not of Johnson but of the American presidency. Their appeal for national unity could not have been more basic. These elderly men, who collectively had led the country through two decades of dangers and triumphs, chose to avoid all the burning questions such as the bombing of North Vietnam and appealed in American terms for unthinking loyalty to king and country. For an Englishman, it revived memories of 1939 but without Churchill or national unity. Americans were not being called to fight a heroic battle with the forces of Nazi evil but to suffer a nasty little war which could not be won and was now hated by many decent Americans.

One was left with the impression of more than personal apprehension. There was the suggestion that something had gone radically wrong with the national security system they had helped to devise. This was more evident among the deserting intellectuals, many of whom had also helped to create the system. It was as much a monument to them as to the great administrators and proconsuls who had moved with such ease and assurance in and out of government office from their law chambers and executive suites. Unlike the establishment men, the intellectuals appeared to be determined to pull down the national security system and destroy Johnson.

There was some extraodinary inconsistency in their attacks, as one of their number pointed out. Richard Rovere, that most serious political writer in that most serious magazine *The New Yorker*, remembered that they had not objected to American involvement in Korea. It was difficult to see why what was morally right then for men such as Fulbright, Schlesinger, and Galbraith should now be morally wrong. He dismissed the idea that Kennedy could have done better, had he lived. "Kennedy just might have managed to run a more tasteful and elegant war." The insistence that Johnson should admit he was wrong, as did Kennedy after the Bay of Pigs, was similarly dismissed. The country would be thrown into worse turmoil than it had known since the Civil War.

Nevertheless, these were danger signals. Johnson ignored them at first and chose to see them as tests of his fortitude and future greatness. He began to make comparisons with the trials and tribulations of Lincoln: of how a dump-Lincoln movement was organized and of the Confederate general who hoped for victory if the superior Union forces were resisted until a peace candidate was elected president. I was reminded by one presidential assistant of the Civil War draft riots and of how the *New York Times* had favored negotiations with the Confederacy. Few Americans were prepared to see Johnson as another Lincoln. Instead, some began to think of the other Johnson, Lincoln's successor, who came within one vote of being removed from office. Max Ascoli of the *The Reporter* magazine saw the politicking against Johnson as the equivalent of an impeachment.

Johnson's unbending attitude could not last. He must have sensed the collapse of confidence. On September 29 he modified the terms under which he was prepared to negotiate a Vietnam settlement. The principle of reciprocity was quietly dropped in a speech given at the National Legislative Conference at San Antonio. He was not yet ready to order an unconditional halt to the bombing of North Vietnam, but he went a long ways toward it. He said, "I am ready to talk with Ho Chi Minh, and other chiefs of state concerned, tomorrow. I am ready to have Secretary Rusk meet with their foreign ministers tomorrow. I am ready to send a trusted representative of America to any spot on this earth to talk in public or private with a spokesman of Hanoi." With this typical Johnsonian rhetoric out of the way, he went on, "As we have told Hanoi time and again, the heart of the matter is really this: the United States is willing to stop all aerial and naval bombardment of North Vietnam when this will lead promptly to productive discussion. We, of course, assume that while discussions proceed, North Vietnam would not take advantage of the bombing cessation or limitation."

There was no evidence that Hanoi had been told any such thing before; reciprocity had been the cardinal principle. Hanoi had been required to offer something in exchange for the cessation of bombing. Now Johnson offered to stop the bombing merely on the assumption that Hanoi would not take military advantage of it. This was a major concession, but few Americans appeared to appreciate it. Rather surprisingly, Johnson at first did nothing to publicize what eventually came to be known as the San Antonio formula. When asked about it the next day at a press conference at his ranch, he even refused to concede that he had changed course. This was rather extraordinary. Before Johnson had left Washington for San Antonio, reporters were called to the White House to be impressed with the importance of the speech. One can only assume that he was loath to emphasize what he must have felt to be a personal defeat. Certainly he was the kind of man determined to avoid the impression that he had given in to public pressure. He knew of the preparations for antiwar demonstrations across the country and that the March on the Pentagon was due before the end of October. He hunkered down again.

Some 60,000 demonstrators converged on Washington. They met for speeches at the foot of the Lincoln Memorial, and about half of them afterward marched across the river to the Defense Department. There were some wild ones among them. One held a sign which read, "Where is Oswald now we need him?" Another tried to urinate on a soldier defending the entrance to the Pentagon, and others were viciously provocative. There were flower children and middle-aged people who could have been veterans of antiwar demonstrations stretching back to the Second World War. Trotskyist and other far-left magazines were peddled, but the vast majority were respectable, well-to-do undergraduates. Their numbers provided a double warning. The educated classes were moving into determined opposition, and the comparative lack of working-class people was a reminder of the deep division in the country.

Johnson and Rusk did not see it that way. They remained convinced that the young students were a minority and of small importance because they rarely bothered to vote when they were old enough to register. The assessment was far too narrow, if understandable. The statistics certainly showed that young Americans were not eager voters. Throughout the fifties students had been quiescent because of McCarthyism. There had been the outpouring of youthful enthusiasm during the Kennedy period, but this had subsided without trace. Johnson had been concerned about the unrest on the campuses, although unlike in Europe and Latin America there was no American history of student militancy. He concluded that without leadership there was little to fear from them except for more violence on the campuses. Leadership was nevertheless available, and from an unexpected source. Three weeks after the March on the Pentagon Senator Eugene McCarthy of Minnesota let it be known that he was thinking of opposing Johnson in some of the Democratic primaries in the following year.

The effect of this challenge on Johnson was quite literally startling. At his next press conference, in the East Room of the White House, he was like a boxer coming out of his corner fighting. For a few minutes he was the old Johnson so many of the reporters remembered, tough, voluble, and thinking on his feet. Asked about the frustration over the war, which McCarthy said should be debated in the primaries, Johnson said, "There has always been confusion, frustration, and difference of opinion in this country when there is a war going on. There was in the Revolutionary War when only about a third of the people thought that was a wise move. A third of them opposed

174

it, and a third were on the sideline.

"That was true when all New England came down to secede in Madison's administration in the War of 1812, and stopped in Baltimore. They didn't quite make it because Andrew Jackson's results in New Orleans came in. They were having a party there that night. The next morning they came and told the president they wanted to congratulate him—that they thought he was right all along, although they had come from Boston to Baltimore in a secessionist move. That was true in the Mexican war when the Congress overwhelmingly voted to go in and later passed a resolution that had grave doubts about it. Some of the most bitter speeches were made. They were so bitter they couldn't be published. They had to hold up publication of them for a hundred years.

"I don't have to remind you of what happened in the Civil War. People were here in the White House begging Lincoln to concede and work out a deal with the Confederacy when word came to him of his victories. They told him that Pennsylvania was gone; that Illinois had no chance. These pressures come to a president. You know what President Roosevelt went through, and President Wilson in World War I. He had some senators from certain areas then that gave him very serious problems until victory was assured. Now, when you look back on it, there are very few people who would think that Wilson, Roosevelt, or Truman were in error. We are going to have this criticism. We are going to have these differences. No one likes war. All people love peace. But you can't have freedom without defending it."

Reporters who had known Johnson from his Senate leadership days went away more than half convinced that the president would once again give the country powerful leadership. Although the challenge from within his own party had come from a relatively obscure senator, it was nevertheless a challenge that outraged both his vanity and his sense of party loyalty. In Texas, Democrats did not buck the system, at least not in Johnson's time. Even the delegates to national conventions were selected by the bosses of the state party. He did not regard the front runners for the Republican presidential nomination as

175

dangerous contenders. Governor Romney of Michigan might have had his own private line to God—he certainly gave that impression—but there were apparently no revelations or else he was too inarticulate to announce them. Governor Nelson Rockefeller of New York was still insisting that he was not in the race. Richard Nixon was quietly traveling the country signing up Republican county chairmen, but he was rarely thought of as the next candidate. For all the delegate votes he was securing, the politically knowing in and out of the Republican party assumed that he would be overtaken by a more attractive candidate.

For Johnson, the enemy was within. If McCarthy was hardly known outside Minnesota and the Senate, he was a possible leader for the liberal dissidents. He read books and wrote poetry. Then he was likely to steal votes from those dreary German and Scandinavian populists in the plains states. He was also a Catholic. There was no anticipation of his becoming the students' hero and leading a children's crusade, but it was enough that McCarthy threatened to divide the party. The Democrats were already worried by the inroads George Wallace was making in the once-solid South and in northern cities. He was expected to take his home state of Alabama and two or three more, and split the votes in other states. Moreover, there was the constant fear of Robert Kennedy.

The situation demanded strong presidential and party leadership, and Johnson had all the awesome power of his office. There was nothing to stop him from taking some dramatic peace initiative in Vietnam. Political patronage still buttressed his authority within the party. If some Democrats in the North did not want to be too closely associated with him in the coming election, party bosses such as Mayor Richard Daley of Chicago were still loyal. And even the dissident Democrats would rally, or would be forced to rally, to him if he exerted leadership. He did nothing of the sort. One of the Kennedy speech writers, when urging the senator to run, said that Johnson had no guts. The young man was wrong. The president had done more than write speeches for another man to mouth. He understood power and was not afraid to use it, but he did not understand national party politics. The party machine always falls into disuse between elections, but Johnson had made no effort to revive it. More than that, he was hung up on Vietnam. His appreciation of the enemy was better than most. He was convinced that Hanoi was not just waiting for an invitation to sit down and negotiate. Alas, he could draw only one conclusion from this. The war had to go on.

As he saw it, there was little more to do than soldier on, but there was another factor, and an ominous one. It was becoming increasingly difficult for him to move about the country without attracting antiwar demonstrators. The sign carried during the march on the Pentagon reading "Where is Oswald now we need him?" was only one indication of potential violence. The Secret Service guard was strengthened, and Johnson became a virtual prisoner of it. More and more often his visits from the White House or the ranch were to military installations where security could be guaranteed. In these circumstances, active leadership for the country and the party was impossible.

It was a cold, wet morning when McCarthy formally announced his candidacy. He was a study in gray, and the tone of his announcement was as gray as the day outside. There was none of the cheerful hoopla or stirring rhetoric that normally attends such occasions. He was concerned that the administration had appeared to set no limits to what it would pay for military victory in Vietnam. There was growing evidence of a deepening moral crisis in America: discontent, frustration, and a disposition to extralegal—if not illegal—manifestations of protest. He was hopeful that his challenge might alleviate the sense of helplessness and restore to many people a belief in the processes of American politics and of American government. He was not for peace at any price, but for an honorable, rational and political solution of the war.

McCarthy spoke on November 30. It took North Vietnam three months to move men down the Ho Chi Minh trail to battle positions in the south. On November 30 the 1968 Tet offensive was therefore well beyond the planning stage. For all the nonsense still being talked of its little but proud president waiting for Johnson to invite him to the conference table, Giap and other North Vietnamese commanders were already implementing the decision to launch one of the most destructive and costly battles in the long history of their fight for independence and national unity. Yet an intelligent dove such as McCarthy still spoke of an honorable, rational, and political solution of the war. There was still the assumption that Hanoi would be content with less than victory. Most Americans could still not understand the determination of those little yellow men in black pajamas. They believed that a change of policy in Washington would do the trick, as John Kennedy once believed that a change of leadership in Saigon would win the war.

This belief infuriated Johnson. There had been four truces during the year, and there was to be a fifth on Christmas Day. Tet, the lunar new year, and Buddha's birthday had been correctly observed, but the military reported that the respites had only been exploited by North Vietnam to supply its forces to the south. McNamara estimated that the enemy had lost 165,000 men that year, but the over-all strength had again increased. According to intelligence estimates it had been increased by half. The breakdown was as follows: 118,000 regular main-force troops, organized in regiments and divisions; 90,000 well-armed guerrillas; 40,000 administrative and logistics troops; 85,-000 in the political cadres; and 150,000 local militia. The Vietcong had complete control over 3 million of the country's 17 million people and substantially influenced another 2 million. The Saigon government controlled some 5 million, in the cities and refugee camps. The remaining 7 million lived in an administrative no man's land, by day at least. At night they were defenseless against the Vietcong, which recruited and collected taxes everywhere, including Saigon.

This was all Westmoreland had to show as the Year of the Offensive wore painfully to a close. In April he had addressed a joint session of Congress and was given a hero's welcome. In November he returned to a different Washington with a different story. He said, "It is conceivable that within two years or less the enemy will be so weakened that the Vietnamese will be able to cope with a greater share of the war burden." Ellsworth Bunker, who had replaced Lodge as ambassador in Saigon, could report steady but not spectacular progress. There was now no doubt that the war would continue throughout the election and beyond. Johnson was driven into a frenzy of frustration and sought some relief in movement. He flew to Australia for the funeral of the prime minister, Harold Holt, and some awful compulsion drove him on—to Thailand, South Vietnam, Pakistan, to Rome and the Vatican.

Those who pursued him felt that they were doomed to fly on forever. But Johnson had to return to reality, which was reflected in cold figures at the end of the year. American casualties for 1967 were twice those of the preceding year. The total for the entire war was 15,774 dead and 99,756 wounded. The Harris Poll reflected the political consequences. The proportion of the poll expressing satisfaction with the conduct of the war was 34 percent.

1968

General Westmoreland expected after the Year of the Offensive that 1968 would be the Year of Decision. Indeed, it was: in Washington, New Hampshire, Los Angeles, Miami, and Chicago as well as Saigon, Danang, Hué, and Khesanh, but the decision went to Hanoi. No doubt there have been other tense and anxious years in American history, but there could never have been one with so many harsh surprises. Apart from the assassins' bullets, one reason was Westmoreland's refusal to believe that the North Vietnamese could take decisive military action against his magnificent army. Another was the increasing isolation of Johnson. He had lost touch with his people at home. In hunkering down to ride out the storm, he was oblivious of the danger signals and cut off from those who were anxious to help.

Physically his isolation was almost complete. He continued to hold his weekly breakfasts for congressional leaders, and there were the usual visitors, but the White House resembled a beleaguered frontier fort in Indian country. The Indians were not exactly at the gate. The U.S. cavalry still maintained some semblance of order in the Territory, but Johnson only occasionally ventured outside. To avoid a watchful enemy, the militant anti-Vietnam demonstrators, the occasional forays from the White House fort were rarely announced in advance. He would be in and out before most people knew he had gone. The same trail was never followed twice, and the Secret Service posse acted as if everybody were an enemy. Depending upon the viewpoint, it was either as breathless as an old western movie or a cause for national shame.

Johnson helped to evoke the old frontier past. I went along to see him one night and found that Lincoln and the Civil War were forgotten. Instead, he referred more than once to the spirit of the Alamo. It seemed an unfortunate parallel. Colonel William Travis and the 150 defenders were all annihilated, but one could hardly point that out to a Texan president. In any case, he remembered only the grim courage of his brother Texans, the ruthless fighting, and Mexican duplicity. It was touching, but appalling. He was as polite as ever, only regretting the blindness of his opponents, but seemed to have little idea of what was going on outside. He clung to the idea that Americans had all the fortitude and loyalty necessary to win the war. Many have such qualities but much depended on the war to be fought. He also forgot what he had said about the Revolutionary War and the War of 1812 only a few weeks before. Or perhaps he believed that he was being betrayed. His isolation went far beyond the White House and the territorial limits of the United States. He had rarely paid much attention to Western Europe, but when he turned that night to Britain and Harold Wilson, the prime minister, his sense of betrayal was painfully obvious.

Johnson described himself as a great admirer of the British people. Apparently it was blood that counted most. He was proud of his English origins and he bought his Hereford cattle from England. He allowed that the island race could work a little harder, but he had always believed that the United Kingdom and the United States would be united in a close working relationship. "It may be an itty-bitty place, but that is where mother came from." That said, he made it quite plain that he had a low opinion of all Churchill's successors. Admittedly he had enjoyed the company of Sir Alec Douglas-Home, who appreciated fine cattle, but there had been the little business of buses for Cuba. If the buses had had to be sold, Sir Alec should have approached him. A market could have been found. The suggestion seemed to be that the corporate arms of various Texas transit lines would have been sufficiently twisted. But the unbelted earl was a paragon of allied loyalty compared to Harold Wilson. Johnson despised the socialist prime minister, and made little effort to stifle his feelings. Wilson's gratuitous advice on the need for restraint in Vietnam, and the earlier insistence that only a narrow gap between the positions of Washington and Hanoi had to be bridged to bring about peace, reduced Johnson to the homely expletives of the Texas hill country.

There was more to Johnson's anger than Wilson's apparent politicking with Vietnam peace initiatives. Britain had just announced that its troops would be withdrawn from Singapore and the Persian Gulf. It was in fact a decision too long delayed. Britain could no longer afford to keep so many men overseas. Nor were there persuasive reasons for keeping up with the superpowers. The colonial empire had gone, and with it the one justifiable reason for maintaining such expensive garrisons. They had contributed to Britain's financial difficulties, and distracted attention from more urgent business, such as improving the export performance. The United States had led the frequent rescue operations for sterling. Johnson had helped to get better offset payments from West Germany for the British Army of the Rhine as well as the American 7th Army, but always on the assumption that sterling was the first line of defense for the dollar and that Britain would retain some of the dimensions of a world power. This help was no less worthy because it served immediate American interests, although the resistance to the devaluation of the pound in 1964 was a cruel mistake. There was a run on the pound when Labour came to power, and the new chancellor of the exchequer, James Callaghan, was advised by most of the central bankers of Western Europe to devalue. The United States, with an overseas balance-of-payments deficit aggravated by the Vietnam war, urged him to hold the line. The responsibility was, of course, Callaghan's. He wanted to have a go, but without American advice to the contrary he might have listened to the other central bankers. The mistake had grievous consequences for Britain. Sterling was eventually devalued, and retraction, long overdue, became unavoidable.

The decision to withdraw from east of Suez, to abandon the defense of the old imperial *glacis*, marked the end of the special Anglo-American relationship. I do not refer to Anglo-American friendship and the many ties joining the two peoples, but to the diplomatic and defense partnership begun during the Second World War. Alas, it had led Britain astray, blinding many of her politicians to the cold realities of the country's diminished power. The United States had found it useful, without attaching too much importance to it publicly, and Johnson was both angered and surprised. He was angry because when Wilson visited Washington soon after coming to power he had assured Johnson that Britain would continue to shoulder the burden of world power. There was talk of British aircraft carriers and Royal Marine commandos keeping peace east of Suez. He had been taken at his word, and a grateful McNamara had fought off the efforts of the U.S navy to station a task force in the Indian Ocean.

Wilson's reluctant decision to forget his Kiplingesque dreams posed serious problems for Johnson, Rusk, and McNamara. The British presence in Southeast Asia, modest though it was by American standards, had been more than a comfort for a country that did not want to appear to be acting alone. Britain had defeated the communist uprising in Malaya and had defended the peninsula after independence in the confrontation with Indonesia. In strategic and economic terms, Malaysia, as it became known after independence, was infinitely more important than Vietnam. Its output of rubber and tin was essential to free-world trade. Singapore was a great entrepôt port, and if the communists had won they could have closed the Strait of Malacca. The free world would have been denied access to much of Asia. In defense of American involvement in Vietnam the Johnson administration afterward claimed that Indonesia was saved from communism. The claim, to say the least, was arguable, but nobody could doubt that Indonesia and much else was saved by the British defense of Malaya. If Britain had failed, Southeast Asia would have fallen eventually to communist insurgency, and Japan, Australia, and New Zealand would have been dangerously exposed.

I never noticed during my years in Washington that Britain's effort was fully appreciated, nor was the fact that she had soldiered on uncomplainingly without American help. The United States had grown accustomed to having British troops stationed in strategic areas, but this only partly explained Johnson's surprise. He and his closest advisers had become too preoccupied with Vietnam to think of larger Asian security problems, and indeed of much else in the world. The true condition of one of her closest allies, perhaps the closest, had been ignored. They were unready for the moment of truth in spite of frequent warnings from London. When George Brown, the foreign secretary, came to Washington before Wilson to announce and explain the final decision, Rusk and others still protested that it was unacceptable. The blow, when all protestations failed, was psychologically damaging. There was the sudden realization of how much American national security policy was based on Britain's presence in Asia. McNamara angrily exclaimed that the United States would not assume the self-imposed white man's burden, but there was no alternative if the forward policy was to be continued. Above all, their isolation over Vietnam was that much increased.

Looking around the world, Johnson could now see few of America's traditional allies who were prepared to support him. France was actively opposed. The smaller Western European countries were appalled, and Sweden was ready to grant political asylum to American military deserters. For their own reasons, Australia, New Zealand, Thailand, Malaysia, and Singapore were reluctant but frightened allies or friends. They did not like the war, but were afraid of a precipitate American withdrawal that would have left them more or less defenseless. Apart from these countries, the only firm support enjoyed by the United States came from the military governments of Taiwan and South Korea. It was hardly something to boast about.

Another dimension of Johnson's isolation, much more serious than the withering of relations with old allies, was evident in his almost complete dependence upon the Pentagon for reports on the situation in Vietnam. Unlike Roosevelt in the Second World War, he sent very few emissaries to the front to make independent assessments. The one or two who were sent were utterly dependent upon the presentations of the armed forces. The embassy was in no position to send independent reports on the fighting or the political situation in Saigon because it had become part of the war machine. The ambassador was not a diplomatic envoy in the accepted sense but a proconsul ultimately responsible for the armed forces and the continued existence of the fragile Saigon government. The Central Intelligence Agency was no less a part of the war machine, actively involved in the military and political intelligence side of the war and also responsible for clandestine operations. Although the director of the CIA had direct access to Johnson, he rarely if ever gave him the independent assessments he was entitled to receive. The agency's biased view of the struggle was made public in 1965 when an article on Vietnam appeared in the quarterly *Foreign Affairs*. The publication of this article was also further evidence of how even distinguished magazines could be misused for official propaganda purposes. *Foreign Affairs* described the author, George Carver, as a former officer in the United States aid mission in Saigon. He had in fact served there as a CIA agent.

It was therefore inevitable that the Tet offensive should come as a bolt from the blue in spite of early reports of enemy troop movements and concentrations. Even before the old year was out there was a general movement of main forces toward Saigon, Danang, Hué, Khesanh, the demilitarized zone, and many provincial and district capitals. During January more reports were received by Westmoreland indicating that a major offensive was to be launched just before or after the Tet holiday. He accordingly modified his own plans to conduct major offensive operations but afterward admitted that he did not anticipate the true nature and scope of the enemy attack. It did not occur to him that frontal attacks would be made against a number of cities, including Saigon.

To some extent, Westmoreland was the victim of North Vietnamese duplicity as well as his belief in American omnipotence and its eventual victory. The Vietcong had perfidiously announced a seven-day truce to celebrate the holiday, and he had agreed to a three-day cease-fire. Large numbers of South Vietnamese troops were allowed to go on leave in spite of the enemy concentrations. The strength of most of their units was reduced by half. American troops were placed on full alert several days before the holiday, but again Westmoreland was misled, and in much the same way as the French were some fourteen years before. Thousands of American troops were concentrated at Khesanh and Conthien near the DMZ. Both positions were difficult to support because of the terrain, and both were exposed to concentrated enemy rocket fire from just across the DMZ. The monsoon also closed Route 9, which meant that Khesanh could only be supplied by air. Low cloud cover made flying difficult. There were strong arguments for withdrawal, but Westmoreland believed that the enemy was hoping to achieve a military-political victory similar to Dienbienphu. He thought that a stand at Khesanh would tie down large enemy forces that otherwise would be used against populated areas, and decided that he could afford to reinforce the fortress with troops, supply it by air, and defeat an enemy far superior in numbers.

In fact, the defense of Khesanh did not weaken the enemy offensive in the south where the local Vietcong and North Vietnamese troops were already poised for battle. Their main objective was to win a military-political victory in the south. Whatever the ultimate intention at Khesanh, the enemy attack was essentially a diversionary operation. This strategy was, alas, a brilliant success. Westmoreland was left to face the main assault with his own troops seriously divided, with about half of the South Vietnamese army on leave and his air forces strained to defend and supply Khesanh and to deal with the major enemy assault against South Vietnamese cities. This amounted to a major miscalculation comparable to MacArthur's advance to the Yalu River in the Korean War. What followed revealed that Westmoreland and his staff had little or no comprehension of Giap's strategy. Equally astounding was that neither the Saigon government nor the CIA, for that matter, knew what went on in their own cities.

Enemy troops and Vietcong, many in civilian clothes, slipped unnoticed into the cities, especially Saigon and Hué. In the capital they were said to have used a funeral procession to smuggle in weapons and ammunition. Other supplies came in farm trucks and sampans. The attack in Saigon began with an audacious assault on the American embassy, the presidential palace, the Tan Son Nhut airbase, and the headquarters of the South Vietnamese general staff. The Phu Tho race track was used as a base area. The South Vietnamese fought well, but nevertheless Westmoreland had to send five American battalions into the city. Some neighborhoods were bombed by American aircraft. So it went on the length and breadth of the country. The old citadel in Hué was seized and held for days against repeated U.S. marine attacks. One provincial capital was liberated only after it was utterly destroyed. Hundreds of thousands of people were made homeless.

After the fury of the battle was spent Westmoreland claimed a great victory. As he saw it, the enemy had been beaten back with crippling losses after failing to hold a single town. Perhaps. It was possible that even a military genius such as Giap was capable of believing his own propaganda. He may well have expected popular uprisings in support of his troops. But whatever the truth or half truth of Westmoreland's claim, Giap won the military-political victory he had always wanted, and at a cost that was sustainable. The American estimate of the number of enemy troops killed between January 29 and February 11 was 32,000. This was much greater than allied losses, but it was not too heavy a price to pay for such a victory.

This was apparently not evident to Westmoreland, but in Washington and throughout the United States the impact was all that Giap could have wished for. Great countries have lost battles before, but defeat has more often than not strengthened the national resolve to fight on to ultimate victory. Such was the case in Britain after Dunkirk, in the Soviet Union after the German advance on Moscow, and in the United States after Pearl Harbor. But not after the Tet offensive. The bazooka that blew a hole in the wall of the American embassy compound in Saigon did not destroy the embassy, but in the United States it blew the top off all the smoldering opposition to the war. Robert Kennedy was the main spokesman for those moving into open opposition. The lesson of the offensive, he said, was that "a total military victory is not within sight or around the corner; that, in fact, it is probably beyond our grasp. Our enemy, savagely striking at will across all of South Vietnam, has finally shattered the mask of official illusion with which we have concealed our true circumstances, even from ourselves . . . no part or person of South Vietnam is safe from their attacks: neither district capitals nor American bases; neither the peasant in his rice paddy nor the commanding general of our own great forces."

Public anger, as much against Johnson as distant foes, was compounded by the spy ship *Pueblo*, which the North Koreans had seized a few days before the North Vietnamese offensive. Rusk described the seizure as an act of war, 14,600 reservists were called up, and a large fleet led by the nuclear-powered carrier *Enterprise* was ordered into North Korean waters. Again there were circumstances in which this awful might was useless. A raid on Wonsan would surely have led to the execution of the *Pueblo's* crew. A punitive air strike could have provoked another Korean war and Chinese intervention. Frustration grew when the deficiencies of the vessel were revealed, and the Defense Department admitted that there had been no American aircraft available to defend it. The fighter-bombers based on South Korean airfields were armed only with nuclear weapons.

In Washington only Johnson and his closest advisers appeared not to realize the enormity of the defeat in Vietnam. The president insisted that the main battle had yet to come at Khesanh. At an impromptu press conference in his office he said, "I am confident that our men and the South Vietnamese will be giving a good account of themselves." Rusk and McNamara were required to appear on television. With cool professionalism, Rusk defended American policies as if the situation remained unchanged. McNamara, who looked as if he could not wait to leave for the World Bank, lightly dismissed possible mistakes in Vietnam with a philosophical quotation from one of T. S. Eliot's *Four Quartets*.

Johnson was, of course, deeply shaken. While still unprepared even to consider the possibility of American defeat, he took the Tet offensive as a personal affront. Once again he was reminded of the Alamo, especially of the Mexican duplicity. He had never trusted the North Vietnamese. He believed that they would never negotiate except to avoid defeat, but he had reluctantly agreed to the Tet truce, without which the enemy assault could not have been so effective. Moreover, only a week before, the defense secretary-designate, Clark Clifford, had further clarified the San Antonio formula. In testimony before a congressional committee, he had said that North Vietnam would not be required to stop the normal supply of men and matériel to the south if the bombing was suspended. The United States only asked North Vietnam not to take advantage of a suspension. When asked what he meant exactly, Clifford said that North Vietnamese activity could continue in South Vietnam until a cease-fire was agreed upon.

This was another major modification of American policy, and Hanoi was informed long before the offensive. The fact that it was ignored was final evidence for Johnson that negotiation was useless, but his critics were not persuaded. Kennedy went on insisting that talks were both possible and necessary, and there were many street demonstrations. Of equal significance was the moral outrage of American clergymen. A group of Protestant, Roman Catholic, and Jewish ministers known as Clergymen and Laymen Concerned About Vietnam met in Washington to protest the brutality of the war. They were a distinguished group led by Dr. John Bennett, president of the Union Theological Seminary, Dr. Robert McAfee Brown, the theologian from Stan-

ford University, Rabbi Abraham Heschel of the Jewish Theological Seminary of America, Father Joseph Mulligan of Fordham
University, and Bishop John Wesley Lord, United Methodist
Bishop of Washington, D.C. They were outspoken. They said,
"American conduct in Vietnam is condemned by those very
standards of conduct which we imposed on a defeated enemy
in the Nuremberg trials. . . . Any nation that cherishes the religious heritage that America claims should set for itself particularly high standards of moral constraint, far beyond the
minimum demanded by international law, and yet the awful
truth is that on occasion after occasion we have failed in Vietnam to observe even these minimal standards." South Vietnam
and the United States were accused of contravening the Geneva convention of 1949, by killing prisoners, torture, pillaging,
taking hostages, and the forced transfer of the civilian population. "When we make a body count of the enemy soldiers we
have destroyed, the high number of bodies with no weapons
upon them suggests that among those we identify as military
personnel are many civilians."

The administration denied the allegations, but among those
who addressed the group was Eugene McCarthy. The senator
was also worried about the morality as well as the practicality
of American intervention in Vietnam. He spoke of the purposes
and objectives, the methods and means, and finally the relative
value of the intervention. Even if the purposes were good and
the methods justifiable, there was still the question of whether
the evil and destruction required to win the war were propor-
tionate to the good that might be achieved. The question worried many other Americans, and the support they gave
McCarthy in the New Hampshire primary election, mixed as it
was, came as the final surprise for Johnson.

McCarthy was an unlikely man to challenge the President of
the United States and the leader of his own party. Indeed, he
did not at first regard himself as a serious candidate for the
Democratic nomination. He was honest enough to admit that
Robert Kennedy could best challenge Johnson, but he repeat-

edly said that he was not a candidate. Somewhat reluctantly, a number of Kennedy men supported McCarthy as an alternative candidate, and a few were willing to work for him. This he saw as sufficient proof that Kennedy was not waiting for a more opportune moment to declare himself. The field appeared to be clear, perhaps too clear. McCarthy's decision to run did not impress other senators opposed to the war. Some were seeking re-election and could not believe that they would ride to victory on his coattail. His senate career had produced few headlines, and he was not then nationally known. His personal staff was provincial in outlook, and there was small evidence that he could attract sufficient campaign funds. The man himself was handsome, but too intellectual, enigmatic, and apparently cold. He could attract and repel people. He looked and sounded like a professor or fashionable priest rather than a presidential candidate. His active supporters who could be identified at the time, especially men such as Allard Lowenstein of the Conference of Concerned Democrats, were likely to do him more harm than good with the party regulars. His quietism offended many liberal Democrats who regarded the presidency as a powerhouse of reform. Above all, no serious politician believed that the party could deny the nomination to an incumbent president. The view was shared by Kennedy.

They overlooked two or three factors, apart from the growing opposition to the war. For a start, student unrest had grown, and the increasingly violent antics of the SDS and other militant groups did not attract the majority. Many were looking for a constructive cause. Young and on the whole idealistic, they responded to McCarthy's challenge. It was romantic. He was taking on the president, the parties, the State and Defense Departments, the CIA, the Joint Chiefs of Staff, and the military-industrial complex. They appreciated his learning and quiet wit as well as his courage. They thrilled when he said that men who challenge the king must be prepared to die. They delighted in remarks such as, "If elected, I shall go to the Pentagon." You could feel their excitement when he spoke of personal commitment, of the need for a renaissance of profession and vocation in modern society. When Mary McGrory of the Washington *Star* described their endeavor as a children's crusade she was closer to the truth than perhaps even she realized.

One small point also overlooked was that New Hampshire is surrounded by universities and colleges, that Harvard, for instance, is only two or three hours by Volkswagen and M.G. from towns such as Manchester and Concord. They came up in the thousands every weekend, and many skipped classes to work on through the week. There was talk of the more way-out students shaving off their beards and hanging up their beads for the duration, but most of the youngsters I met were conventional enough and accustomed to neat collegiate dress. They were well behaved and organized. All the old electioneering tricks were revived and improved upon. At least one of them had a long memory. On the wall of the campaign headquarters in Concord, the state capital, was tacked an old front page of the Boston *Globe* reporting the defeat of Truman by Kefauver in the 1952 primary.

Their effectiveness was evident long before polling day. The regular Democratic candidate, Governor John King, who was standing in for Johnson, took sudden fright. I can remember reporting at the time that both Kennedy and Governor Nelson Rockefeller of New York were reconsidering their positions. Rockefeller was encouraged by Governor Romney's withdrawal from the race, and Kennedy, or his men, were obviously reading the signs. They all pointed to unexpected success. McCarthy also had a lot going for him in the last days of the campaign, especially the Tet defeat. Three days before polling day the *New York Times* reported that Westmoreland had requested 206,000 more troops. This would have raised the troop levels to nearly 750,000, and the implication was that war would be fought at an even higher level of violence. Nevertheless, the political acumen of some of the young McCarthy campaigners was extraordinary. I asked Joel Fagenbaum, one of the students in the backroom of the Concord headquarters, how many votes the candidate would win. Fagenbaum, who was a graduate student in theoretical physics at Cornell, said 42.5 percent of the

Democratic poll. This was an astonishing figure, much higher than the public-opinion polls had reported, and when I mentioned it to McCarthy later he appeared no less astonished. But sure enough when the votes were counted, McCarthy had won 42 percent of the vote. With the write-in votes, he came within 230 votes of defeating Johnson's surrogate.

This was not the near-victory suggested by the returns but a complete triumph. The entire political climate was changed overnight. For the first time something of the true temper of the country had been revealed by the electoral process. Not all of it was an antiwar vote, but Johnson's political future was gravely threatened. Kennedy publicly admitted that he was thinking of running, and naturally public attention switched from the lone challenger to the reluctant hero, but the larger significance of the victory of McCarthy and his children's crusade should not be overlooked. His candidacy may have been quixotic. Politically he may have been destined to die after striking at the king, but the children's crusade revealed much that was wrong with American politics. To sum it up quickly, but I think accurately, representative politics as normally understood had hardly functioned from the moment Johnson took office.

Part of it was the nature of the man—secretive, a wheeler-dealer of great skill and experience who was reluctant, perhaps unable, to participate in and give a lead to the processes that representative politics require. His overwhelming victory in 1964 made him unassailable for two years or more, but as discontent over the war eroded his position it became clear that he was not the only reason why the American political system came close to failure in 1968. McCarthy embarked upon his desperate venture, as it was, because Congress and the party had also refused to respond. In McCarthy's words, there were too many congressmen who saw politics as a career and not as a vocation which, like medicine and the law, requires its practitioners to take risks and observe standards. Too few had the guts to stand up and say what they and many of their constituents thought about the war. It can be argued, of course, that this was the proper function of the Republican opposition, but in 1968 the Republicans offered no alternative. Richard Nixon was reluctant to speak about the war and was remembered as a hawk. Rockefeller was not yet in the race but had little new to say about Vietnam. He sounded hawkish. Governor Ronald Reagan of California was hovering in the wings but looked like another Goldwater in studio make-up.

Within the Democratic party, Kennedy had long been billed as tough, a winner, and devoted to the public interest, and he said much about moral courage. In his book *To Seek a Newer World* he wrote, "Only those who dare to fail greatly can ever achieve greatly." And again, "Moral courage is a more rare commodity than bravery in battle or great intelligence. Yet it is the one essential, vital quality for those who seek to change a world that yields most painfully to change." Nevertheless he attacked Johnson only from the safety of the sidelines. There were various explanations for this refusal to act, or to dare. He had only to wait until 1972, when the presidency would be returned to him as the heir apparent. He also could not afford to divide the party. Whatever the reason, there was no alternative to Johnson's Vietnam policy until McCarthy's candidacy and victory in New Hampshire. Representative politics began to work again only because of McCarthy, who probably saved it from grave damage. Even then Kennedy would have preferred to wait until 1972, and this obsessive caution was evident when he presented Johnson with an ultimatum. He would not run for the Democratic nomination if Johnson would accept a commission to re-evaluate Vietnam war policies. The president was also to state publicly that a complete revision of policy was necessary.

Johnson was approached by Theodore Sorensen, one of the Kennedy men, on Monday, March 11, the day before the New Hampshire election. Kennedy and Sorensen saw Clifford three days later. The Defense Secretary was told that Kennedy would not run if Johnson established a commission and appointed to it members who were anxious to seek a wider path to peace in Vietnam. Kennedy's list comprised himself; Roswell Gilpatric, a former deputy secretary of defense; Edwin Reischauer, a former ambassador to Japan; Kingman Brewster, president of Yale; General Lauris Norstad and General Matthew Ridgway, both former supreme commanders in Europe; and Carl Kaysen, a former assistant to President Kennedy. Clifford asked why no senators were included, apart from Kennedy, who then suggested Mike Mansfield of Montana, John Sherman Cooper of Kentucky, and George Aiken of Vermont.

The ultimatum was so breath-taking in its disregard of constitutional practice and of presidential self-respect that Johnson had no other course than to dismiss it. To protect himself, he also let the details leak to the press, saying that the ultimatum was rejected on four grounds. It would be a political deal, it would usurp the powers of the presidency, it would boost the morale of Hanoi, and the proposed commission would not be an objective group. Kennedy expressed surprise that the traditional rules of confidence governing White House conversations were no longer respected. The administration's version, he said, once again fell short of the truth. "This incident reveals in the sharpest possible terms why the American people no longer believe the president and the White House; why the credibility of our political leadership has been so critically eroded; and why it is clear that the only way we are going to change our policy in Vietnam is to change the administration in Washington."

The fact of the matter was that Kennedy's version was not so very different from that of the White House, and he continued to attack Johnson with morbid intensity. Addressing women party workers at Kings Point, New York, on March 15, the day before his candidacy was announced, he said, "Maybe it is personal animosity because he [Johnson] feels that I think John Kennedy should still be the President of the United States. That is what President Johnson has been saying." At that time, Johnson was saying nothing of the sort. He was telling callers that he was determined to fight the war to a finish. He told me that, regardless of the effect on his popularity, he would do everything necessary to ensure an American victory short of using nuclear weapons. He saw the war as a contest of presidential wills with Ho Chi Minh. He said that the outcome might depend upon how long each of them could accept the punishment, and he was in no doubt as to who would prevail. Ho, he recalled, was seventy-eight. Westmoreland would be given all the troops he wanted. The military strategy remained one of attrition, and more bloody fighting was to be expected. On the day that the military headquarters in Saigon announced that total American casualties had exceeded 20,000 dead, he said he would not be deterred by the attacks of the enemy or by dissent at home. "Peace is our goal. Let no one mistake our resolve, peace will be won." Vice-President Humphrey announced that the administration had ordered an intensive review of the war, and Johnson continued to give the impression that it could only be intensified.

A joke heard in congressional corridors after Kennedy entered the race was that Democrats had an ornithological choice of a hawk, a dove, and a vulture. It had a point, as such jokes often do, but during the last few days of March Johnson appeared in public more as the superpatriot than as a mere hawk. He had decided earlier that the heroic role of wartime leader hard pressed at home and abroad was the best for the election campaign, and now he stepped into the part publicly and played it with considerable spirit. In one speech he said, "The enemy has reached out to fight in the hearts and minds of Americans. He has mounted a heavy and calculated attack on our character as a people, on our confidence as a nation, on the continuity of policy and principle that has so long and proudly marked America as the champion of man's freedom. . . . We cannot fail those anxious and expectant millions in Asia. We must not break our commitments to freedom and the future of the world. We have set our course and will pursue it just as long as aggression threatens us. Make no mistake about it. America will prevail."

Publicly there seemed to be every reason to expect that Johnson at least would prevail. There was the nature of the man, and some cold calculation was seen behind the rhetoric. For him the results of the New Hampshire primary were not all bad. The Irish-American and French-Canadian wards had remained loyal, although badly organized. This loyalty suggested that with good organization he could depend upon the ethnic and labor votes in the large industrial states. George Meany, the president of the AFL-CIO, was an old friend and a doughty cold-war warrior. Johnson would have to share the Negro support with Kennedy, but this had small representation at national conventions. In any case, the Kerner report on civil disorders, which he had refused to endorse, was seen to have done him a lot of good. Its blanket condemnation of white racism had made good headlines. The scourging may have been beneficial if drastic therapy for the consciences of middle-class liberals who did not have to compete with Negroes for jobs, but it had infuriated the urban, working-class, and suburban rednecks. Hence Johnson's refusal to commend the report, hence his added emphasis on law enforcement. Pacificism, crime, civil disorder, foreign communism, and even dissent could be seen as one and the same thing: an attack on the America of flags and superpatriotism, or Americanism. Americanism was not the recent invention of the right-wing radicals. Its nativism went back earlier to the Know-Nothings and the Native American and American parties. The ethnic minorities, against whom it was first directed, had also embraced and vulgarized it further.

Johnson was not prepared to go back on civil rights to rally the South. He remained utterly loyal to the cause, but this superpatriotism was seen to weaken George Wallace, whose American Independent party had wrapped its stand against segregation in both the Union and Dixie flags. It looked as if the country was in for an ugly election, perhaps a dangerous one. It seemed that two kinds of McCarthyism were to be heard in the campaign, the dispassionate voice of the junior senator from Minnesota and the slime that flowed out of Wisconsin in the early fifties. The outlook was bad for moderates and liberals in spite of the bright promise of the student volunteers. Apart from the war, although it was certainly a decisive factor, racial prejudice and violence was also expected to sway the election. Martin Luther King, Jr., had emphasized the obvious connection between Vietnam and the lack of funds and attention for his hard-pressed people and the urban ghettos. There was some talk of his running for the presidency as a peace-party candidate with Benjamin Spock, the baby doctor, in second place on the ticket. This in turn increased the anger and hatred on the right and in the South.

What was then known of the reappraisal of Vietnam also suggested that Johnson was determined to fight on. It began in late February and was concerned only with military requirements. General Earle Wheeler, the chairman of the Joint Chiefs of Staff, reported from Saigon that the enemy had suffered heavy casualties but was proving to be tenacious. More than about two out of five American maneuver battalions were engaged in the northern provinces, and there was no reserve to ensure the continued survival of Saigon and other southern cities. Westmoreland required 206,000 more men, 107,000 before May. He also requested seventeen air force fighter squadrons to reinforce the thirty squadrons already in South Vietnam. The last request was extraordinary because even some air force men thought that there were more than sufficient aircraft already available. McNamara calculated that Westmoreland's demands would mean raising force levels to nearly 4 million men. Another $12 billion would have to be added to the Vietnam bill, which was already about $30 billion a year. He ordered the Joint Chiefs to review the requests, but his instinctive response, as always, was to reduce the military demands and not to consider alternative strategies.

Fortunately, McNamara was on his way out, and Clifford was already preparing to take over. Just before he was sworn in as defense secretary, Johnson established an *ad hoc* task force, with Clifford as chairman, to examine Westmoreland's requests in the light of the domestic situation. In other words, he was to decide what could be sent without further alarming an uneasy electorate. Clifford has given his own version of the task force's work.* He said that he had supported the original involvement and that as a member of the President's Foreign Intelligence

---

*Clark Clifford, "A Vietnam Appraisal," *Foreign Affairs*, July 1969.

Advisory Board had agreed with the domino theory accepted by Eisenhower and Kennedy. He had opposed the thirty-seven day bombing halt, but was later worried by the lack of enthusiasm for the war in Southeast Asian and Pacific countries. For instance, New Zealand sent 70,000 troops overseas during the Second World War but only 500 to Vietnam. "Was it possible that our assessment of the danger to the stability of Southeast Asia and the western Pacific was exaggerated? Was it possible that those nations which were neighbors of Vietnam had a clearer perception of the tides of world events in 1967 than we? Was it possible that we were continuing to be guided by judgments that might once have had validity but were now obsolete? In short, although I still counted myself a stanch supporter of our policies, there were nagging, not-to-be-suppressed doubts in my mind." He had therefore welcomed Johnson's San Antonio formula for stopping the bombing.

As defense secretary, Clifford was given no assurances that the 206,000 men requested would win the war. The hope was that bloody attrition would eventually persuade North Vietnam to stop fighting, but no general would dare surmise when this could be expected. American public opinion was also seen to be a cause for concern, and Clifford was convinced that further fighting was hopeless. He decided that the primary goal was to level off American involvement and work toward a gradual disengagement. Johnson had to be persuaded, and reminded that the original American objective in South Vietnam had been limited to prevent its subjugation by Hanoi and to enable its people to determine their own future. He argued that this had been largely accomplished. Clifford finished his version of those tense days by saying that Johnson had listened to his and others' advice and in the closing hours of March announced his decisions to the American people.

Clifford's version was of interest in revealing how the well-disciplined if conventional mind of a man in and out of government for many years could see and accept the inevitability of change. It did not reveal much of what went on at the Pentagon and in the White House during the interdepartmental battle for the mind of the president. Clifford was much too discreet a man. Townsend Hoopes went a good deal further.* Hoopes was under secretary of the air force, and he reported how Dean Acheson, the former secretary of state and a cold-war warrior, had intervened in late February. He told Johnson of his loss of confidence in the military. "With all respect, Mr. President, the Joint Chiefs of Staff don't know what they're talking about." Johnson was shocked and asked Acheson to study the situation further. There were special briefings by representatives of the State and Defense Departments and the CIA, and Acheson decided that Johnson was being led down the garden path. Westmoreland was demanding the impossible. The war could not be won without totally unlimited resources, and then perhaps only after five more years of fighting. He added that the president's speeches were unrealistic, believed by no one at home or abroad. In his judgment, the country was no longer supporting the war.

Johnson was not altogether persuaded, although a week before Clifford had resisted an air force recommendation to intensify the bombing against North Vietnam, including Haiphong, the dikes upon which local agriculture depended, and the railway marshaling yards within the Chinese buffer zone. Nevertheless, the first report of his task force assumed that the war would be continued at a higher level of violence. Johnson was advised to send about 20,000 men immediately, and to provide the remaining 186,000 requested by Westmoreland by calling up the reserves, increasing the draft calls, and extending the tour of duty in Vietnam. There was little more the task force could have done because of its narrow terms of reference, but Clifford's anxieties were by then acute. There had been no mention of negotiations or of the political implications of providing so many more men. Johnson had to be reminded that Vietnam was not the only battlefield and apart from Acheson few other men could have spoken so forthrightly. Johnson and Clifford had been friends and political allies for many years, they had risen together in Washington, but Clifford's honesty

*Townsend Hoopes, *The Limits of Intervention* (New York: David McKay, 1969).

was not welcomed. Johnson expected loyalty above all else, especially in support of his Vietnam policies which dominated his life. Nevertheless, Clifford pressed for time for further study of the political and economic implications, and Johnson reluctantly agreed.

This also provided time for dissent to surface outside the administration. The newspapers and public-opinion polls reported public disenchantment and worse. The Senate Foreign Relations Committee hearings put Rusk on the defensive. Television viewers perhaps admired his fortitude but must have noticed that he had nothing new to offer. Paul Nitze, the deputy secretary of defense, was on the point of resigning, and there were other significant defections. McGeorge Bundy, the president's former special assistant for national security affairs, had already gone over to the doves. Arthur Goldberg, the permanent representative at the United Nations, also argued for a complete bombing halt in the expectation that negoiations would follow. This advice arrived on March 15, the day Acheson had said that the war could not be won without totally unlimited resources, and Johnson was furious.

In spite of the former secretary's remark about unrealistic speeches, Johnson stormed off to deliver another truculent address on March 16, the day Kennedy declared his candidacy. He said, "As your president, I want to say this to you today: we must honor our commitments in the world and in Vietnam. We shall, and we are going to win . . . make no mistake about it— I don't want a man in here to go back home thinking otherwise —we are going to win." The next day, in Minneapolis, he said that he did not plan to surrender, pull out, or allow the country to be divided in an hour of national peril. "The hour is here. This government has the best diplomats. This government has the best generals. This government has the best admirals. This government has the best resources in every corner of the globe. [We] are trying to preserve this American system, which is first in the world today. I want it to stay first, but it cannot be first if we pull out and tuck our tail and violate our commitments." And so it went on, from one emotional height to another, until

without any warning he relieved Westmoreland of his command on March 22. Johnson refused to explain this action, but
for those who could read the signs he was obviously preparing
the ground for a dramatic change of policy. Westmoreland had
long before been promised all the men and matériel he wanted
to win the war, and with the general's departure this vainglori-
ous promise no longer held.

No one knows for certain why Johnson changed his mind on
Vietnam or decided not to run for re-election. His memoirs are
still awaited, and he may well decide to follow Clifford's discreet example. Certainly there were several factors. Only a few
have been established, but the rest can be surmised. There was
the awful thought of years of war and the bitter knowledge that
American strategy had failed. The public was aroused, and
abroad American prestige could not have been any lower. The
Democratic party was deeply divided by McCarthy's and Kennedy's candidacies, and the coming campaign trail looked like
another battlefield. I do not think that he was afraid. He had
more than his share of brute strength and courage. He would
have carried on if he had remained convinced that it was his
duty to do so. There can be no doubt about that. But the shock
of the Tet offensive and the arrival of Clifford had forced him
to look beyond his narrow circle of advisers. Necessarily he had
to listen to other men, to Acheson, and to the *ad hoc* task force,
and the Senior Advisory Group on Vietnam, which represented
the cream of the American establishment. These were the men
who had advised presidents and helped to formulate and apply
policy from the earliest days of the country's superpower responsibilities.

Their names read like a roll call of American leadership: Dean
Acheson, secretary of state under Truman; George Ball, under-
secretary of state for Kennedy and Johnson; General Omar
Bradley, the first chairman of the joint chiefs of staff; McGeorge
Bundy, then president of the Ford Foundation; Arthur Dean,
the chief negotiator in the Korean peace talks; Douglas Dillon,
ambassador to France under Eisenhower and secretary of the
treasury under Kennedy; Averell Harriman, ambassador to Mos-

cow under Roosevelt, governor of New York, and ambassador at large and much else under Truman, Kennedy, and Johnson; Henry Cabot Lodge, former United States senator, permanent representative at the United Nations under Eisenhower, Republican vice-presidential candidate, and twice ambassador and proconsul in Saigon; John McCloy, president of the World Bank and high commissioner for Germany under Truman and special representative in Europe and the disarmament field for Kennedy and Johnson; General Matthew Ridgway, UN commander in Korea and supreme commander in Europe; General Maxwell Taylor, chairman of the Joint Chiefs of Staff under Kennedy and ambassador and proconsul in Saigon; and Cyrus Vance, secretary of the army under Kennedy and deputy secretary of defense and special troubleshooter under Johnson. There was also Goldberg down from the UN, Robert Murphy, ambassador and troubleshooter under Truman and Eisenhower, and Abe Fortas, an associate justice of the Supreme Court and a personal friend and adviser to Johnson.

Most of these men had supported the war. Only Ball had opposed the war before the Tet offensive, but by the middle of March the majority had swung behind Clifford, and for much the same reasons. Taylor, Fortas, and Murphy were the tiny majority favoring further escalation. Johnson could not but be impressed. He knew the worth of these men and what they stood for. If he had preferred the company of Senate committee chairmen, he had depended upon many of the establishment men for advice before Vietnam had closed his mind. He had occasionally felt uneasy with them, but had never questioned their loyalty to the presidency and the country. In the special circumstances of modern presidential rule, dependent as it is upon layers of advisers, the long experience and shrewdness of such men was indispensable. Lincoln could afford to ignore his cabinet, but a modern president could hardly ignore the almost unanimous opinion of these informal advisers. Some already believed that they had betrayed their special trust by remaining silent too long. I suspect that a few had their moments of private shame. They had, of course, not been privy to many of the

203

decisions to escalate. Most were what is known as in-and-outers: distinguished men who move in and out of government in official and advisory capacities as required by presidents. But when their collective moment came they spoke out, some perhaps more cautiously than others, but their advice called for a radical change of policy. Nevertheless, it was not decisive. The final credit for that and the decision not to seek re-election must go to Mrs. Johnson. Rusk, whose views had also changed, insisted afterward in private conversation that she was ultimately responsible.

The First Lady was a formidable woman. Handsome, charming, and intensely loyal, she was a shrewd businesswoman and an astute politician. She had been with her husband from the beginning of their climb from obscurity to power and knew his weaknesses and strengths. She had suffered his occasional crudities. Another reason why McCarthy had grown to dislike Johnson was that Johnson had cruelly slighted her in his presence, but Mrs. Johnson had remained the devoted wife. She also had all the old-fashioned patriotism of a southern lady. In 1964 she had urged him to run for re-election, quite unnecessarily one must suppose, because Goldwater appeared to threaten much that was good in American life and vital for American security. Now four years later the time had come for another decision. She had enjoyed her years in the White House, during which their two daughters had married happily, but both their husbands were in Vietnam, one of them as a marine officer. She must have hated their departures and the disturbed nights when Johnson had been awakened because of the continuing Vietnam crises.

The night of the little monks was something of a joke in Washington but not for the Johnson family. It was the night when American bombers had attacked oil depots in the Hanoi and Haiphong areas, and unlike most commanders in chief Johnson could not leave it to his generals and enjoy a good dinner and a night's rest. He stayed up into the small hours awaiting the first reports. His daughter Luci recognized his highly emotional state and suggested that they should go to a

Catholic church in southwest Washington to pray. Johnson's main memory of this apparently was of priests hovering with some bewilderment in the background. Hence his reference to the little monks. This was only one aspect of Johnson's personal involvement in the war. All presidents and prime ministers must feel some responsibility for the wars their countries are engaged in, but Mrs. Johnson knew that every American death diminished her husband. The anguish was a severe strain, and she became increasingly worried for her husband's health.

The bad heart attack when he was Senate majority leader, and the periods in the hospital as president were never far from her thoughts. The prospect of the coming election campaign was appalling. Johnson was an enthusiastic campaigner and had not spared himself in 1964. He was oblivious to personal danger, and the assassination of John Kennedy could not have been forgotten. Johnson was also bone-tired after nearly five years of the most active presidency in the history of the country. If he ran again and won, he would serve more than nine years in the White House, longer than any president except Roosevelt—if he survived. It was an impossible thought in view of his health, the war, and mounting resistance at home. She considered retirement. The possibility had been discussed between them before. Bill Moyers knew of earlier occasions when he was press secretary at the White House, but this time Mrs. Johnson was in earnest, and Johnson finally capitulated. He appeared before the television cameras on Sunday, March 31, and announced that there would be no more bombing attacks against North Vietnam except in the area north of the demilitarized zone, where the enemy build-up threatened allied forward positions.

Then he said, "With America's sons in the fields far away, with America's future under challenge right here at home, with our hopes and the world's hopes for peace in the balance every day, I do not believe that I should devote an hour or a day of my time to any personal partisan causes or to any duties other than the awesome duties of this office—the presidency of your country.

205

"Accordingly, I shall not seek, and I will not accept, the nomination of my party for another term as your president."

Johnson afterward said, "A man finally gets tired of being hit over the head," but there were to be more hard knocks for president and people as the country moved into one of the darkest periods of its history. The bombers continued to attack the North Vietnamese panhandle to within eighty miles of Hanoi, which dismayed many people and suggested that Johnson was up to his old tricks again. His announcement had been somewhat misleading, but the limits placed on the bombing reflected the proposal made the year before. Only raids north of the 20th Parallel, where the overwhelming majority of the population lived, had been stopped. The angry charges of duplicity were quickly cut short, however, when Hanoi announced its readiness for talks. The words were hardly encouraging or friendly. Alleged American imperialism was condemned, and there was a demand for a final settlement based solely on the program of the National Liberation Front. Hanoi was prepared only to discuss the complete and unconditional cessation of the bombing and other acts of war against North Vietnam. The tone was that of a victor. There was to be no compromise. The United States, the largest and most powerful country in history, was meekly to accept the demands of a small country whose existence it did not officially recognize.

It was a bitter pill to swallow. The San Antonio formula was ignored, and Johnson knew that the enemy meant what he said. Moreover, for all the talk of meeting Ho Chi Minh at any time, in any place, and under any conditions, he was at first loath to accept because he could see a repetition of the Korean experience. History had two lessons for American policy makers: Pearl Harbor, where the navy was surprised, and Panmunjom, where talks to end the Korean War dragged on for two years while American casualties doubled. Successive administrations had sworn that neither would happen again, but the United States had been surprised by the Tet offensive, and now there seemed to be no way of avoiding protracted talks and mounting casualties. Johnson knew that the situation at home and abroad could not be controlled if he refused Hanoi. There was no alternative, and he announced his reluctant acceptance on April 3. He also said that he would fly on the morrow to Honolulu once again for talks with his generals. Then on the night of April 4 when the aircraft were about to take off (with a hundred or more other reporters I was sitting in the press plane at the end of the runway) Martin Luther King was murdered in Memphis.

The murder of King was worse than criminal. The Nobel Peace Prize winner had represented the hope of a reasonably civilized solution to the racial problem. If his authority had been challenged by younger and more militant black leaders, he was still idolized by the black community and respected by the whites. Nobody knew who was responsible for the murder, and everybody feared for the future. There was the assumption of a white racist conspiracy and the dread of a black uprising. Events began to outpace the wildest rumor. Angry blacks were already roaming the streets of Washington's ghetto, looting stores and molesting white passersby. Perhaps only heavy rain prevented instant combustion. Reports from other cities read as if civil war was inevitable, but Johnson's nerve held. As on the night of President Kennedy's assassination, the country should have been grateful to him.

Ramsey Clark, the attorney general, was dispatched to Memphis to take charge of the investigation. Clark Clifford was ordered to alert troops. More than 350,000 troops and National Guardsmen stood by. Before dawn twenty-one civil rights leaders were invited to attend an emergency conference at the White House. April 7 was proclaimed as a day of national mourning, and all flags were to fly at half mast until after the funeral. All that could be done to show proper respect, avoid disorders, and take prompt action should they occur was done quickly and efficiently. The larger danger was avoided, but not outbreaks of violence. Rioting, looting, and burning broke out in the Negro districts of more than a hundred cities. In Washington, there was the extraordinary sight of looters smashing windows of stores within three blocks of the White House as terrified civil servants clogged the streets in a wild escape to their suburbs. It was as if the city were being abandoned to an invading army. Clouds of smoke hung over the Potomac, evoking memories of the London blitz but not of its fortitude. I wandered through the ghetto streets that afternoon, and clearly Washington could have been taken by the mob if Johnson had not acted firmly but with circumspection. The national toll was thirty-nine people killed, and nearly 20,000 were arrested. Property damage was estimated at more than $30 million, but the trouble could have been infinitely worse.

I can remember watching Johnson emerging from the basement situation room of the White House after it was all over. Security precautions were strict, and correspondents had to wear their passes suspended from the neck on little chains provided for the purpose. There were few other signs of nervousness, but Johnson was red-eyed and taut with fatigue. He appeared to be on the point of exhaustion. Admiral George Burkley, his physician, hovered in the background, and no wonder. It had been an impossible week.

Johnson had announced that he would not run for re-election, limited the bombing, responded to Hanoi's answer, got ready to fly to Honolulu, and then taken charge of a dreadful internal crisis. That was not all. As he looked to the future—and on that morning staff assistants were already waiting with papers and worried expressions—the prospect was grim. A dozen and more problems demanded quick action. Inflationary pressures were worse than worrying. The Advisory Commission on Inter-governmental Relations had just reported that the crisis in the cities was threatening the American political system. The conclusion was that the danger was unprecedented since the Civil War. Campus unrest was increasing, and at Columbia University students had seized buildings and were beginning to stage a month-long strike. His party was more divided than the country. There were to be difficult and tortuous negotiations with an implacable enemy during what promised to be a violent election campaign. Richard Nixon, the Republican presidential candidate, had proposed a moratorium on campaign criticism of

Johnson's peace-seeking efforts, but McCarthy and Kennedy continued to snipe from the hustings. There was the extraordinary situation where bipartisanship in foreign policy existed between the leaderships of the two parties, but not between the two wings of the Democratic party. In Vietnam, the relief of Khesanh was in sight, but elsewhere there was no de-escalation. Men and matériel were still moving southward down the Ho Chi Minh trail. Hanoi was also to demonstrate its awkwardness over the choice of conference sites. It proposed Phnom Penh, the Cambodian capital, which was clearly unacceptable because of the lack of communications, accommodation, and reasonable security. A dozen foreign cities were proposed and rejected before agreement on Paris was finally reached in early May. And this was only the beginning. Johnson was convinced that Hanoi was not prepared to negotiate a compromise agreement. As he saw it, the enemy had gained one objective and was determined to win the next—a complete cessation of the bombing—before negotiating the withdrawal of American troops. Beyond that there was no indication of its intentions. Few other Americans assessed the situation as accurately as he did. Kennedy and McCarthy still assumed that a compromise was possible if Johnson would only be more flexible. But after leading his country into the Big Muddy, he had a more realistic appreciation of the difficulties of getting out of it.

For a president who was to be in office for only nine more months, Johnson had more than enough to do. Nevertheless, he yearned for some more legislative victories. He acted as if there were still overwhelming Democratic majorities in both houses of Congress, and the extraordinary thing was that he did so well. Another historic civil rights bill was passed. It prohibited discrimination in the sale and rental of housing, which with education was one of the major areas where integration was resisted. Another noteworthy success was the housing and urban development bill. This provided for federal subsidies to encourage house ownership among low- and moderate-income groups and included measures for the participation of industry and nonprofit groups in slum clearance and the provision of property insurance in riot-torn ghetto neighborhoods. The relationship established between bad housing and violence was a factor ensuring the passage of both bills, but Johnson's leadership was again indispensable. He also succeeded in defeating efforts to reduce the funding of most of his Great Society programs.

But there were some rebuffs and defeats. With inflation, the mounting cost of the war, and a budget deficit of about $25 billion, economy in government spending was a dominant issue. Congress insisted upon a ceiling for expenditure as the price for accepting the tax surcharge. About $6 billion was cut from the estimates. Some programs were excluded from heavy pruning, but foreign aid was reduced to $1.8 billion. Conservation and consumer-protection bills fared reasonably well. Aid to vocational and higher education was expanded, but riders attached to a number of bills penalized students involved in riots. Johnson's omnibus crime-control and safe-streets bill was also savagely rewritten. The gun control provision was weakened, police wiretapping and bugging was extended to criminal cases, and the rights of suspects during police interrogation were restricted. Funds requested for the Law Enforcement Administration under the general direction of the attorney general were instead given as block grants to the states. Another bill which was passed made the desecration of the national flag a crime.

Much of this reflected the mood of the country. To put it mildly, the white majority had long been impatient with Negro agitation and student unrest, and the April riots had frightened many. The unrest on university campuses was no less disturbing. The troubles at Columbia and elsewhere in no way approached the serious political threat of the student movements in France and West Germany, but the senseless violence was appalling. There was also the widely publicized smoking of marijuana in student dormitories, and many Americans, presumably frustrated by Vietnam, were ready to seek some kind of vengeance against blacks and students. This tough attitude was reflected as much in the omnibus crime bill as in the punitive riders attached to others. Moreover, in the heated atmosphere of that year, crime, riots, and campus unrest were all seen to be threats to established order, and somehow connected. The rumbling discontents of the previous year were exploding. Johnson, and good sense, prevailed to the extent that the civil rights and housing bills were passed and aid to education extended, but the reaction of the extreme right and southern and suburban rednecks could hardly be controlled when millions of citizens were disturbed. Mayor Richard Daley of Chicago ordered his police in the future to "shoot to kill arsonists and shoot to maim looters." This was inflammatory, as the country was soon to discover, but much else was understandable and to be expected. The country did seem to be falling apart. The old standards and verities were being shamelessly flouted. The national flag was being burned and defiled. Crime statistics were frightening.

There comes a time in the lives of most nations when the majority, what Nixon was afterward to describe as the great silent majority, responds resentfully to the importunities of a minority or minorities. Generally the condition or complaint of the minority is not the governing factor. Both can be recognized, but if the minority tries to move too quickly, offends the conventional wisdom, or takes to the streets, further trouble is almost unavoidable. Such was the situation in the summer of 1968 all over the United States. It was useless for black leaders to argue that their people had waited too long, for more than a hundred years. Most white Americans had been unaware of their plight until after King launched his movement in the late fifties. In the eyes of many whites too much had been done for the blacks. Indeed, the antipoverty programs and recent Supreme Court decisions were seen to give them unfair advantages. This was cruel nonsense, of course, but there had been excesses on both sides and the national temper was such that many Americans were no longer willing to listen to reason. It was also an election year and Nixon, the Republican front runner, sensed the mood. Even Kennedy, campaigning in Indiana, recalled how firm he had been in maintaining law and order when he was attorney general. Crime and violence became burning issues, perhaps even more than Vietnam. Nixon held

Ramsey Clark, the attorney general, responsible for most domestic ills. It was an oblique attack against Johnson, Clark was only a convenient Aunt Sally, and the attacks did redound upon the president.

In fact, Johnson had charted a shrewd and courageous course between the requirements of law and order and social justice. He had been ably assisted by Clark, a new and enlightened southern populist and one of the best Americans of his generation. He also happened to be a Texan, which should have been a sufficient warning against accepting the stereotypes mentioned earlier in this book. He had sufficient comprehension of the revolutionary forces convulsing America and had said: "The poor in this country are no longer willing to accept poverty. Nor are they willing to accept the injustice that has always accompanied it. Events no longer give us a choice about having or not having true criminal justice. Without it, we won't survive." Clark also argued that the country should strike at the roots of these and other problems instead of turning itself into a police state. This was not academic liberalism. Clark enjoyed the confidence of Quinn Tamm, the president of the International Association of Police Chiefs, who thought that the attorney general had done more to help law enforcement than any of his predecessors. He had introduced the Strike Forces the year before. They were groups of lawyers and investigators who cooperated with local authorities in combating organized crime, and they had been successful in Buffalo and other cities. Clark was also eager to help train the police and to improve their status in society. Both were necessary if law and order was to be better maintained. He had been stanchly supported by Johnson, who also cherished the rights of the individual and had not been inactive in trying to deal with crime. In fact, crime had increased at a greater rate during the Eisenhower administration, when Nixon was vice-president, than during the eight subsequent Democratic years.

Johnson struck the right balance again with the Poor People's March on Washington, which began in April. The march was quite unnecessary. The original objective was to demonstrate support for the civil rights bill, and this had been enacted. It was also dangerous coming so soon after the riots. Resurrection City, a shantytown built of plywood and canvas near the Lincoln Memorial, was an affront to many whites. The assembly of so many thousands camping out in the heart of the nation's capital posed obvious health and security problems. The leadership of the Reverend Ralph Abernathy, who succeeded King as president of the Southern Christian Leadership Conference, was occasionally inept. There was grandiose talk of educating the government, and much of it ended in tragic farce. Deputations clad in the blue overalls of field workers met congressmen and heads of the federal departments, and most of the meetings were merely happenings. The tense relations with the white majority were further aggravated, and memories were revived of Coxey's Army and the Bonus Marchers. The situation actually provided more cause for alarm than frightened Washington matrons supposed. The camp was penetrated by militants determined to provoke a confrontation and a violent response from the authorities. But no general mounted on a white horse was allowed to disperse the camp as MacArthur did on the Anacostia flats so many years before. Patient diplomacy, generally conducted by Clark and Abernathy, avoided trouble until after two months Johnson decided that the camp dwellers had had more than their say. One swelteringly hot morning the police quickly and peacefully evacuated the camp. Johnson's sure grasp of the situation was once again ignored by blacks and whites. He was apparently doomed to acrimony until his departure.

He was not the only unhappy man in the Democratic party. Kennedy had begun his campaign well in Indiana but had discovered that he had lost much of the support of young people. His advance men ensured that his airport arrivals were celebrated by the usual crowds of squealing teen-agers, but he missed the more serious and involved students. They had remained loyal to McCarthy, disgusted by Kennedy's reluctance to enter the race until their man had demonstrated the precariousness of Johnson's position. This hurt Kennedy far more than he was prepared to admit. Apart from dented pride, he genu-inely cared for young people. He enjoyed their company far more than did McCarthy, who kept them at arm's length as if he were still an economics professor slightly jaundiced by their adolescent enthusiams. Then came Oregon. McCarthy's victory was laughed off. The state was said to be unrepresentative and not important, but defeat was doubly painful. The Kennedy mystique, founded on youth and success, was damaged almost as much as the candidate's pride, and mainly by the young people he claimed to represent.

Kennedy had seen defeat coming for at least a week before polling day, and he showed his dismay. His speeches were often parodies of campaign oratory. He mouthed the set phrases hap-hazardly, with little obvious connection, and made jokes about himself. They were both appealing and painful. He was lovingly and ably supported by his wife, Ethel, and friends and advisers, but appeared to be a lonely man. California, the last state to have a primary, was also far from certain. Its primary was the most decisive, but the Kennedy advance men had had too little time to organize. He won, but only by a few percentage points. McCarthy had done very well in the circumstances, and else-where Vice-President Humphrey had the support of most of the party regulars and many of the trade unions. Unlike in 1960, the primary trail was not to be the royal road to the presidency for another Kennedy. The Democratic National Convention would meet in Chicago as divided and undecided as before. Alas, there was no time for calculations. Kennedy was shot in a hotel kitchen after the victory celebration in Los Angeles and died the next day.

The tragedy for the Kennedy family was grievous for decent men everywhere. No American had to be reminded of their sad history—one son killed in the war, a daughter killed in an air crash, the assassination of John Kennedy, and now the murder of their third son. For Kennedy followers, the hopes of a restora-tion had been cruelly dashed on the bloodstained floor of a hotel kitchen, and other men also felt that this was a tragedy for the country. They believed that the United Stated needed strong leadership if the fissiparous forces continued to pull it asunder. Such was the power of the Kennedy name that the young senator was thought to be the only man who could provide this leadership. Millions believed that only he could persuade the young, the blacks, and the discontented to move from damaging dissent to wholehearted cooperation. This was not unanimous, of course. A minority had always hated the Kennedys, their success, their presumption of power, and their gaiety. Republicans not unnaturally had other ideas. Those with a larger faith in the United States disagreed, but without reflection upon Kennedy. The old Jacksonian faith in the ability and availability of men of good will to do their duty was still strong, but coming so soon after the death of Martin Luther King, the murder of Robert Kennedy was terrifying.

There was a widespread sense of helplessness as well as grief, rage, and suspicion of conspiracy. Political violence had always been part of American history, but the sixties had been particularly grim. John Kennedy, Medgar Evers, George Lincoln Rockwell, Martin Luther King, and Robert Kennedy were only the better known victims of political violence. With the talk of revolution and urban guerrilla warfare, political assassination threatened to become an integral part of American life. Assassination threatened the will of the people, even of the few miserable American Nazis, and endangered the democratic process. Not only the country's leadership, but also its institutions were under attack. It hardly mattered that there was no evidence of conspiracy. The death of Robert Kennedy at the hand of another rootless and confused man was for many Americans an indictment against their society.

The pain passed. The presidential election had to be won. Only the free and open election of a new president offered some respite from violence and the hope for a better future. The candidates returned to the hustings. Hope was renewed within the Democratic party that the antiwar forces could unite behind McCarthy, but the Kennedy men appeared to regard the Minnesotan as a worse enemy than Johnson, Humphrey, or Nixon. Some withdrew from active politics. Others, in spite of the lateness of the hour, looked about for a surrogate. They formed up behind Senator George McGovern of South Dakota, an intelligent but largely unknown man. There was the suspicion that some had hopes of a draft for Senator Edward Kennedy, the last surviving son of the family. In any event the peace forces were divided, and the nomination was left largely to Johnson, the bosses, and the party hacks.

About this time Johnson began to show regret over his decision not to run. To more than one correspondent he indicated the belief that with Kennedy and Rockefeller out of the race he could win the nomination and election. His contempt for Nixon had grown no less with the passing years, and certainly the Republican had aroused little enthusiasm within his own party. Perhaps one will never know how close he came to reversing his decision. There was a precedent of sorts. Konrad Adenauer, the West German chancellor, had earlier decided to seek the presidency rather than run for re-election and reversed himself when he belatedly discovered the extent of the constitutional limitations on that largely ceremonial office. He again successfully ran for the more powerful office of chancellor despite protests within his party. Many would not have put it past Johnson. He had an immense capacity for recuperation, and the gall to do it. His opinion of Humphrey, now the Democratic front runner, was not much more complimentary than his view of Nixon. He did not despise his vice-president. Indeed, he appeared to like him, but Humphrey was not regarded as a worthy successor.

Johnson was also engaged in high diplomacy. He had never given up hope of persuading the Russians to negotiate the limitation of strategic nuclear armaments, and they finally agreed. There were plans for a summit conference. This was a diplomatic coup that might have ensured a Democratic victory in November. It was not to be. The Czech crisis deepened as the Democratic National Convention approached, and one night Anatoly Dobrynin, the Soviet ambassador in Washington, called on Johnson and informed him that the Soviet invasion of Czechoslovakia had begun. He also gave assurances that Rumania would not be invaded. The ambassador's call was further proof of the extraordinary relationship developing between the two superpowers. Each country was determined to pursue its national security policy and act independently within its sphere of influence—the Russians in Czechoslovakia as the Americans in Cuba—but they were equally determined to avoid a super-power confrontation. Hence the use of the hot line in the previous year, and Dobrynin's visit. This was cold comfort even though the Russian's information preceded that of the CIA. There could be no diplomatic coup, no summit conference even to launch disarmament talks, while Russian tanks rolled into Prague.

As for Johnson's second thoughts on seeking re-election, there was no evidence that he did more than toy with the idea. It was much too late, and in any case the news from Chicago was grim enough to dispel it. Vietnam still convulsed a large part of the nation, and antiwar demonstrators and the radical left were preparing for a confrontation in Chicago. Johnson's security advisers doubted that the President of the United States and the leader of the party could safely attend the Democratic National Convention. They finally agreed that he could attend, even as a spectator, only at the peril of his life.

The convention was another terrible blow for American self-respect and confidence. Even before the opening speeches, some six thousand regular troops were airlifted into the city. They came equipped with rifles, flame throwers, and bazookas. An equal number of the Illinois National Guard was activated to support the twelve-thousand-member police force. On the other side of the barricades, there was the foul language of the wild ones, the anarchists and revolutionaries. The behavior of the flower children, openly making love in the city's parks, offended the Irish puritanism of the mayor. Nevertheless, the Walker Report concluded that "the vast majority of the demonstrators were intent on expressing by peaceful means their dissent either from society generally or from the administration's policies in Vietnam." It was the police who rioted, and much of their violence was beyond the range of the television cameras, which were supposed to have encouraged the wild minority in the crowds. As a foreign correspondent, I have covered riots and other civil disorders in cities as far apart as Berlin and Calcutta, Singapore and Beirut, Washington and Aden, but never before have I seen such cruel and sustained official violence. Inevitably one looked back to Hitler's stormtroopers for comparison.

The situation was not much better inside the convention hall. The public galleries were packed with Daley's men displaying placards with the legend "I love Mayor Daley." The police controlled the entrances to the floor, and refused entrance to or evicted delegates as they or Daley saw fit. The mayor controlled the business of the convention from the floor. This was a raw display of police power utterly alien to democratic tradition. The will of the party was shamelessly flouted. Johnson's Vietnam policy was brutally steamrollered through. Even so the peace plank was supported by two-fifths of the delegates. The two largest delegations, New York and California, draped their areas in black crape and held up signs reading "Weep for America." In this atmosphere of brute force and cynical manipulation, wild rumors swept through the hall. A draft mounted for Edward Kennedy, and McCarthy privately offered to stand aside for him, but Kennedy refused to run. Humphrey was finally nominated the candidate of a divided party, but Daley was not satisfied. His police raided McCarthy's headquarters in the Conrad Hilton Hotel without a warrant and savaged many of his student helpers.

Unbelievably, this violence ended in prayer. I came out of the hotel very early on the Friday morning to get the stink of tear gas out of my nostrils. The commuter traffic was beginning to speed along Michigan Avenue, still lined with National Guardsmen, when Bishop Crowther (formerly Bishop of Kimberley) appeared in the park opposite. Dressed in Episcopalian cope and miter he celebrated Communion for the exhausted young demonstrators by the flickering light of a bonfire. His congregation squatted or stretched out on the trampled grass, unshaven, their smutty faces at peace. No one could persuade me that

218

these American youngsters were anything but men and women at peace. There was, or course, the release from the horrors of the previous night, when the police, after a benediction from Daley, had once again clubbed the crowd and tried to disperse it with tear gas. There was a new horror, or at least new to me. The National Guard had equipped the fronts of their jeeps with steel frames across which were stretched close strands of barbed wire. The tactic was to drive the jeeps in close formation into the crowd. Those who could not get away, and the press of people denied rapid retreat, were lacerated by the barbed wire. It was worthy of the Wehrmacht's Einsatzgruppen in Poland, the unhappy land from which many of the guardsmen's families had come.

But that was over, and they listened to the bishop wearing the device of the New Christianity, the cross and CND circle. His rich voice had acquired a slight American accent, but the big, confident, Church of England face would have been recognized by any English schoolboy. A young delegate from California came up to the pulpit, a park bench, and the bishop said that he had last seen him in Savannah. He had gone down there "to bail him out after the usual thing," a casual reference to the civil rights campaign. The delegate asked that they pray for their brothers in Prague, and they prayed silently. The bishop prayed for Robert Kennedy, and a black girl prayed for Martin Luther King and Dick Gregory, who was in prison somewhere in Chicago. The sun was coming up through the trees when the bishop said he wanted them to do something special. He wanted them to go over to the guardsmen and pray for them.

A slight girl in a blue woolen jumper and a seersucker mini-skirt jumped up, with white teeth flashing in a dirty and irre-pressibly gay face. "Wait for it," the bishop cautioned. "You must do this strictly by the book. No rushing, no touching. I want no trouble. Go over there slowly, look into their eyes and say, 'The peace of God be upon you.'" The little ragged army, dressed in jeans and jerseys, blazers and flannels, sandals and construction boots, rose to its feet and went slowly over to the line of soldiers and formed a second line. I stood behind the girl, her head wrapped in a flimsy piece of silk. She looked into the eyes of a Negro sergeant and said, "The peace of God be upon you." The sergeant, his eyes red with fatigue and rifle still at the port, smiled slowly and said, "Thank you, m'am." The black soldier doing his duty and the white girl who had come to exercise her inalienable American rights were for one brief moment joined. Alas, that morning they represented the only apparent unity in these United States.

The temper of the country at the time was such that the police violence in Chicago was widely applauded. The Institute for Social Research at the University of Michigan discovered that even among whites who had taken a clear dovish position on Vietnam almost 70 percent rejected the suggestion that the Chicago police used too much force. About 40 percent believed that not enough was used to suppress the demonstrations. There was, of course, the connection, previously noted, between the riots and the increasing crime rate. For many Americans, public political dissent, although guaranteed by the First Amendment, was as bad as black rioting in the ghettos. Police suppression was seen to be the only answer. It mattered not that the troublemakers at Chicago were a tiny minority, certainly no more than two hundred, or that police violence at the beginning of the convention week made confrontation inevitable. Few were prepared to listen to an inspector from the Los Angeles Police Department, in Chicago as an official observer. He said, "There is no question but that many officers acted without restraint and exerted force beyond that necessary under the circumstances. The leadership at the point of conflict did little to prevent such conduct and the direct control of officers by first supervisors was virtually nonexistent."

This fevered atmosphere was partly responsible for one of Johnson's most stinging personal defeats. Earlier in the year, he had nominated Associate Justice Abe Fortas to succeed Earl Warren as Chief Justice of the United States. They had been close personal friends since the thirties when they were young and poor and beginning to make their way in Washington. The friendship had blossomed with success, and Fortas and Clifford were probably Johnson's closest advisers. Fortas was a liberal, dedicated to the rights of the individual, and his appointment would have ensured an extension of the liberal era of the court which began in 1954 with the school desegregation decision. This was Johnson's intention, but he was asking for trouble. His critics said that he had no right to make such an important nomination at the end of his term. Be that as it may, the court had long been under attack from the southern Democratic–conservative Republican coalition, and they seized their opportunity. A filibuster was launched in the Senate to block consideration of the nomination, and finally on October 1 action was taken on a motion to invoke cloture. Debate can only be brought to an end when two-thirds of those present are in favor. The vote was 45 to 43, or 14 less than required. The defeat was staggering, and Johnson withdrew the nomination within the week.

The hearings of the Senate Judiciary Committee had in fact been embarrassing for Fortas. It was established that he was paid $15,000 for a series of university lectures in circumstances that raised many eyebrows. His role as a presidential adviser was seen to offend the principle of the separation of powers. Fortas was also an arrogant man, and in 1969 further revelations were to force his resignation from the court, but at the time there could be no doubt that the temper of the country had contributed to his and Johnson's defeat.

The impatient demand for what was known as law and order was also to decide the election. It was seen as a move to the right, but curiously enough the move, although obvious enough, was at variance with the deep, underlying trends in the country. For instance, the Institute for Social Research established that in 1968 only 30 percent of white Southern Democrats demanded strict segregation of the races compared with 52 percent in 1964. The proportion favoring desegregation rose from 12 percent to 18 percent, a small enough gain but nevertheless part of a broad national trend. The cold-war attitudes were also being eroded. Rusk tried to frighten his fellow countrymen with a yellow peril that would be unleashed should they fail to do their duty in Vietnam, but they would have none of it. Nixon, an old cold-war warrior, was applauded when he called for negotiation and not confrontation with the Soviet Union. The so-called Castro threat was almost forgotten. The administration, after negotiating the nuclear nonproliferation treaty, was commended for its eagerness to limit strategic weapons. More remarkable, in view of the war and dissent at home, there was little of the old hysteria over the alleged internal communist threat.

The John Birch Society still frightened old women of both sexes and all ages, but Gus Hall's announcement that the communist party would run a presidential candidate attracted almost no attention. Both were seen to be utterly irrelevant to the election. This old anticommunist phobia was always beyond the comprehension of Europeans who lived with sizable communist parties and on Russia's doorstep, and its passing was surely of great significance. One could argue, of course, that nothing much had really changed, except that the country now had something really to worry about. Perhaps, but Vietnam was not an anticommunist crusade. It could have been if the old cold-war attitudes had remained unchanged. For all the violent reaction to antiwar demonstrations, individual pacifists had a less unpleasant time of it than in previous wars. Many Americans were apprehensive when draft cards were first burned. The burnings were a symbolic act striking at the heart of society. The intention could be a brave gesture of conscience or of plain disloyalty. One could never be certain, but there was remarkably little violence or demagogy. Benjamin Spock and his men were tried and found guilty of the part they played. Theirs was an unhappy trial, but again there was little violent reaction and their appeals were successful. In general, there was only a puzzled silence and profound sadness that such men felt required to act as they did. The racial conflict would also have been more violent if Americans had believed the hints of black communism dropped by J. Edgar Hoover and his unreconstructed FBI.

Extremism still flourished of course, on the left and right, among blacks and whites. Violence was not far below the surface in many northern cities and some parts of the South, but the failures in Vietnam and the assassinations at home produced no witch hunts. It seemed that most Americans had done with the old fears and easy answers. Certainly the rhetoric of the two major candidates was restrained. Nixon was remembered by his political enemies as the master of the innuendo and the smear, but whether or not there was a new Nixon he made no attempt, outside the law-and-order issue, to inflame his listeners. One obvious reason was the third-party candidacy of George Wallace. He was enough to disturb decent men, and none of the major candidates could have competed with his appeals to racial prejudice. His vice-presidential candidate, Curtis LeMay, the former general, had a peace platform based on the bomb. His message was that nuclear bombs were beautiful and nothing to be afraid of. There was no difference between being killed by a rusty knife in Vietnam and by a nuclear weapon. Given the choice, he would lean toward a nuclear death. It was apparently much cleaner. He railed against the antinuclear phobia of a public allegedly fed on propaganda, which was handicapping the country and jeopardizing its safety. A nuclear war would not mean the end of the world. Twenty years after the Bikini tests the fish were back in the lagoon, the coconuts were growing again, and the rats were bigger, fatter, and healthier than ever before. "Under President George C. Wallace, America will assume her rightful place, a nation dedicated to peace and the freedom of men, a world power both respected and admired."

Wallace and LeMay had the effect of sanitizing the campaign. The alternatives they offered were extreme enough to make the most impatient Americans pause and consider. Yet it was not a good campaign. The issues—war and peace, social justice, and the urban crisis—were not clarified. The trend toward moderation lost momentum. The national purpose was not redefined. The obvious reason was the national distemper after five years of Johnson rule, the main symptom of which was the demand for law and order. But his five years had also divided the Democratic party. The deep divisions over the war, the succession of candidates for the nomination, Kennedy's death, the partial withdrawal of the liberal intellectuals, and the convention violence combined to defeat the usual processes mentioned above. The party's Roosevelt coalition was to survive, except for the South, but the leadership was divided, and confusion among the rank and file was complete. For instance, there was more to the New Hampshire primary than the politicians and columnists had supposed. Clearly McCarthy's success there was a Democratic protest vote against Johnson, but not all his supporters wanted a negotiated peace in Vietnam. There was a joke among journalists covering the election that some of the taciturn locals mistook Gene for the late Joe. True or not, the Institute for Social Research afterward established that a majority wanted to end the war by escalating it. Furthermore, a plurality of the support for McCarthy voted for Wallace in November. The institute found that the McCarthy-Wallace people were against desegregation, in favor of an increased military effort in Vietnam, and indignant over the lack of law and order.

The general confusion persisted until election day, partly due to Nixon's refusal to discuss most of the issues but mainly because of the havoc Johnson had wrought among Democrats. As he approached the end of his term the criticism and calumny heaped upon him reminded one of Truman's last days in office. Then the Korean War, twenty years of Democratic rule, the tales of corruption, the ugly response to Joe McCarthy's slanders, and the nomination of Eisenhower made a Republican victory inevitable. In 1968 there was no Eisenhower, only Nixon, and he almost lost the election because the Roosevelt coalition, strengthened by labor's political muscle and money, held together. I wondered at the time what would have happened if there had been an Adlai Stevenson available. He might have won. Certainly he would have defined the issues, and the fact that this was not done left Johnson fairly free to pursue his policies to the end. The lame-duck president was given an unexpected new lease on political life.

This was patently clear in Vietnam. Alternative policies were never debated. A working consensus was not established. Not

224

a single significant roll-call vote was taken on Vietnam in Congress. Until the very end nobody had a clear idea of what the electorate wanted, or what kind of compromise would be generally acceptable. These extraordinary circumstances allowed Johnson to make war with a new intensity, although the March 31 decision and the beginning of peace talks in Paris led most people to assume that the military role would be reduced to a holding action until agreement was reached. Johnson, of course, remained convinced that nothing could be expected from Paris without military pressure, and the number of troops in Vietnam rose from 486,600 before the Tet offensive to 535,500 by late summer. The new authorized level was 549,500. General David Shoup, the former Marine Corps commandant, said that the United States could not win without an invasion of North Vietnam. Even Westmoreland admitted before leaving Saigon that victory in the accepted sense was impossible, but Johnson persisted. The enemy at first was no less aggressive, and casualties mounted alarmingly. There was also an intensification of the bombing.

Johnson told Clifford that his objective was to leave to his successor "the best possible military posture in Vietnam." The defense secretary protested that a better inheritance would be "negotiation, firmly committed to ending the war and reducing the American involvement in Vietnam." In fact, Clifford was not optimistic about Paris. I saw him in his office at the Pentagon soon after Johnson's March 31 announcement, when he had little confidence in the outcome of the talks. His main hope was for mutual troop withdrawals, with or without formal agreement. The principle of parallelism, when two countries adopt similar policies without consultation and for their separate purposes, was referred to. At the time American troops were being reinforced to re-establish the strategic reserve, and mutual withdrawals were for the future. Clifford had formulated the policy known as "Vietnamization." The South Vietnamese army was to be enlarged and re-equipped and then gradually take over the responsibility of the war. Then mutual withdrawals of American and North Vietnamese could be expected.

The prospect of the South Vietnamese successfully defending themselves was hardly bright. They were a tough people, but they had been at war for too many years and remained politically divided. The military junta which passed as the Saigon government appeared incapable of inspiring national unity. Moreover, "Vietnamization" would be a protracted process. American air and logistical support would be required for years after its completion, and there was the impatient opposition to war in the United States which had frightened Clifford. Launched earlier, the policy would have had some chance of success, but 1968 was very late. Clifford knew this. At times he appeared to be the only realist in the Johnson administration, but he saw no alternative. An admission of defeat was impossible for Johnson and for many Americans. The United States had also assumed some responsibility for South Vietnam by intervening in its affairs. The country could not in good conscience be abruptly abandoned, not without incalculable repercussions elsewhere. "Vietnamization" could be said to serve the American war aim of an independent South Vietnam free to decide its own future without interference. It at least provided more time for the Saigon government to strengthen and extend its authority outside the capital.

With this in mind, Clifford could address himself to the distant possibility of the mutual withdrawal of troops. Again there were dangers. There was no indication that Hanoi would be prepared to cooperate. If its troops were withdrawn, they could return more easily than the Americans. In any event, they would leave behind their politicomilitary infrastruture, manned by the Vietcong. This was a risk that had to be taken, but there could be no progress at Paris while North Vietnamese targets were still being attacked by American bombers. A complete halt to the bombing was essential. This was well understood by Averell Harriman and Cyrus Vance, who led the American delegation to Paris. They pressed for a bombing halt, without success, for many months, and Clifford discovered that his "Vietnamization" policy had been taken up by the hawks. They saw it as a convenient cover for further military pressure, which they felt could still persuade Hanoi to negotiate an agreement. The harmony within the administration established by the March 31 announcement was short-lived. The contest for the president's mind broke out once again.

Johnson remained ambivalent but inclined toward the hawks. The presidential election and its confusions had diverted attention from Paris, and at first he felt he could afford to wait upon the results of continued fighting. The only reward was more American casualties. The battle remained as indecisive as ever. Humphrey's campaign was going badly, and his loyalty to Johnson was under immense strain. Time was running out. Eventually, in early October, Harriman was allowed to tell the North Vietnamese delegation that the bombing of North Vietnam would stop on condition that they did not seek to take advantage of it. Specifically, he said that they must observe the neutrality of the demilitarized zone and not attack South Vietnamese cities. The National Liberation Front could join in the peace talks if Hanoi accepted South Vietnam. Apart from the proposal to enlarge the conference, there was little more to this than what Clifford had suggested earlier in the year to a congressional committee. Hanoi's first response was cool. It refused to modify its old demand for an unconditional bombing halt. The bickering dragged on through the month, and just before the election Johnson capitulated. He would order a complete bombing halt only on the understanding that Hanoi would not take advantage of it.

It was too late to save Humphrey, although a few more days might have made all the difference, and at first little was seen to have been gained in Paris. The North Vietnamese said that they were only prepared to discuss the evacuation of American troops. It must have been infuriating for Johnson, and final evidence of the uselessness of negotiations, but after all the years of stern, almost Calvinistic inflexibility the North Vietnamese slowly began to respond to Harriman's diplomacy. The distinguished envoy, who had long prided himself as the only American capable of negotiating with Russians and similarly difficult people, was in fact a master of the art. He had just celebrated his seventy-seventh birthday, but age had not closed his mind. He was still very spry, physically and mentally, but the years were closing in and Johnson had only a few more weeks in office. Understandably, Harriman wanted a final success. The North Vietnamese found that they could also afford to be a little more flexible. A tiny nation of 17 million people had forced the President of the United States to accept their basic terms. This was a famous victory, and they could now be not so much magnanimous as patient. They still demanded the total evacuation of American troops, but mutual withdrawals, if not too prolonged, were as good a way as any of achieving this objective. Harriman found them a little easier to talk to. They were willing to begin troop withdrawal when the fighting was diminished. He also had one or two aces in his own diplomatic hand. The North Vietnamese understandably hated the B-52 bombers which were still raiding their troop concentrations in the south. They indicated that the pace of withdrawal could be quickened if the raids were stopped. In any event, the bombers were a card to play should the talks run into difficulties again. The North Vietnamese were also interested in American aid. Johnson's Baltimore speech had not been forgotten. The development of the Mekong river valley, with its promise of hydroelectric power, was of particular interest.

The talks did not at first lose their momentum when Nixon won the election. Johnson was to remain in power until January 20, 1969, and Harriman continued to edge toward an agreement. Nevertheless, the process of handing over to the new administration was quietly begun, and the passing of power and the possible change of policy was anticipated in Saigon. The military junta became more intransigent, and refused to attend the Paris talks. Clifford said that Johnson had a constitutional responsibility to continue without them. On December 10, only forty-one days before Nixon was to be inaugurated, Clifford said that he would like to see the withdrawal of troops begin within forty days. "I think there is an opportunity to agree with Hanoi on a mutual withdrawal of troops during that period." The North Vietnamese had in fact pulled back some of their troops, and Harriman pressed Washington to reciprocate. Gen-

228

eral Creighton Abrams, who had succeeded Westmoreland, redeployed his troops but continued to press the enemy. Johnson remained ambivalent, and the moment passed. The war was to go on.

The remaining days of the old year were brightened by another success in space. Apollo 8 circled the moon and returned safely to earth. It was a wonderful moment, and Johnson should have shared some of the credit, but Americans and people all over the world were now looking to Nixon and the men being appointed to serve him. North Korea also released the crew of the *Pueblo,* for which Johnson had worked hard, but the homecoming did not much reduce public anger over the incident and the failure to prevent it. Nevertheless, he continued to work hard. He tried to influence the policy of his successor by releasing a special report compiled by Wilbur Cohen, Secretary of Health, Education, and Welfare. It said that the advances in the last five years were unprecedented but much remained to be done. A list of twenty-five goals for 1976 was included, the first being the abolition of poverty.

If it was not to impress the incoming administration, the report was a suitable valediction for Johnson. The accompanying statement said,

The report disclosed that during President Johnson's Administration: 62 "landmark laws" in health, education and welfare and social service, including Medicare and Federal aid to education, were enacted by the Congress. Poverty in the United States declined by 38 percent. The Federal investment in health services and research tripled—to nearly $14 billion in fiscal 1968. The high school drop out rate dropped 27 percent; the number of college students receiving Federal financial aid quadrupled. The average social security benefit to persons 65 years old or older rose by 60 percent. . . . I can think of very few documents that I have seen during my Presidency that have given me more satisfaction than Secretary Cohen's report. The events and actions recorded here—in leadership, in legislation, and in administration—are the events and action by which the administration will be remembered.

The report and statement were released from the Bethesda Naval Hospital, which Johnson had entered again, this time suffering from a cold. He went to the ranch for Christmas, from where he addressed the armed forces. One passage said, "This will be my last Christmas message to you as your Commander in Chief. But I will remember you all the days of my life, as the patriots who manned the watchtowers in a time of peril, so that we might live as free men." He was soon back in Washington to press again the cause of better education and to hold another press conference. Asked what he wanted most to achieve before leaving office, he said, "The one thing that would make us all happier than anything else is to have a truce in Vietnam and to have substantial progress towards peace. . . . It would just be paradise if we could end that thing. But we must end it with honor." That evening Mrs. Johnson was asked in a television interview if she was happy to leave. She said, "The horrendous ring of that telephone at four o'clock that drags you to consciousness and you know on the other end that it is something significant. And it is never good when it rings at that time. It is —and then, the sense of responsibility. It is not my responsibility but it does spill over into the whole climate of your life. And then deadlines, and eighteen-hour days."

These statements in a way sum up the Johnson administration: the undeniable triumphs at home; Vietnam; the emotional patriotism, and the refusal to accept defeat; and the killing pace he set for himself and his wife. They left out a good deal, of course, especially the final bitterness. I was reminded of it at a reception in the State Department. It was a farewell party for Rusk. The atmosphere was suitably friendly and nostalgic, but the secretary of state, who had been as firm as a rock for eight years, suddenly broke down. We had all had enough to drink, and he came over and asked me why Britain had not sent troops to Vietnam. He knew well enough, but rather lamely I began to repeat the obvious. He cut me short and said, "All we needed was one regiment. The Black Watch would have done. Just one regiment, but you wouldn't. Well, don't expect us to save you again. They can invade Sussex, and we wouldn't do a damned thing about it."

1969

Johnson was a worried man during the last few days of his administration. He feared the turn to the right and distrusted Nixon. This was made evident by Ramsey Clark in an interview with *Congressional Quarterly*. The outgoing attorney general said that the federal government must vigorously enforce civil rights legislation, especially the laws prohibiting segregation and discrimination in schools, employment, and labor unions. Police misconduct came in for some sharp comment. Clark was crying in the wind. His successor, John Mitchell, looked like Judge Jeffreys, the hanging judge of the Bloody Assizes, and in his case looks were not altogether misleading. But Johnson was still not powerless. One of the oddities of the American political system is that the outgoing president prepares the budget for his successor's first fiscal year. It is unavoidable because of the congressional calendar, and the incumbent can thus influence the first eighteen months of the new administration. The new president can make changes, but structural alterations are difficult if only because of the lack of time and the new man's inexperience. The outgoing president also reports on the state of the union and the country's economic condition. These can be more easily ignored, but Johnson seized every advantage to extend his influence beyond retirement.

The State of the Union message is essentially a list of legislative proposals, rather like the Speech from the Throne in Britain. They were modest by Johnson's standards, but enough to keep any Congress in session until Christmas. Many of the proposals were built into the budget—for instance, the continuation of the 10 percent tax surcharge. Somewhat ominously, the Vietnam War estimates for the coming year amounted to more than $25 billion. Clearly he expected the war to continue undiminished.

In those crowded last days Johnson also had a few things to say about himself. He gave a final press conference in the National Press Club and was rather sullen. He was better at a farewell dinner in New York. He recognized David Dubinsky and recalled how he had been inspired by the old trade union leader to be one of the three southerners to vote for a minimum wage of 25 cents an hour in 1938. He also recalled his earliest hours at the summit of authority, when he decided that the curse of John Kennedy's assassination could only be expunged by making America a better land. What really mattered was not the ultimate judgment of history but whether there had really been a change for the better in the way Americans lived. He spoke of his achievements. He did not know what future generations of Americans would say, "but I do believe—in fact, I know —that they will say we tried."

That was on January 13. Johnson had only one more week in office, but the stream of presidential announcements, reports, and appointments continued. Even on January 20, but a few minutes before noon, he added another 300,000 acres to the National Parks system, and made three final recess appointments. Then with Mrs. Johnson he drove for the last time from the White House to the Capitol and listened to Nixon's inaugural speech. He looked mildly interested as the new president spoke about a lowering of voices but, politician-fashion, continued to recognize faces in the crowd. The last impression I had of him that day was of the politician so long accustomed to power that he still could not grasp that it had passed to another man. Nixon could have been one of the thousand and more speakers Johnson had been required to listen to in nearly four decades of public life who would soon step back into the obscurity from which they had been allowed to emerge for one brief moment. But it was all over. The moment Nixon had sworn the oath of office, the thirty-sixth president of the United States was plain Mr. Lyndon B. Johnson of Johnson City, Texas.

After the ceremony, he took luncheon with a few friends at Clark Clifford's house in nearby Maryland, and they saw him off to the ranch from Andrews air force base. It was here that Johnson had first landed as president on November 22, 1963, with the body of John Kennedy. Andrews had subsequently been the point of countless arrivals and departures, and it was here that Johnson had once walked toward the wrong helicopter. A young air force officer rushed forward to announce the fact, and Johnson had looked down on him and said, "Son, all of them are mine." That assertion of proprietary right vividly demonstrated how he had taken the presidency, the government, and the country as his own, but that was all over, too. Except for the few loyal friends, nobody wanted to remember his five years and sixty-nine days in office. He was leaving Washington as he had arrived from Dallas on that dreadful night. There was then no hail to the new chief, and on this day there was no farewell. Nixon had provided the presidential aircraft, Air Force One. There was a band but a minimum of ceremony and no public attention. Whatever one thought of the man and his works, the occasion was immeasurably sad, and the sadness was emphasized by the slow departure of the plane. Only a few days before, even a few hours, its clearance would have been given top priority. The superb machine, with its staterooms, offices, communications equipment, staff, and accompanying reporters, would have been roaring over the woods and fields of Virginia within minutes. Instead, it seemed to creep slowly toward the runway like a shuttle plane on a busy day at La Guardia. The band went on playing and the lonely clump of friends went on waving, and even they must have been only too thankful when it finally disappeared in the direction of Texas.

The Johnson years were over, and the change in the atmosphere was immediate and for the better. The inauguration had worked its magic again, with the promise of national renewal, but there was something very special about the ceremony in 1969. Even Republicans could not pretend that Nixon was the most popular man to have been elected president. The war continued, and the domestic problems remained, but the country had survived a terrible year. There had been the murders of Martin Luther King and Robert Kennedy, the riots in Washington and other cities, the pitched street battles in Chicago, the ugly brutalities of the campus disorders, and the antiwar demonstrations. Some of the onlookers standing in the freezing cold as Nixon was sworn in remembered the bitter divisions, the loss of confidence, and the fear that the country was coming apart. Yet at the end of the year the presidential election was held, and there was no violence as 69 million Americans went to the polls. The enormous power of the presidency passed peacefully from one man to another. American political democracy had once again performed its most important function as by law ordained.

I can remember musing on this as the inaugural parade went past the White House. I then thought that the United States was a great nation not only because of its size, power, and wealth. It was a great nation because of the political institutions and the spirit of the people. Together, they had worked in creative tension over the decades and had achieved much. They had had their crises, and 1968 was one of the worst years, but they had once again emerged fundamentally sound and willing to try again. Nixon had few solutions to offer, but he could depend with complete confidence upon sufficient support to govern. This was part of the greater glory of the Republic, but the inauguration did not entirely explain the new atmosphere. Undoubtedly a good deal of it was due to Johnson's departure. The country was glad to see him go, and for a year at least some of the tensions in American life also went. There was no hot summer. No major urban area went up in flames. The war went on, but there were few violent antiwar demonstrations. Even the campuses were quieter. Nixon departed for Europe and Southeast Asia and in the summer removed himself for a working vacation to a distant Pacific promontory as if he had all the time in the world. Toward the end of the year his popularity rating went up to 68 percent. All the evidence suggested that the majority, the so-called silent majority, was solidly behind him. It must have been galling for Johnson, who had tried so hard to do so much for so many people.

There were about 190 million Americans when he succeeded Kennedy, and they were producing goods and services valued at $562 billion a year. About 34 million of them were officially described as living in poverty. Only 78 had died in Vietnam. The population was 202 million when he left the White House, and the gross national product was $892.5 billion, or $726 billion in 1963 dollars. If inflation was self-evident, there had been a real growth rate of 29 percent. The number of Americans designated as poor had dropped to 24 million, and casualties in Vietnam had risen to 30,000 dead and nearly 200,000 wounded. Unemployment had declined from 5.7 percent to 3.6 percent, and per capita income, allowing for higher taxes and inflation, had increased by 21 percent. Casualties and property damage caused by racial and other civil disorders had grown from insignificant to alarming proportions.

Johnson was responsible neither for all the violence nor for all the affluence, but he had done more than most of his predecessors to improve the material well-being of the country. Certainly he had done more for the oppressed, but only the war and the domestic violence were remembered. It must have been all the more galling because Nixon was no less determined to avoid an obvious defeat in Vietnam. Troop withdrawals were begun in 1969, but at a slower rate than Clifford had planned. The policy of "Vietnamization" was essentially the same as that inherited from the Johnson administration. The level of the fighting and the number of casualties were reduced, but the end of the war was still nowhere in sight. The negotiations in Paris were at a standstill, and the hopes of men such as Harriman and Vance had faded. In Washington there was even some talk of re-escalation and military victory.

Johnson's work for civil rights was also apparently forgotten. Mitchell proposed that his guidelines for the desegregation of schools be ignored, and he sided with Mississippi when that state again resisted a court order to desegregate. Robert Finch, the new secretary of health, education, and welfare, requested a federal court to postpone the order, and eventually the executive branch appeared before the Supreme Court in the unprecedented role of a defendant charged with violating the law of the land. Mitchell threatened to prosecute "hard-line" militants who crossed state lines to incite riots, although the law was almost certainly unconstitutional. He almost persuaded Nixon to take a strong public line against student dissenters until Father Theodore Hesburgh interceded. The president of Notre Dame University and chairman of the U.S. Commission on Civil Rights warned Nixon that he would alienate an entire generation. Nevertheless, the police dispersed a student demonstration at Berkeley, California, with tear gas sprayed from a helicopter, fired buckshot at the fleeing crowds, and killed an onlooker. Mitchell refused to investigate or prosecute, although the civil rights of the students had been clearly violated. Preventive detention of criminals arrested on suspicion of committing another crime was also proposed. Senator Sam Ervin of North Carolina said that the measure was unconstitutional and smacked of a police state because the traditional presumption of innocence would be suspended. Mitchell said that legislation was imperative because of the high rate of crime among defendants out on bail, and Nixon's popularity continued to increase.

At the time of writing, this and much more suggested to many Americans that Nixon was currying favor with the electorate by appealing to its meanest instincts. Most Republicans naturally saw it somewhat differently. Nixon was doing what every first-term president did, ensuring his re-election, and others went further. The United States, they said, was after all a democracy where only the will of the people should count. This was an advance on Goldwater, who always insisted that the United

States was a republic rather than a democracy, but those who looked to the president for moral leadership were cast down by the new turn taken by Republican politics. Known as the southern strategy because of the efforts to establish the party in the South, the label was nevertheless a misnomer. The 10 million Americans who had voted for Wallace in 1968 lived all over the United States, and their support was the main objective. They were not to be educated out of their prejudices but attracted by programs and promises similar to those made by the racist former governor of Alabama. These were seen as essential to the emerging Republican majority, and the tactics were explained in a book of that name by Kevin Phillips.* Nixon denied the purpose of the book, but Phillips had worked for Nixon in the campaign and had been rewarded with a job in the Justice Department. The actions of the attorney general were sufficient evidence that Nixon wanted a lily-white Republican vote in the South and would not object to a political division along racial lines in the North. The Negroes, Mitchell said, were not a Republican constituency.

The proposed realignment was described as ethnic polarization, the hallmark of American politics and not an unprecedented and menacing development. If this was a reference to ethnic politics, as practiced so successfully by the Democrats, it was a travesty of American political history. Ethnic politics, as mucky as it often was, had in fact helped to assimilate, at least politically, millions of immigrants. It was a great unifying force and had helped to make the United States the largest and most stable pluralistic society the world has ever seen. The old Democratic machine bosses were unconscious of this historical process; they sought only votes, but they did help to unite people of all races, colors, creeds, and ethnic backgrounds.

Phillips, of course, was proposing the reverse, the seeking of power by dividing the nation between the so-called silent majority and the liberals, blacks, and other oppressed minorities. This went beyond historical travesty. His calculations and

The Emerging Republican Majority (New Rochelle, N.Y.: Arlington House, 1969).

acceptance of what was seen to be the lowest common denominator, fear or hatred of blacks, led him to reject much that was truly splendid in his own country. The prospect was disturbing. With the blacks more or less in political limbo, their rights and demands could be ignored. The domestic crises would inevitably deepen, and violence could increase. The following prophecy of the National Commission on the Causes and Prevention of Violence could come true:

The central business districts of most cities will be largely deserted except for police patrols during the night-time hours. High-rise apartment buildings and residential compounds protected by private guards and security devices will be fortified cells. . . . Ownership of guns will be almost universal in the suburbs, homes will be fortified by an array of devices from window grilles to electronic surveillance equipment, armed citizen volunteers in cars will supplement inadequate police patrols in neighborhoods closer to the central city. . . . Private automobiles, taxicabs, and commercial vehicles will be routinely equipped with unbreakable glass, light armor, and other security features. . . . The ghetto slum neighborhoods will be places of terror with widespread crime, perhaps entirely out of police control during the night-time hours.

It was ominous that a national commission under the chairmanship of Dr. Milton Eisenhower, president emeritus of Johns Hopkins University and the youngest brother of the late president, should have given such a warning. It was no less ominous that in the last days of 1969 the Nixon administration and what appeared to be a majority of Americans paid little attention to the warning. Nixon was applauded. Vice-President Spiro Agnew became a folk hero when he attacked the press and television. This posed some interesting questions about Johnson's presidency. Had he in fact misjudged his fellow countrymen? Were they prepared to see men locked away without due process? Were they indifferent to the plight of the oppressed, the poor, and the hungry? Indeed, did the promise of American life mean little or nothing to those who had made it in one way or another? Was Johnson responsible for bringing the country to this sorry pass?

238

The answers must surely be no. The United States, with other countries, had passed through more than one cycle of progress and reaction. Johnson had made many mistakes, but they could not have precipitated this new wave of reaction unless other forces were at work. The real answer, I think, helps to explain much of the divisions and violence of his later presidential years. I do not subscribe to the theory of historical determinism, but powerful forces were at work within the United States which would have taxed the leadership and administrative capacity of any president. Vietnam obviously exacerbated the situation, which may prove to be the final tragedy of that war. Johnson was almost certainly doomed from the moment he decided to fight it with American troops.

There can be few major politicians who were exposed to as much change as Johnson. He grew up in Texas when it was for the most part a poor state and populism was the best stance for the young aspiring politician. By the time he was established in Congress the great oil finds had changed the state and its politics, and defense of the oil-depletion allowance had become the first duty of the Texas delegation. He remained a genuine populist, but the new loyalty, which he could not reject, helped to explain his ambivalence and perhaps some of his personal insecurity. For instance, he could never have forgotten the day in 1960 when campaigning on the Democratic ticket with John Kennedy he was spat on in his own state by outraged Protestant conservatives. But the changes in Texas were nothing to those which were beginning to transform the country when he succeeded to the presidency.

The second industrial revolution, as I suppose one must describe the extraordinary technological, electronic, and nuclear advances of recent years, was under way. The general expectation was that the results would on the whole be benign. The benefits of economic growth and material affluence in the sixties were obvious, but the industrial revolution was accompanied by a cultural revolution. The scope and dimensions of both were unprecedented, and they reshaped the lives and life styles of most Americans. Almost every field of technological, human, and spiritual endeavor was affected. To put it simply, the hippies arrived as God died and man prepared to fly to the moon.

The Johnson years thus coincided with the beginning of what will surely be the most revolutionary period in history. Two characteristics of change are instability and violence. Revolution also provokes counterrevolution. One has only to recall the Reformation and the Counter-Reformation, which provide better parallels for the cultural revolution and the reaction it provoked than do most political revolutions. This historical process was accentuated in the United States because of the Vietnam War and the old problem of race. Race was indeed part of the cultural revolution. The country had also lagged behind other industrial democracies in social reform, and Johnson's efforts to catch up contributed to the counterrevolution. The United States was, and remains, a conservative country. Beyond the intellectual excitements of a few cities were millions of fundamentalist Christians whose views of life had not changed much since the early settlements. For every scientist and philosopher working on the outer frontiers of knowledge, there were millions who clung to the simplistic beliefs of the Harding and Coolidge years.

For the majority, and indeed for some of the educated and cultivated minority, the acceleration of change threatened to sweep away much that they held most dear. Institutions, authority, morality, sexual taboos, religious beliefs, society itself were questioned, attacked, and defended with a new vehemence. The strife was complex because so many forces were involved, and was often triggered by events that had little apparent connection with the act of violence. One example was the frustration over the course of the war and attacks against young men wearing their hair long. Unbeknown to millions, the increasing interdependence of modern society was dislocating their motivation and sense of personal identity. Rationalism seemed to be in retreat as affluence eroded the old disciplines. For the sensitive and intelligent, man's ability to control scientific progress appeared increasingly unlikely as pollution and haphazard urbanization disfigured the environment. Representative government came under attack, admittedly only from a minority, because the American system seemed incapable of teaching slum children to read and write or of providing simple municipal services such as garbage collection. The Vietnam War cast doubt on the validity of national security policies and even on American humanity. The last apprehension grew because more than 20 million went hungry amidst plenty. The confidence of the reformers buckled as programs appeared not to improve the condition of the blacks and other distressed minorities.

No other decade had been so thoroughly reported. For the average American watching television the kaleidoscope of news was often bewildering and occasionally brutal. Everything seemed to go wrong after the assassination of John Kennedy, in spite of Johnson's legislative successes. Looking back one can remember without trying the Negro nonviolence ending in white violence, the slaughter in Vietnam, drugs, the apparent unending confrontations on the streets and campuses, the cop-outs, dropouts, acid heads, and more dreadful assassinations. Much of the good of the Johnson years was forgotten, and the new—pop art, space travel, go-go girls, nudity on the stage, the songs of social protest, self-immolation in Saigon, see-through clothes, the first heart transplants, black power, and the glorification of brutality in *Bonnie and Clyde*—was often disquieting, frightening, or degrading. One could go on, but this book is primarily concerned with the political consequences. Of course not every modern ill or social tension was brought about by the twin revolutions. Not many Americans were aware of their true significance, but the combination of forces and the clash of ideas swept the country to a point where the national equilibrium was in danger of being lost. Politics was polarized. The loose coalitions of the two major parties were put under immense strain.

I can remember attending a seminar at the Hudson Institute just before the 1968 elections when the revolutionary and counterterrevolutionary forces in the country were discussed. Seven

distinct political groupings were identified. Working from the
left to the right, there was the Revolutionary Left, the militant
wing of the New Left. Fundamentally moved by youthful anger
over racism and poverty, they despaired over the discrepancy
between western man's idealism and his reality. Some of them
retreated into a fantasy world. The Weathermen, a splintering
from the Students for a Democratic Society, gloried in violence.
Youngsters such as these were largely responsible for the campus disorders. Next came the confrontationist left, the nonviolent New Left. Romantic, anarchical, and antitechnocratic, its
young members were intensely humanist but revealed elitist
traits. Some worked for Eugene McCarthy, and others dreamed
of participatory democracy. They were the rank and file of
peaceful antiwar demonstrations. Others also retreated into fantasy, often with the help of drugs.

The third group, the liberals, were pragmatic, optimistic, and
generally committed to the economic solution of social and political problems. The New Deal was their genesis, and they had
fathered the Fair Deal, the New Frontier, and the Great Society
programs. They had long been the dominant political force in
the country. The center, much beloved by Republicans and
Democrats alike, had become the revisionist center. This was
seen as an inchoate alliance of many of the followers of
McCarthy, Robert Kennedy, John Lindsay, and Nelson Rockefeller. They sensed that the New Deal approach was becoming
inadequate. They were anti-Vietnam for a variety of reasons,
and neoisolationist in that they believed in the priority of
domestic problems. Generally humanist and antitechnocratic,
they were sympathetic to many of the New Left ideas but
distinctly conservative in their commitment to preserving the
political system which they saw to be in danger.

On the right were the conservatives, the chief political chal-
lengers to the liberals. Similarly pragmatic and optimistic, they
were inclined toward economic and social *laissez-faire.* They
were committed to developing a decentralized and individual-
istic response to the domestic crisis but were restrained by their
political alliance with the romantic conservatives. These were

the insurgent force within the Republican party. They were frankly hostile to the New Left and antitechnocratic, and they stood for social order and traditional values. They were ambivalent in foreign policy, essentially isolationist but also aggressively internationalist in defense of world order against communism. Lastly there was the revolutionary right, who were invariably racist. They violently rejected the political system as it existed, usually in the name of the American system as it was romantically alleged to have been in the glory of the past.

One could argue about these arbitrary groupings. I shall lump the last two together as the counterrevolutionary right, but their characteristics could be recognized. Only the revolutionary left and the confrontationist left were new, and they had taken the place in the political spectrum of the communists and Marxists, whom they despised. The liberals were on the whole Democrats, and the conservatives were Republicans. The revisionist center included members of both parties, but Democrats were in the majority. The romantic conservatives were Republican, with roots in American political history going back far beyond Goldwater. The revolutionary right, which would have been known as fascist in Western Europe, belonged to both parties. They were a latter-day version of the Know-Nothings and voted for Wallace in 1968.

With the exception of the New Left, the groups were traditionally American and had in the past coexisted under the umbrellas of the two major parties. Neither party had been ideological, except to the extent that Democrats tended to favor a strong federal government and Republicans preferred a weak one. Few hard lines could be drawn between them. For most Americans, political loyalty depended largely upon their place of birth and the politics of their fathers. Some Democratic congressmen were more conservative than most Republicans, whose liberal wing could be to the left of a majority of Democrats. The southern Democratic–conservative Republican coalition was an obvious example of how party lines could mean little or nothing. Nevertheless, the two parties had retained their identity and cohesion. Since the thirties, and with the exception of the Eisenhower years, the liberals and much of the center had ensured a run of Democratic successes at the polls. The conservatives had led the Republican party and, except for 1964, had managed to restrain the romantic conservatives.

This was not the case in 1968 because of political polarization. The Democrats and Republicans of the revisionist center could not carry their own parties. They were weakened by Robert Kennedy's death, the one-issue campaign of McCarthy, Humphrey's fatal attachment to Johnson, and Rockefeller's tardiness in declaring his candidacy, but there was more to their failure than that. The liberal movement, which had established the modern mixed economic and social system, was in decline throughout the Atlantic world. One reason was comparative success. The components of the system—representative government, welfare-state projects, centralized planning in varying degree, and a humanist concern for the unfortunate, to mention only the obvious—had worked as well as could be expected in an imperfect world. The system had reached a kind of plateau in Western Europe. Apart from marginal improvement, further movement if not progress could be achieved only by greater control of the means of production and distribution. The dreary history of nationalization in Britain, and the failures of the Soviet consumer economy, were not encouraging. There were more fundamental doubts, concerning personal freedom and the right of property. More important, the steam had gone from the movement because those who had benefited most from it had become more conservative. There were arguments over whether or not a fat communist was safer to live with, but none about the conservatism of a contented trade unionist.

The United States had lagged behind in social reform, and the Great Society programs were Johnson's efforts to catch up. He did extremely well for almost everybody except those whose needs were largest, the blacks and the poor generally. Again the contented trade unionist was partly responsible, but the liberals must share some of the blame. One verdict was that they tried to build the Great Society with New Deal methods. As in Western Europe, there was certainly a dearth of new ideas, and even less enthusiasm for tinkering with the economic system. Nevertheless, the inadequacy of New Deal methods was recognized by some liberals, as were the beginnings of the twin revolutions. This led to a new departure, the so-called new politics, but alas this proved to be further provocation for the counterrevolution.

Some practitioners of the new politics saw themselves as a ginger group within the Democratic party, but in fact they had been polarized. Their concern for the blacks and the poor led them to ignore the balance of power and groups within the party. They offended organized labor, which, with a few exceptions, was even more conservative than the Western European unions. Their arrogance was occasionally monumental. One appalling example was provided by McGeorge Bundy after he left the White House for the Ford Foundation. In so doing, he exchanged partial responsibility for the Vietnam War for an unofficial but powerful place in the war against poverty and its social ills. One of his major targets became the New York City school system, once among the best in the country but then incapable of teaching many of its students. Bundy threw himself into the fray with what was still known as Kennedy vigor. He was an intelligent man. He knew that little could be achieved while the country continued to spend half of its revenue on defense and space, or before the relationship between the federal government, the states, and the cities was reformed. He could not wait. Something had to be done, of course, but he chose to decentralize part of the school system. The idea was derived from the maximum feasibility principle of the community action programs of the Office of Economic Opportunity. The people—the blacks and the poor—were to make the decisions.

The Ocean Hill–Brownsville project was thus supposed to be an experiment in participatory democracy, but the tactics chosen were those of confrontation. Much could be said for creative tension (a cliché of the new politics), but between whom? In that Brooklyn neighborhood it was not between the established system and the proletariat, nor between the rich and the poor. The rich did not send their children to ghetto schools. The representatives of the system under attack were the schoolteachers, for the most part Jews of liberal persuasion. The leaders of most of the parents were more interested in fomenting racial unrest and civic nihilism than improving education. Dr. Kenneth Clark, the well-known black educator, said that the project was retrogressive. Certainly the teachers' strike was only one consequence. The larger were an increase in racial tensions, further alienation, and a loss of confidence in liberal solutions.

Bundy was typical of the new generation of in-and-outers, those men who move in and out of government from university common rooms and law chambers. He had indeed taught many of them at Harvard. They could not be condemned as a group. Many were motivated by the desire to serve their country. Washington, and especially the White House, could hardly function without them, but some were gravely flawed. Regarding themselves as an elite, they had small regard for Congress, politicians generally, and, for that matter, people. As is often the case with reformers, people were impersonal masses to be influenced and engineered rather than individuals to be led and persuaded. Their intellectual arrogance could be self-damaging. They prided themselves on being tough and hard-nosed and on their ability to solve problems. They all gloried in being pragmatists, but for educated men their definition of pragmatism was, to say the least, narrow. Their definition was the vulgar one of not being doctrinaire. There was little of the old Anglo-Saxon humanism. They tended to tackle problems in isolation and often for electoral purposes. The intellectuals' contempt for the working and lower middle classes was enhanced as they worked for the blacks. No wonder the counterrevolutionary right found recruits among the rank and file of the Democratic party.

The counterrevolutionary right was, of course, a minority, but the majority rarely rules in its own name. It gives credentials to contending minorities, and the mood was such that in 1968 the pendulum swung to the right. The swing was long in coming. Resistance within the Republican party to its moderate wing, the so-called eastern establishment, had been building up steadily since the late forties. There was the opposition to Eisenhower in 1952 from those who rallied behind Taft. In 1960 Goldwater was convinced that the counterrevolutionary right could take over the party. His success was short-lived in 1964. He was inept as a candidate, and the conditions of the times demanded national unity behind Johnson, but he deserved a better reputation as a psephologist. Much of what Phillips was to write later, and which was accepted by the party leadership, was sensed by Goldwater years before.

He knew that the continental tilt, politically and economically, was gradually sloping westward. The John Birch Society had been doing its mission work among the counterrevolutionary right since the late fifties. Many people laughed at it, but a hundred of the delegates to the 1964 Republican national convention admitted to being members. At a rally held before the convention, attended by groups such as the John Birch Society, the Conservative Society of America, the Liberty Lobby, the Christian Crusade, and We, The People, top priority was given to purging the moderates from the party. By 1968 there were nearly 5,000 right-wing organizations. Some were of little account, and there was considerable overlapping, but their combined annual budget was proved to be at least $40 million and was suspected of being closer to $50 million. This was more than the official budgets of each of the two major parties for the presidential election. H. L. Hunt alone financed five hundred radio broadcasts a day.

They worked on hidden veins of fear, racism, and resentment. They exploited the failures of the liberal approach to modern human and social problems. As one observer afterward remarked, "Just as Americans are beginning to be emancipated from the Main Street mold of parochialism and Puritanism, the old prototype of George F. Babbitt is reclaimed as the accepted norm for society."* Nixon, although conservative, was not necessarily one of them. The counterrevolutionary right would have much preferred Governor Ronald Reagan of California as

*The National Committee for an Effective Congress, annual report, 1969.

presidential candidate, but Nixon was accepted as a compromise candidate. He successfully campaigned on the law and order issue, the slogan which expressed so many of the fears and frustrations of millions of Americans. The election was close, but only because of Wallace's 10 million votes. Many Democrats remained loyal to the party, but the right-wing minority was decisive for the first time in the history of modern presidential elections. The twin revolutions continued, but 1968 was a victory for the counterrevolution.

Some Americans believed that the Kennedys, John or Robert, could have better controlled the consequences of the twin revolutions. I believe that John Kennedy would have done better than Robert. The transformation of the younger brother from the shadow of McCarthyism to the new politics was undoubtedly real. His concern for the blacks and the poor had once been good Democratic politics, but his compassion was beyond question. He was stronger than his older brother. He really believed that he had an almost divine right and responsibility to rule, but I think that he would have been too divisive. Some of his young advisers were far to the left of the intellectual liberals who had served John Kennedy. The New Left did not much like him, but the counterrevolution could have been more vicious than it was.

John Kennedy would have done better because of what he was and not because of what he was supposed to be. For all the talk about the New Frontier, he was influenced by his conservative Catholic background. He was a Democrat because he was an Irish-American from Boston, but born elsewhere he might have been a Republican. There was not much to choose between him and most youngish Republicans of wealth. He was an honorable and kindly man, but in the old biblical words he had little fire in his belly for change. His association with the liberal intellectuals was quite accidental. My understanding is that Kay Halle, the most handsome, shrewd, and delightful of all Washington's political hostesses, brought them together. Certainly he had previously shown little interest in things of the mind and social reform. He was described as a meat-and-potatoes man

248

and during his congressional years spent more time at George-town parties than at party politics. Nevertheless, he was a born politician. Soon after his death, one of his advisers gave him the supreme accolade. He said, "Kennedy was an old pro." His old Boston friends, the so-called Irish Mafia, were closer to him as president than the intellectuals, with the possible exception of Sorensen.

This background helped to explain his cautiousness in domestic politics. He did not give priority to civil rights legislation because the political dangers were recognized. It would have come, had he lived, but he would have been more cautious. I think that he would have been content with one civil rights bill. The reaction of the right could have thus been much less than it was to Johnson's program. To put it another way, he would have avoided trouble because of his conservatism. Nevertheless, the majority of blacks loved him. All those I knew preferred Kennedy to Johnson in spite of the latter's record. They knew that Johnson had done more for them, that he met and listened more to their leaders, but they still mourned the other man's memory. This might have curbed some of the violence in the ghettos, and I think that he would have dealt more effectively with the eruptions that would have inevitably occurred. He would have sent in personal emissaries, men such as John Doar, who did such splendid work for him in the South. Communication between the blacks and authority would not have broken down so completely. At the same time, I believe that he would have acted more promptly in putting down violence. Federal troops would have been deployed sooner. He had a strong sense of the dignity of the presidency, and violence not only disturbed the domestic tranquillity but also offended his office.

Equally important, Kennedy was much better attuned to the political heart of America, in part because of his lace-curtain Irish conservatism but also because of the Irish facility for politics. He, his father, and the Irish Mafia knew among them every Democratic boss and leader in the country. They were taken care of, listened to, and this extraordinary political machine, the Kennedy machine really, was also a vast intelligence network.

It helped him to keep in touch with what people thought, both white and black. He knew what could or could not be done safely. He erred on the side of caution, but that was where safety was to be found. Robert Kennedy realized the importance of the law-and-order issue only when he arrived in Indiana to fight the primary. John Kennedy, I am sure, would have known long before. I am reminded of his decision to negotiate the nuclear-test-ban treaty. Most of the early groundwork had been done before by Hubert Humphrey in the Senate. Before Kennedy's inauguration, Jerome Weisner, his scientific adviser, and Walt Rostow returned from a Pugwash conference convinced, after their talks with Russian scientists, that a treaty could be signed. The negotiations were long and tortuous, the Russians broke the moratorium, and there was also a resumption of American testing, but the long delay was due as much to Kennedy's cautiousness as the experts' differences over nuclear thresholds. He decided to act only after the Pope gave the treaty his blessing—not because he was under papal influence or any such rot, but he knew that millions of American Catholics, most of them conservative and suspicious of the Soviet Union, would not argue with the Pope.

If this was not the Kennedy of popular mythology, it was the real man and explains why I think he would have done better at home than Johnson or his brother. Kennedy would also have been better with the nation's youth, and not only because he was a younger man than Johnson. Again he was not a favorite of the New Left, whose members quickly recognized his conservatism and machine connections, but their depredations could have been less damaging because of his appeal to the majority. The campuses were still fairly quiet when he died, although I can remember hearing a warning of the early stirrings from one of his advisers long before the press and television were aware of them. He would have been forewarned, and more important he could have communicated better with them. He also understood better the new life styles just then being fashioned by the cultural revolution. He might well have managed to influence them.

I am not so sure that he would have done better in Vietnam. One witness who believed that he would have fought the war as did Johnson has already been quoted. Rostow was not impartial, but the record would appear to support his conclusion. Kennedy began where Dulles had left off, as much because of his conservative Catholic background as the hard-nosed young men he brought from the Charles River to the banks of the Potomac. Dulles, for all his talk of massive retaliation and agonizing reappraisals, helped to involve the country in nothing more serious than the Lebanese landings. Kennedy accepted all the rhetoric and acted upon it. Unlike in domestic affairs, he was aggressive and romantic abroad. After the fiasco of the Cuban invasion, he reaffirmed the Monroe Doctrine as legitimate authority for United States domination over the Americas. This was an extraordinary assertion of imperial power, no less than the doctrine expounded by Leonid Brezhnev after the invasion of Czechoslovakia. I, for one, resented the Cuban missile crisis. The world was taken to the nuclear brink although Khrushchev was prepared to remove the missiles from Cuba if Kennedy took American missiles out of Turkey. It was an obvious solution, but one of Kennedy's biographers, Arthur Schlesinger, Jr., wrote of Kennedy's consternation when Radio Moscow broadcast the text of Khrushchev's letter. The offer was rejected, but the reason was never explained. The crisis took place just before the midterm elections, and another biographer, Theodore Sorensen, indicated that they were much in Kennedy's thoughts when he demanded what amounted almost to unconditional surrender.

There was no consultation with the NATO allies, who were closer to the brink than the United States. Lord Harlech, the British ambassador and an old friend of the Kennedys', was warned of the coming crisis the day before Kennedy announced it on television. They met at the White House swimming pool, and the momentous news was broken between dips. Harlech naturally wanted to inform his prime minister, Harold Macmillan, but Kennedy was reluctant to give permission. As I understand it, Harlech was allowed to report only the barest details. The reaction of de Gaulle was misrepresented. Dean Acheson was sent to Paris to explain what was afoot and reported that the French president was suitably loyal and quiescent. Three years later when de Gaulle ordered American forces out of France, he mentioned Cuba as one reason why his country could no longer risk being associated with the United States.

Nevertheless, the Kennedy charisma was a great gift. As the world saw him, he emerged from the Cuban crisis as a cool leader whose calculated boldness had saved the world from incineration. This suggested that Kennedy, had he lived, might have had an easier time over Vietnam, but I am not so sure. The missile crisis lasted only six days. Vietnam could have been his problem for eight years, and when he died there was no way of knowing what he would have done when all the liberal counterinsurgency ideas came to nothing in 1964. I could not see him admitting defeat, especially in an election year. One only knew that he left to his successor a terrible mess the like of which few presidents had inherited since the other Johnson succeeded the murdered Lincoln. I. F. Stone thought Kennedy died just in time. Stone, who began as a great admirer of Kennedy, wrote the following in his *Weekly* soon after the assassination:

He died in time to be remembered as he would like to be remembered, as ever young, still victorious, struck down undefeated, with almost all the potentates and rulers of mankind, friend and foe, come to mourn at the bier. For somehow one has the feeling that in the tangled dramaturgy of events, this sudden assassination was for the author the only satisfactory way out. The Kennedy Administration was approaching an impasse, certainly at home, quite possibly abroad, from which there seemed no escape. In Congress the President was faced with something worse than a filibuster. He was confronted with a shrewdly conceived and quietly staged sitdown strike by the Southern committee chairmen determined to block civil rights even if it meant stopping the wheels of government altogether.... Never before in our history has the Senate so dragged its heels as this year; never before has the Southern oligarchy dared go so far in demonstrating its power in Washington. The President was caught between these old men, their faces set stubbornly towards their white supremacist past, and the advancing Negro masses, explosively demanding "freedom now." Mr. Kennedy's death, like those of the Birmingham children and of Medgar Evers, may some day seem the first drops portending a new storm which it was beyond his power to stay.

Stone was more prophetic than he could have known. The storm squarely hit Johnson, and unwittingly Kennedy left him another inheritance. The Kennedy legend, fostered by Robert, haunted him until the end like some terrible ghost. It divided the Democratic party and contributed to the fissiparous political forces already mentioned. After the early years Johnson could never be certain of party loyalties, an uncertainty which must have fed his insecurity. The constant attention given to the murdered president and his surviving brothers wounded his psyche. It nurtured youthful fantasy. One had the impression at times that both the left and the right avoided the harsh present, the right in the American past and the left in Kennedy's Camelot. The revival of this idiotic Tennysonian fantasy, by Theodore White, who ought to have known better, was a measure of the resentful escapism that plagued Johnson.

He did his best. After it was all over, one of his assistants said, "He was an extraordinarily difficult man to work for. He had no outside interests. He was not interested in the theater. He was not interested in playing cards. He was not interested in reading, or in the arts. He was interested in one subject and that was being president. Politics were his vocation, avocation, and his relaxation, and you were expected to be available twenty-four hours a day. Your family life almost completely disappeared." One does not have to weep for Johnson's assistants. They all did well enough afterward, with the exception of Rusk, whose subsequent misfortune helped to explain Johnson's cruel predicament. The former secretary of state began his career as a college professor. His years of experience in government—as secretary of state and before that as assistant secretary for Far Eastern affairs and for United Nations affairs and as special assistant to General Marshall—should have assured safe tenure at any of the best universities. There were no offers because his association with the Vietnam policies would, it was feared, have kept the campuses in a constant turmoil. Yet when he was first approached to join the faculty of the University of Georgia, his home state, white supremacists were opposed because of his liberal attitude to the blacks.

There could have been no more hard-working president than Johnson. He was shrewd, experienced, and knowledgeable. He had enormous physical strength, and a deep and abiding love of country. He knew all about the earthiness and occasional corruptions of American politics, as did John Kennedy; but his personal vision, perhaps more idealistic than Kennedy's, was to a surprising degree undistorted by his political manipulations. Johnson's personal habits and behavior were less attractive. He could never hope to be loved outside his own family. He was too old to inspire youth. Mrs. Johnson was a splendid woman, in many ways a much better First Lady than the then Mrs. Kennedy, but the public interest she aroused was minimal. There was therefore little to stem the tide when opinion began to turn against him, but this lack of personal charm did not in itself make the White House untenable. Millions of Americans did not afterward vote for Wallace because of the memory of Johnson lifting a dog by its ears. The South was not in a state of near-rebellion because he exposed his stomach scars to the public view. The northern ghettos did not erupt in flame because of his cornpone humor. American society, and not Johnson, alienated the hippies and the flower children.

Johnson was not well equipped to meet the many challenges, but the most powerful man in the world could frequently be almost powerless at home, a fact often forgotten by Americans who complained about the concentration of power in the White House and still demanded instant presidential action. There was not much that could be done quickly for the blacks, who had little or no share in the benign consequences of the second industrial revolution. The liberal failures have been noted, but he could not have moved quickly enough even if a resistant Congress had made the money available. The ghetto blacks could rarely be found in the political groupings mentioned in this chapter. They belonged to an apolitical substratum that had little or no connection even with local Democratic bosses. They became a mob in being, reminiscent of the anarchy of European cities in the Middle Ages, and the modern mobs to be found in Middle Eastern and other unstable countries. Their nether world was of course part of the price paid for the second industrial revolution. Castoffs of an industrializing South, they had migrated to the North only to find that they were utterly unprepared for survival in the new world being created. Families collapsed, with all the dreadful consequences for the children's welfare and neighborhood peace. Much of the increasing crime was committed by blacks, mainly by youngsters between the ages of fifteen and twenty-four, and blacks were the main victims. The fact that so many danced with glee among the flames of burning cities surprised only those who had closed their eyes to what was going on in their country. The very ignorance of conditions in the ghetto was further evidence of a divided society, but the shocked surprise only increased tension, prejudice, and strife, and to Johnson's detriment.

He was particularly powerless in the maintenance of law and order. The Constitution awards that responsibility to the states. The only law enforcement agencies under his direct command were the FBI and the Secret Service, and their functions were, and remain, strictly limited. He was slow to dispatch federal troops to riot-torn cities, but the motives could not be questioned. He had a respect for the authority of state governors. Many police departments had become part of the counterrevolution and in some areas were a political force in their own right. "Support your local police" became a rallying cry for the counterrevolution. At first the police and National Guard had little or no training in riot control and frequently exacerbated already dangerous situations when they intervened. Improvements were made eventually, but better police methods were not the final solution unless the maintenance of order rather than social justice was the ultimate goal.

The United States was and remains a free society, and Johnson could not hope to control the cultural revolution, as Kennedy might have done. He diverted billions of dollars to education but could not influence student thinking. His munificence in education quite unwittingly created yet another problem. With 40 percent of the nation's youth in universities, the gap between the educated and the rest became more marked. The educated young, with their liberal elders, also held the working class in contempt, reserving their sympathy for blacks, who evoked guilt feelings. Those not clever or rich enough to go to college lost status and were alienated by the campus goings-on. For those without a trade, the future was economically insecure. Joseph Califano, an assistant to Johnson, remarked that it would soon be necessary to have a degree to dig ditches. They were already being dug by machines, which continued to replace men in factories as the second industrial revolution produced more electronic controls. Feeling on both sides was often high, and Richard Scammon, the psephologist, saw all the manifestations of a class struggle in the making. Certainly a high proportion of Wallace supporters came from the younger generation of the working class.

Johnson could do little or nothing about increased drug addiction. Local law enforcement agencies were primarily responsible for tracking down dope peddlers, and in the field of rehabilitation existing legislation tied the hands of responsible government. He could do nothing about long hair, fantastic clothes, and the rock culture which also helped to provoke the counterrevolution against its white enemies. He was powerless to do anything about pornography, blue films, and sexually explicit plays once the Supreme Court had handed down its decisions. Nothing could be done about the Pill and its erosion of sexual morality. All this provided more fuel for the counterrevolution. Then there was Vietnam.

I have touched upon many aspects of it, but too little attention has been given to the public acceptance of the war during most of the Johnson years. The antiwar demonstrators were vocal, but a minority. Much was heard of deserters and youngsters fleeing to Canada to avoid the draft, but the overwhelming majority

quietly did what was required of them. I can remember driving
down to Charlottesville, Virginia, after the 1967 March on the
Pentagon. On the way I stopped at Culpeper for a cup of coffee
and was attracted by the sound of martial music. About thirty
young men were boarding a bus for a military induction center.
A high school band played, volunteers handed out coffee, cokes,
and doughnuts, and parents and girl friends clustered about the
bus. There were some tears, and pride. Above all there was
acceptance. The young men were going away to do their duty,
as their fathers had done before. I saw similar scenes a dozen
or more times across the country, and there must have been
thousands of them. As far as I know, they never attracted the
television cameras, and local papers are rarely if ever read in
Washington or New York.

Most of my American friends accepted the inevitable. They
were happy if their sons earned a draft deferment by going on
to graduate school, but one of them accepted the death of his
son, a helicopter pilot, grievously but without obvious anger. He
was not alone. I think that the critics forgot how young men
have always marched off to war, and until almost the end of the
Johnson years many American accepted the official objectives
and explanations. Certainly about half of college students did in
1967. The Gallup poll then asked students the following question. "People are called 'hawks' if they want to step up our
military effort in Vietnam. They are called 'doves' if they want
to reduce our military effort in Vietnam. How would you describe yourself—as a 'hawk' or as a 'dove'?" The results were:
hawks, 49 percent; doves, 35 percent; no opinion, 16 percent.
The poll asked students in November 1969 if they approved of
Nixon's handling of the situation in Vietnam. His policy was
well understood by then, to withdraw American troops gradually but to avoid defeat. He was adamantly against a precipitate
withdrawal. Those who approved of his policy amounted to 50
percent. Only in the East was there minority approval.

In the nation as a whole, the hawks ranged from the simple
patriotic to the counterrevolutionary right, which wanted to
bomb North Vietnam into the Stone Age. They complained

bitterly against the territorial limitations Johnson placed on the war, and some against the refusal to use nuclear weapons. Johnson could not ignore them. An early reversal of strategy, say before the 1968 Tet offensive, might well have provoked a revulsion of national feeling. Johnson was well aware of this, and if he traded on it to continue his strategy of military victory, other men shared his apprehension.

That said, Johnson clearly did not possess what is required for national leadership, and with John Kennedy lying in Arlington National Cemetary it did not matter, alas, whether he was better endowed. There is more to being president than churning out a never-ending stream of legislative proposals, no matter how good they are. There is more to national leadership than charisma, although it is easier to recognize than to describe. Americans have only to remember Franklin Roosevelt in 1933. The British need only look back to 1940 and Churchill. Johnson remembered and looked back frequently. The two men were his heroes. He saw himself with them as an immortal trinity. If the thought is farcical for some, Johnson had the larger task and, I think, the larger ambition. The challenges his two heroes met were grave but essentially simple, economic desolation and despair for Roosevelt and national survival and a hateful enemy for Churchill. These were challenges which united the two nations. The problems which crowded in on Johnson were infinitely more difficult, not only because of their variety, but because they were divisive. The sum of his challenge was greater than the parts. It demanded greater leadership, and this Johnson could not provide.

Late in 1969, Johnson gave his version of his inadequacies in a television interview with Walter Cronkite of CBS News. Much of it was pure fiction, but his attempt to rewrite history was self-revealing. He denied that he was an ambitious man who enjoyed power and whose greatest desire was to be president. He did not want to seek the office in 1960 or 1964. He ran in 1964 only because his wife said that it was his duty. He could have won in 1968 but had decided four years before not to run again. He had never really believed that he was the man to be

president. He suffered from too many disadvantages—poor upbringing, limited education, and being a southerner—to inspire
and unite all Americans. This was typical southern "poor-
mouthing," but there were a few grains of truth. The deep
affection he and Mrs. Johnson had for each other was true. As
already noted, she did want him to run in 1964, although he
needed no urging. It was also true that he talked occasionally of
not running again in 1968. One of his advisers told me of this
as early as the spring of 1965, before the commitment of American troops in Vietnam, when Johnson was literally on top of the
world, and most Americans thought that all was well with the
world because he was in the White House. He was also fully
aware of the contempt the liberal intellectuals and some of the
Kennedy people had for him because of the Texas background
and speech, and his old alma mater, the Southwest Texas State
Teachers College, but none of this diminished his lust for power.

The talk of not seeking re-election was at best protective—his
wife was always anxious for his health—and at worst an example
of his nasty weakness for playing cat and mouse with people.
His background hurt him but not his inadequate education.
Whatever he lost in not going to a decent university, to Harvard,
Chicago, or Berkeley, he more than made up during the years
of public office. His vision of a better America was not impaired
by the lack of a good degree, although the sneers of the intellectuals further increased his personal insecurity. His southernness
was a stigma, but the greatest weakness revealed in that television interview was Johnson's refusal to be honest with the country, and himself. There was the disdain for facts as most rational
people see them and the belief that anything and everything
could be fixed or explained away. Nobody ran him off the range.
He saddled up and rode off in his own good time. He did not
fail to achieve peace in Vietnam. He implied that if Humphrey
had not spoken that night in Salt Lake City in October 1968 all
American boys would have been out of Vietnam soon after
Christmas. All this was patently untrue, but his performance was
not an aberration. This was the true Johnson as congressmen,
officials, and journalists remembered him: the accomplished

schemer, wheeler and dealer, and fixer, who had practiced his skills for so long and with such success that he hardly knew when to stop.

These skills explained why he was such a superb majority leader in the Senate, where there were skeletons in many cupboards and the sharpest instinct was for political survival. He knew when and why his colleagues could or could not give him their votes and how to extract them when wanted. The objective facts of Johnson's congressional world were rarely as outsiders saw them. More often than not, they were the knowledge of other men's weaknesses, their need for protection, and the cajolery, threats, rewards, flattery, and questionable compromises required to establish a majority rather than the substance of the legislation.

This is not necessarily corrupt politics but is essential if the Congress is to be made to function. In spite of what Edmund Burke said to the voters of Bristol in 1774, congressmen are not representatives of independent judgment. To reverse his election address, the Senate and the House of Representatives are a congress of ambassadors from different (and occasionally hostile) regions, states, and districts, whose interests each must maintain, as an agent and advocate, against other agents and advocates. It cannot be otherwise, because Congress has become the final cockpit of group and regional competition, which American domestic politics is all about.

Johnson made the Senate work reasonably effectively. Legislation was ground out, often more useful than could be expected because of his genius. As he saw it, the president was only a more powerful majority leader who also had to deal with other politicians and special interest groups to establish a national consensus. To some extent he was right, hence his brilliant legislative record, but modern presidents have to deal with another set of objective facts. Power had flowed from the Capitol to the White House because the congressional system could not always meet the nation's needs. In reconciling internal interests, Congress maintained the Union but at the expense of indecision and the avoidance of urgent problems. Nationwide problems could only be solved at the national level and by a branch of government above the congressional cockpit—the president. Theodore Roosevelt was one of the first presidents to recognize the new imperative of presidential initiative, and he formulated the principle of the president as the steward of the people. Franklin Roosevelt firmly established it, and over the years the American people came to look to the White House when they had aspirations to be met and wrongs to be redressed. Johnson understood this and desperately wanted to be president of all the people. He was less prejudiced than most Americans. He was color blind, and ethnic origins meant little or nothing to him apart from his pride of family. One heard a great deal about the Texans on his staff, but Italian-Americans occupied important positions in the White House for the first time during his presidency. He had compassion, a rough variety perhaps, but suitable enough for the rough and tumble of politics. He ought to have been a good president.

He narrowly missed being one because the president is more than majority leader. He must deal with 200 million Americans as well as a hundred senators. His final strength lies in the leadership he can provide and the trust he can inspire. He must have the power to persuade a majority to do something they might not want to do. This was beyond Johnson. The natural gifts which made him the most successful Senate majority leader in history rendered him unfit to lead the nation in times of crisis. National leadership could not be exercised from a back room, with cajolery, fixing, and the rest of his tricks, and Johnson knew no other way. He rose above the smell of the Senate cloakrooms. He soon learned that he had to deal with a different set of objective facts—with, for instance, resentful blacks, militant students, pacifists, and frightened suburbanites instead of committee chairmen, but they could not be fixed. He reached them occasionally. His civil rights speech with the theme of "We Shall Overcome" was an obvious example, but he could not sustain such moments. The old congressional habits were too strong. The credibility gap was real because he could not be honest with the nation at all times. Other presidents had been required to be less than honest on occasions, but the good ones had been invariably honest about their ultimate intentions. They had used plain language when necessary, and this Johnson could do but rarely. One did not have to plow through Professor McLuhan's works to know how fatal this had to be in an age of instant and visual communications. It was sufficient to watch the CBS interview. His face was secretive, brooding, and calculating, as it had been in the Senate or the privacy of his White House office. In spite of the incredulity in the face of the interviewer, he visibly calculated how much the millions watching would take before reason rose in revolt. For all his years in public life, he could never treat people as people. He never understood national politics. He had no feel for anything much beyond his family and the closed politics of Texas and the Senate.

Nevertheless, Johnson just might have survived 1968, unloved but grudgingly respected for the talents behind his tricks, if it had not been for Vietnam. Nations can be extraordinarily patient, especially in a period of considerable affluence. The presidency is an office that commands immense respect. He had powerful allies in business and labor. The real leaders of Congress, the Dirksens and the Russells, were old and loyal friends, and he could take care of the rank and file. The old American establishment knew his worth. He might have ridden the storm, but Vietnam was one problem too many. After twenty-three years of foreign reporting, east and west of the Iron Curtain and north and south of the Equator, I am convinced that no government, no president or prime minister, can deal effectively with more than two or three problems at a time. Britain failed to join Europe at the right time because government and people were too involved in their quiet internal revolution and getting rid of a vast colonial empire. It was just too much to expect them also to accept a startling new concept such as European unity. In 1964 Johnson knew that he had his hands full. He was engaged in his own quiet internal revolution. He was aware of the second industrial and cultural revolutions, and of black militancy and white backlash. Vietnam was one of the catalysts of the American sixties, but still avoidable. He must have remembered what

Korea did to Truman. Why, then, did he choose to fight?

There were many explanations, and certainly many contributing factors, but three sufficed. First was his simple patriotism, of which one example should be sufficient. Soon after the Santo Domingo intervention in 1965, Johnson addressed a conference of the building and construction trades department of the AFL-CIO in Washington. In a long rambling speech, which touched all political bases, he said, "We covet no territory, we seek no domination over any one. All we want to do is to live in peace and be left alone, if they will do it. But if they are going to put American lives in danger, where Americans go, that flag goes with them to protect them." He paused dramatically, and pointed to the flag behind the podium. He then recited, "I have seen the glory of art and architecture. I have seen the sunrise on Mont Blanc, but the most beautiful vision that these eyes ever beheld was the flag of my country in a foreign land." He meant every word of it.

The second was another part of the Kennedy legacy, the liberal intellectuals who stayed on in the White House and in government. Their presence was necessary during the period of transition, but theirs was a new and harsher patriotism. They were convinced that American national security depended upon the maintenance of a global nuclear, territorial, and ideological balance of power. The balance had to be maintained, and by armed intervention in the last resort. With Kennedy, they began where Dulles had left off. Massive retaliation was rejected as too dangerous. Perhaps it was too simple. They addressed themselves to what were seen as fundamental causes of conflict, and believed that Americans could engineer the world and reshape the lives of other peoples to ensure an American peace. The admixture of arrogance and ignorance was appalling. Rather than rethink and change Dulles' policies, as Senator Fulbright proposed at the time, they were prepared to change the world. This was American omnipotence and omniscience with a vengeance. In the words of William Pfaff of the Hudson Institute,* "It took a visionary liberal administration fully to

*Commentary. October 1969.

translate the globalism of American rhetoric into a program of national action. Vietnam was deliberately made into a test of liberal international reform."

The third was brought home to me one night in the fall of 1969. I was invited to Blair House, the president's guest house, to witness the swearing in of the new national advisory council for the Arms Control and Disarmament Agency. It was hardly a newsworthy occasion, but I went along because I like Blair House, a pleasant early-nineteenth-century building with a good deal of the charm of the late Federalist period. It must be the only house in the United States where midmorning callers are always offered sherry or madeira, both excellent. The rooms have the casual, lived-in atmosphere of an exclusive men's club. The houskeeper, very superior but friendly, and the attentive servants complete the illusion.

The illusion was very strong that night. The council was for the most part a branch of the American establishment, and for a brief hour I was reminded again of how the United States has been governed or influenced by a small group of men on intimate, clubby terms with each other. The company included, among others, John McCloy, Dean Rusk, Douglas Dillon, General Lauris Norstad, Llewellyn Thompson, Cyrus Vance, William Foster, Dr. James Killian, Harold Brown, and Kermit Gordon. Between them, they had run Germany, NATO, the State Department, the Treasury Department, the air force, the World Bank, and the President's Foreign Intelligence Advisory Board and had manned embassies from Paris to Moscow. They had served five presidents in a hundred and one other capacities. They and their like were the dramatis personae of the display of American superpower since the Second World War. They had advised presidents on the deployment of that power around the world, confident that their advice would be heard, and more often than not acted upon. As far as I knew, only one man present had run for public office.

Most of them were getting on, but their advice would be heard for a few more years. They were very much concerned with the strategic arms limitation talks, the first serious attempt to control offensive and defensive nuclear missiles. Some had been involved in the design, procurement, and deployment of these weapons, but they saw no irony in the new situation. There was a determination to do everything possible to prevent another lap in the arms race, but not at the expense of national security. The approach to armaments was remarkably cool. For these men, missiles, divisions, and fleets were only weapons of superdiplomacy. One of them chose NATO as an example. Back in the late forties, he said, nobody believed that the Russians would invade Western Europe. NATO was organized to fill a vacuum and to organize Western Europe. He could have added that NATO was a weapon of American superdiplomacy, a convenient way of establishing American authority up to the Elbe, but good manners probably prevented him from going that far in the hearing of an Englishman.

I was about to ask if all the billions of dollars, pounds, marks, and francs spent on NATO armaments had been really necessary when quite matter-of-factly he said that there was still much to be done. The Russians were in the Mediterranean. The southern flank had been turned, and Africa, as well as the Middle East, was exposed to Soviet influence. The atmosphere remained cozy. The affidavits of their new office remained unsigned on a sideboard among the whisky and martini glasses. For most of them, these were the facts of life. There was no escape, but still no reason why the company of old friends should not be enjoyed. They were men of good will, cultivated, and well informed. The easy conversation went on, about the Soviet Union, China, and the urban crisis. For them life was a matter of priorities and resources. They had their differences, and were accustomed to winning and losing a trick or two in the subtle battle for the mind of the president. But after two decades of power and influence they instinctively knew, or thought they knew, what had to be done.

I thought, over the second martini, that the world had much to thank these men for. They had helped to hold it together for twenty years, and with civilized restraint until Vietnam. The final qualification had long bothered me. I had understood the

No Hail, No Farewell

liberal intellectuals' lack of restraint. That could be explained by the acceptance of American omnipotence and omniscience, and unquestioned faith in impersonal concepts, but these mature men were different. They came from the older universities before the days of centers for strategic studies and had grown up in a more humble world for all the rich furnishings of their board rooms and law chambers. They had had infinite experience. They were not only ornaments of the American establishment but the flower of American civilization. Perhaps they were too cut off from the campuses and ghettos, the farms and factories, the tenements and suburban housing developments of America. The only one of them who had run for public office was William Scranton, former governor of Pennsylvania and a poor candidate for the Republican presidential nomination in 1964. They might have achieved power and influence too easily, although McCloy was fond of recalling that he was born on the wrong side of Market Street in Philadelphia. Perhaps in the absence of political disciplines they had also wielded that power too easily. In early 1968 some of them had advised Johnson to stop the bombing of North Vietnam and seek a negotiated settlement, but until the Tet offensive they had loyally supported the war.

Before the party broke up I recalled the extent of their experience and the greatness of their collective achievements in the maintenance of world peace and western freedom. There were a few deprecating gestures, but they waited for the question. I went on to recall their civilized restraint, and avoidance of danger in Hungary, the Middle East, and Czechoslovakia. What went wrong in Vietnam? There was a short silence, and a looking into now-empty glasses. Then with disarming candor, one of them said, "We thought we would win."

Index

267

Index

Index

Index

Index

About the Author

Louis Heren, whose career in journalism began as a copy boy for the *Times,* was born and educated in London.

After service in the British Army, he rejoined the *Times* as a foreign correspondent. His special assignments included a one-man search for Hillary when he was lost in the Himalayas.

From 1956 to 1960 Mr. Heren was chief correspondent for the *Times* in Germany and in 1961 became its chief Washington correspondent. He is now the American Editor.

In 1967 he was given the Hannen Swaffer International Reporter of the Year prize, a British award comparable to the U.S. Pulitzer Prize.

The New American Commonwealth, Mr. Heren's first book, was awarded the John F. Kennedy Memorial Award.

70 71 72 73 10 9 8 7 6 5 4 3 2